Blyden at the height of his powers

WEST AFRICAN HISTORY SERIES

General Editor: GERALD S. GRAHAM

Rhodes Professor of Imperial History, University of London

EDWARD WILMOT BLYDEN

Pan-Negro Patriot

1832–1912

HOLLIS R. LYNCH

OXFORD UNIVERSITY PRESS

LONDON   OXFORD   NEW YORK

OXFORD UNIVERSITY PRESS

Oxford   London   New York
Glasgow   Toronto   Melbourne   Wellington
Cape Town   Salisbury   Ibadan   Nairobi   Lusaka   Addis Ababa
Bombay   Calcutta   Madras   Karachi   Lahore   Dacca
Kuala Lumpur   Hong Kong   Tokyo

Preparation and publication of this series has been made possible by the generous financial assistance of Overseas Newspaper Group, Freetown, Lagos, London and West Indies.

Printed in the United States of America

To all strivers, past and present,
after the Pan-African ideal

Preface

'He was a great man; so great indeed as to require the writing of a full-length biography of him, as one of the greatest sons of Africa.'[1] The man referred to in the above quotation was Edward Wilmot Blyden (1832–1912), the brilliant and controversial West Indian-born Liberian who spent his entire adult life championing and vindicating his race. The person who offered the opinion is Dr. Davidson Nicol, an outstanding African scientist and writer, who is at present Principal of the University College of Sierra Leone. And since Blyden's death such has been the opinion of educated Negroes everywhere, indeed, of practically everyone acquainted with the outlines of his career.

Blyden was easily the most learned and articulate champion of Africa and the Negro race in his own time. To his educated Negro contemporaries his achievements as litterateur, educator, theologian, politician, statesman, diplomat and explorer, were the most convincing refutation of the oft-repeated white charges of Negro inferiority. His teachings, incessantly propounded, that Negroes had a history and a culture of which they could be proud, and that with the help of New World Negroes a progressive civilization could be built in Africa, gave members of his race a new pride and hope, and inspired succeeding generations of African nationalists and New World Negro leaders.

All this is not to suggest that contemporary Negro admiration for him was unqualified. He was, in fact, a highly controversial figure. A 'pure Negro', Blyden showed open and unrelenting detestation for mulattoes both in Liberia and the United States: he claimed that they used their privileged positions (stemming from blood affinity with the ruling white race) to exploit the Negro masses whom they scorned; and far from working for the advancement of Africa and the Negro race, they hindered such advancement. Moreover, Blyden was a failure as a leader and practical

[1] Abioseh Nicol, 'Great Sons of Africa: Dr. Edward Blyden', *Africana: The Magazine of the West African Society*, Vol. I, No. 2 (April 1949), p. 20.

man of affairs: he possessed little organizing ability. He failed to command his admirers and make them do his bidding. He saw himself as a race champion and prophet with a divine mission, and this resulted in his being tactless and impatient of other viewpoints. There were those, too, who felt that he did not use his influence with the colonial rulers to the best advantage of Africans. But even those contemporaries most critical of him honoured him as the supreme symbol of Negro intellectual ability. It was a source of immense satisfaction and pride for his educated Negro contemporaries that in the very process of destroying false stereotypes about the Negro and Africa, Blyden became one of the first Negro-Africans to win full recognition in the English-speaking scholastic and literary world.

This study is only a partial attempt to meet the plea of Dr. Nicol and others, for it is not 'a full-length biography' but rather an examination of Blyden's pan-Negro ideas: it is primarily intellectual history. This consideration has dictated the largely thematic form of the organization of the material. The first obvious break in the chronological sequence comes with Chapter Four, 'Vindicator of the Negro Race' which discusses the major ideas in Blyden's thought. This chapter might at first appear as an arbitrary interruption of the narrative, but there is, I think, justification for it. By 1871 Blyden's ideas had reached maturity, and it seemed to me that the exposition in Chapter Four would make for a full understanding of Blyden's subsequent conduct and activities. In particular, both Chapters Five, 'Race Work in Sierra Leone', and Six, '"Pure Negroes" Only for Africa', are meant to follow logically from Chapter Four. Because I have not used a strictly chronological approach, I have thought it useful to provide readers with a biographical sketch of Blyden.

This book, like practically all historical works, is, in reality, the product of several minds. While, of course, I alone bear full responsibility for it, I should like to record my sincere thanks to the following people who have read the manuscript in whole or in part and have offered valuable criticism: Mr. D. H. Jones of the School of Oriental and African Studies, University of London; Professor George Shepperson of the University of Edinburgh; Mr. Kenneth Robinson, Director of the Institute of Commonwealth Studies, University of London; Professor E. Essien Udom of the University of Ibadan; and Mrs. N.

Ademola, Secretary of the Institute of African Studies, University of Ife.

I owe a special thanks to Professor John D. Fage, Director of West African Studies, University of Birmingham, who provided invaluable help and encouragement to me in the early stages of my research.

I benefited, too, from conversations with Miss Edith Holden of Greenwich, Connecticut, U.S.A., the grand-daughter of Rev. John Knox who had an important influence on Blyden's early life. Miss Holden has spent some three decades collecting material on Blyden which she has compiled into an invaluable source book. Unfortunately, this was not available for perusal before my manuscript went to press.[1] Help from conversations also came from Edward Wilmot Blyden III of the University of Nigeria, Nsukka, and from Miss Isa Blyden of Freetown, who at eighty-five still has vivid recollections of her father.

For their unfailing courtesy and help, I am greatly indebted to the staff of the following: the Public Record Office, the British Museum, the Archives of the Church Missionary Society, the New York Public Library, including the Schomburg Collection in the Harlem branch, the Archives of the Maryland Historical Society, Baltimore; and the Library of Congress, Washington, D.C.

This study was made possible by the grant of a three-year British Commonwealth Scholarship tenable at the School of Oriental and African Studies, University of London. The Central Research Fund of the University of London provided me with a travel grant to make a six month research visit to the United States.

Finally, to the editors and publishers of the *Journal of African History*, *The Journal of the Nigerian Historical Society*, *Présence Africaine*, *Nigeria Magazine*, and the *Boston University African Studies Papers*, I am indebted for permission to use material which in a different form has already appeared as articles.

---

[1] Miss Holden's work, *Blyden of Liberia. An Account of the Life and Labors of Edward Wilmot Blyden, LL. D. As Recorded in Letters and in Print*, was published in New York when my own work was already near publication.

H.R.L.

February 1967

CONTENTS

ILLUSTRATIONS

ABBREVIATIONS

A.C.S.   American Colonization Society

C.M.S.   Church Missionary Society

P.B.F.M.   Presbyterian Board of Foreign Missions

Biographical Outline

1887	Publication of *magnum opus*, *Christianity, Islam and the Negro Race*
1889/90 August–March	Seventh Visit to the United States; two months' tour of 'Deep South'
1890/91 December–February	First Visit to Lagos
1892	Liberian Ambassador to the Court of St. James
1894 April–July	Second Visit to Lagos
1895 July–September	Eighth and last visit to the United States
1896–1897	Agent of Native Affairs in Lagos
1898–1899	Spent mainly in Sierra Leone as a private teacher
1900 January–1901 March	Professor at Liberia College
1901–1906	Director of Mohammedan Education in Sierra Leone
1905 June–September	Liberian Minister Plenipotentiary and Envoy Extraordinary to London and Paris
1906–1912	Spent mainly in Sierra Leone 'in retirement'
1912 February 7	Died

1. The Negro World of the Nineteenth Century and the Making of a Race Champion

The nineteenth was probably the most humiliating century in the history of the Negro race. The African slave trade which had reached new high proportions in the eighteenth century continued to flourish, despite the well-intentioned efforts of the British to stop it and the legal prohibitions imposed upon it by European and American nations.[1] A vast contraband trade supplied the enormous demands for slaves on the plantations of the Americas. On the western coast of Africa this was not effectively brought under control until the 1860's; and in these same years in East Africa, the Arab trade in ivory and slaves caused widespread and unprecedented devastation. Not until the last decade of the century was the traffic successfully combated. Africa had 'bled her life's blood at every pore', and needed resuscitation.

In the New World, the beginning of the century saw the vast majority of Negroes in slavery. Although the system had been abolished in the British West Indies in 1834, and in the French and Danish West Indies in 1848, it continued a vigorous life in the United States, Cuba and Brazil. So entrenched was slavery in the southern United States that it took the Civil War (1861–1865) to bring about its downfall. In Cuba and Brazil, final emancipation did not come until 1886 and 1888, respectively. And even after their emancipation, Negroes of the New World were, for the most part, regarded and treated as inferior members of society.

The lot of the United States Negro was the worst. In Latin American countries slaves possessed rights both by law and custom, and manumission was widespread. In territories under Anglo-Saxon rule, slaves had no rights either in law or custom: they were

[1] See W. L. Mathieson, *Great Britain and the Slave Trade,* London 1929; A. McKenzie Grieve, *Last Years of the African Slave Trade,* London 1949; and Daniel P. Mannix, *Black Cargoes,* London 1963, chap. 5.

mere chattels.[2] West Indian Negroes were fortunate in being the
first in the New World to gain their emancipation. In contrast, the
lot of the Negro in the U.S.A. was steadily to worsen from
the beginning of the century to the outbreak of the Civil
War.

The founding fathers of the American nation had been troubled
by the incongruity of having successfully fought for their own
freedom, and yet denying it to Negroes some of whom had fought
valiantly to help to secure that freedom; and they and all enlightened Americans had hoped that the institution would die a
natural death. After American independence, state after state in
the North abolished slavery, and by 1804 slavery in those areas
had virtually come to an end. In the South, too, during the immediate post-Revolution years, there had been signs that the
institution would wither away: there had been more than enough
slaves for the declining tobacco plantations of Virginia and the
ricefields of South Carolina. But then came an economic revolution in the South starting from the last years of the eighteenth
century as a result of the invention and use of the cotton gin. This
led to the remarkable spread of the 'cotton kingdom' especially
towards the southwest. The successful cultivation of sugar cane
in the hot and humid Mississippi delta, and the westward
expansion of the tobacco plantations to new and fertile lands,
also served to re-energize the hitherto waning institution of
slavery. Manumission, which in the years after American independence, had not been infrequent, virtually came to a halt. But
already a large free Negro population[3] had grown up which was
regarded by the South as an anomaly in, and a threat to its society.
In the North the free Negro fared very little better. For as the
South, newly rehabilitated as a slave society, began taking
measures intended to facilitate the return of free Negroes to
slavery, or to drive them out, the North, fearful of an influx,
seemed to vie with the South in making their lives difficult.

But perhaps the greatest wrong inflicted on the Negro race in

[2] For a comparative study of slavery in Latin and Anglo-Saxon territories, see
Frank Tannenbaum, *Slave and Citizen*, New York 1947; Stanley M. Elkins, *Slavery*,
Chicago 1959; Eric Williams, *Capitalism and Slavery*, London 1964, chap. 1.

[3] In 1800 there were 108,435 free Negroes in the United States. By 1830 this had
risen mainly by natural increase to 319,599, and to 488,070 by 1860. The free Negro
population remained at roughly one-tenth of the entire Negro population. See
Negro Population of the United States, Bureau of Census, Washington 1918, 57.

the nineteenth century was the successful building up of a myth
that the Negro was inherently inferior to other races—a myth that
had been originally elaborated in an attempt to justify Negro
slavery, and later, European imperialism in Africa. In the seven-
teenth and eighteenth centuries, there was no necessity to justify
Negro slavery on specious grounds. The indenture system, which
had once practically enslaved Europeans themselves, was a
marked feature in the early beginnings of European overseas
colonies. At that time, slavery and exploitation was regarded
merely as man's inhumanity to man. But with the easy availability
of Negroes for the expanding plantations of the Americas, and
their easily identifiable physical characteristics, which made their
escape from forced labour difficult and hazardous, Negroes alone
came to be associated with slavery.

But it was the vigorous humanitarian campaign for the abolition
of slavery which spurred slave-holders and their supporters to
defend the institution by asserting that the Negro was an inferior
being, and that slavery was actually for him an elevating process.
By its repetition, the myth-makers and their descendants came
actually to believe that the myth was true. The rise of social
Darwinism in the later part of the nineteenth century with its
theme of the survival of the fittest, provided ready justification for
European imperialism in Africa, and helped further to strengthen
and perpetuate the myth of inherent Negro inferiority.

It was the humiliating lot of the Negro as a human being,
which drove Edward Wilmot Blyden to becoming the greatest
Negro champion of his race in the nineteenth century. Edward
was born, the third of seven children, on 3 August 1832, on the
then Danish West Indian Island of St. Thomas.[4] 'Of ebony hue',
he later claimed to be of 'pure Negro' parentage from the Ibo
tribe in eastern Nigeria. He was of relatively privileged birth. Both
his parents were free and literate. His mother, Judith, was a
school teacher, his father, Romeo, was a tailor. The family lived
in a predominantly Jewish and English-speaking community in
the capital—Charlotte-Amalie—and Edward romped with
Jewish boys on Synagogue Hill, and later proudly pointed out

[4] Biographical details of Blyden's childhood are drawn from the following
sources: Edward W. Blyden, *Liberia's Offering*, New York 1862, introduction;
Edward W. Blyden, *The Jewish Question*, Liverpool 1898, 5–6; Harry Johnston,
Liberia, London 1906, Vol. I, 231; *Lagos Weekly Record*, 1, 29 Nov. 1980; *Sierra Leone,
Weekly News*, XXVIII, 10 Feb. 1912.

that Judah P. Benjamin, 1811–84, the eminent American statesman and jurist, was born in the same neighbourhood. The
Blydens attended the integrated Dutch Reformed Church, and
young Edward went to the local primary school but also received
private tuition from his mother.

In 1842 the family left for Porto Bello, Venezuela, where
Edward, who eventually became a linguist of a high order, first
discovered his facility for learning foreign languages. After two
years, by which time he was fluent in Spanish, the family returned
home. The sensitive and intelligent Negro youth noted and
puzzled over the fact that not only was the majority of his race in
slavery in St. Thomas, but that, in Venezuela, too, Negroes did
most of the menial work. On his return, he attended school only
in the morning, and in the afternoon served a five-year apprentice-
ship as a tailor.

In 1845 a new and important influence came into Edward's life
when the Rev. John P. Knox, a white American, went to St.
Thomas for reasons of health, and assumed the pastorship of the
Dutch Reformed Church. Knox was impressed with the studious
and pious boy of pious parents and became his mentor, encouraging his considerable natural aptitude for oratory and literature.
Mainly because of his close association with the able and kindly
Knox, Edward decided to become a clergyman, an aspiration
which his parents encouraged.

In May 1850, Edward accompanied Mrs. Knox to the United
States and attempted to enrol in Rutgers' Theological College,
Knox's *alma mater*. But he was refused admission because he
was a Negro. Efforts to get him enrolled in two other theological Colleges also failed. In addition to this disappointment,
he had the traumatic experience of seeing the Fugitive Slave Law
(1850) come into operation.[5] In the battle between the slave-
holding South and the abolitionist North which during the previous two decades had yearly grown fiercer and more bitter, the
new measure represented a major triumph for the slave states. It
gave Federal commissioners unlimited powers for the apprehension
and return of runaway slaves. But the bonus rewards for returning
alleged fugitives, plus the fact that they could not summon wit-

---

[5] Blyden recalled this many years later: Blyden to Coppinger, 13 Sept. 1884,
A.C.S. Papers, Vol. 21. Some free Negroes were seized as runaway slaves, see Benjamin Brawley, *A Short History of the American Negro*, New York 1950, 84.

nesses or testify on their own behalf, meant, in effect, that free
Negroes, too, were at the mercy of unscrupulous slaveholders and
commissioners. Understandably, Blyden, like most other free
Negroes, had 'a great fear of being seized for a slave'.

In the United States, Edward came under the influence of
prominent Presbyterians who were associated with the Negro
colonization movement, among them, John B. Pinney, Walter
Lowrie, and William Coppinger; and these men, together with the
Knoxes, helped him to make immediate future plans. Both Pinney
and Lowrie had been prominently associated with the American
Colonization Society since the early thirties. Indeed, Pinney, had
been a Presbyterian missionary in Liberia and had filled the
position of Governor for a few months in 1834. In 1850 Pinney
was on the executive board of both the American Colonization
Society and the New York Colonization Society, one of its sub-
sidiaries, whose *Journal* he edited. Lowrie was an executive of the
Presbyterian Board of Foreign Missions; and Coppinger was the
22-year-old Secretary of the Pennsylvania Colonization Society,
later becoming Secretary of the parent Society in 1864, in which
capacity up to his death in 1892 he maintained a regular correspondence with Blyden.

Because of his own frightful experiences, and the increasing
discrimination against free Negroes, it was out of the question
that young Blyden should remain in the United States. What were
the feasible alternatives for him? He might return to St. Thomas
but opportunities here were severely limited. He could, like many
free Negroes, emigrate to Canada, and bide his time in hopes that
the abolitionist cause would eventually triumph. But this course
did not appeal to the ardent race-proud young Negro. His
colonization friends had, of course, told him about Liberia, which
in 1847 had become an independent Negro state, and which, they
argued, with the support of young Negroes of his calibre was
bound to become a vigorous nation. The idea of helping to build
a great Negro nation in Africa appealed tremendously to the race-
pride and imagination of Blyden. He unquestioningly accepted
the current view that Africa was the 'dark continent' and that a
new and progressive civilization would be created through the
influence of westernized Negroes. Writing to Pinney from Croton
Falls, New York State, in December 1850, Blyden expressed the
opinion that with adequate support from American Negroes,

Liberia would soon 'include within its limits the dark regions of Ashantee and Dahomey and bring those barbarous tribes under civilized and enlightened influences'.[6] He was not concerned to question the motives of the Society; he was confident that its operation could bring only good to Africa and the Negro race. And so, with encouragement from the Knoxes, he accepted an offer from the New York Colonization Society to pay his passage to Liberia. In mid-December Blyden left New York for Phila-delphia where he was the guest of Coppinger who accompanied him to Baltimore from where on 21 December 1850, he sailed aboard the packet *Liberia*. He was thankful to arrive safely in Monrovia, the capital of Liberia on 26 January 1851, after a stormy Atlantic crossing during which he at times despaired of ever reaching his destination.[7]

In order to view his life and work in perspective, it is pertinent briefly to take note of his pan-Negro predecessors, and the ideas which influenced them. For, even before Blyden, other New World Negro leaders had devised or supported plans which they hoped would bring dignity and respect to their race. Because the lot of the Negro in the U.S.A. had been the worst, it was from among them and West Indian Negroes who had experienced American discrimination that pan-Negro nationalism emanated.[8] In the first three decades of the nineteenth century four outstand-ing leaders—Paul Cuffee, Daniel Coker, Lott Cary and Jamaican-born, John B. Russwurm—advocated the emigration of free American Negroes to Africa, held visions of progressive nations rising on that continent, and all but Cuffee played prominent roles in the early history of Liberia.

The vision of a regenerated Africa originated in the late eighteenth century with the influential British evangelical and humanitarian movement which directed its energies against slavery and the slave trade and towards the 'civilization' of Africa through Christianity and commerce. The founding of Sierra Leone in 1787 was the first practical manifestation in Africa of this influence. Its founders optimistically regarded Sierra Leone as a centre from which Christianity and commerce would radiate

    [6] *New York Colonization Journal*, 1 Dec. 1850.
    [7] Blyden to Lowrie, Feb. 1852, *P.B.F.M. Papers*, Vol. 3.
    [8] For a fuller discussion of this, see Hollis R. Lynch, 'Pan-Negro Nationalism in the New World before 1862', *Boston University Papers on Africa*, Vol. II, 1966, 149–79.

in Africa primarily through the agency of westernized Negroes. To the first colonists, among whom were 377 Negroes from Britain, were added 1,131 Negro emigrants from Nova Scotia in 1792, and 500 Maroons from Jamaica in 1800.[9] In 1804, the Church Missionary Society began work in the colony. In 1807 the British Government outlawed the slave trade and on 1 January 1808, assumed from the Sierra Leone Company the direct control of the colony for use as the centre for the suppression of the slave trade in West Africa, as well as for settling and civilizing liberated Africans. By this time Sierra Leone had a population of nearly 2,000 westernized Negroes and had become a logical focus for further New World Negro emigration.

Significantly, it was in 1808 that Paul Cuffee, the first American Negro leader to champion 'repatriation', made his first enquiries about Sierra Leone.[10] Cuffee was influenced by the prevailing ideas for the 'regeneration' of Africa. Among his plans were the promotion of selective American Negro emigration to Sierra Leone, the suppression of the slave trade, and the inauguration of a vast trade between Negro America and West Africa designed to enhance the wealth and prestige of the race; and an intensive programme of Negro education as a necessary prerequisite for the building of sovereign new nations in Africa. He made two trips to Sierra Leone: the first in 1811 was exploratory; on his second in 1815 he brought over thirty-eight Negroes largely at his own expense.

Cuffee's trips had important consequences: they demonstrated the feasibility of colonizing free American Negroes in Africa, and the idea was earnestly taken up in America by a curious combination of the humanitarians and the slave-holders. The humanitarians believed that such a colonization scheme would give American Negroes genuine freedom as well as constitute them agents of civilization in Africa, while the slave-holders were interested in getting rid of free Negroes who posed a possible threat to the institution of slavery. These two incongruous elements founded the American Colonization Society in 1817, and

[9] R. R. Kuczynski, *Demographic Survey of the British Colonial Empire*, London 1948, 40–3; Christopher Fyfe, *A History of Sierra Leone*, London 1962, 13–19.
[10] For Cuffee's biography, see Henry Noble Sherwood, 'Paul Cuffee', *Journal of Negro History*, VIII, April 1923, 153–229; also Henry N. Sherwood, 'Paul Cuffee and his Contribution to the American Colonization Society', *Proceedings of the Mississippi Valley Historical Association*, VI, 1913, 370–402.

their efforts led to the establishment of Liberia.[11] Cuffee had been earmarked for the leadership of the Society's colony but died before the first expedition could leave, and shortly before his death cautioned American Negroes against too eager co-operation with the Society. In expressing this view he was reflecting the strong feeling of the majority of American Negroes against the Society which they regarded merely as the tool of slave-holders.

But Coker, Cary, and Russwurm all came to regard the motives of the Society as irrelevant; for them what was important was the opportunity of building civilizations in Africa which might command the respect of the world. Indeed, Coker[12] was among the first eighty-eight Negroes sent out by the Society in 1820, and it was he rather than the three white officials whom the emigrants regarded as their leader. Before emigrating, Coker had been the schoolmaster and the religious leader to the free Negro community of Baltimore. In a pamphlet written in 1810, he had angrily denounced the institution of slavery and had asserted that despite its handicap, 'the African Race . . . had given proof of talents', Coker's strong race pride led him to play an important role in the Negro breakaway from the Methodist Episcopal Church which resulted in the formation in 1816 of the African Methodist Episcopal Church. Elected its first bishop, he declined the honour in order to go to Africa to help in the laying of the foundation of a Negro nation. In the two years of hardship and uncertainty before the emigrants finally settled at Cape Mesurado —the first beginnings of Liberia—the leadership of the colonists devolved largely on him.

Lott Cary, who was among the second group of emigrants, played a versatile role as clergyman, doctor, militiaman, builder, and pioneer in agriculture.[13] He had given up a position as a well-to-do Baptist preacher in Richmond, Virginia, to go to Africa to 'labour for his suffering race'. Russwurm was one of the first

[11] The two major works on the Society are: Early Lee Fox, *The American Colonization Society, 1817–1840*, Baltimore 1919; and P. J. Staundenraus, *The African Colonization Movement, 1816–1865*, New York 1961.

[12] See *A Dialogue Between A Virginian and an African Minister, Written by Daniel Coker, a Descendant of Africa,* . . . Baltimore 1810; *The Journal of Daniel Coker, A Descendant of Africa . . . in the ship Elizabeth, on a Voyage for Sherbro in Africa . . .* Baltimore 1820.

[13] Johnston, *op. cit.,* 135; Archibald Alexander, *A History of Colonization on the Western Coast of Africa*, Philadelphia 1846, 241–54; J. B. Taylor. *A Biography of Elder Lott Cary, Late Missionary to Africa*, Baltimore 1837

Negro graduates from an American College, and in March 1827, co-founded and edited the first American Negro newspaper, *Freedom's Journal*.[14] Two years later he announced his conversion to the view that the free American Negro could help himself and his race best by giving strong support to Liberia. He emigrated in late 1829, and in 1830 founded the pro-colonization *Liberia Herald*. He also held the positions of Superintendent of Education and Colonial Secretary. From 1836 until his death in 1851, he was Governor of Maryland, a colony adjacent to Liberia to the south, which was founded by the Maryland Colonization Society in 1834. As the first 'coloured' governor of a West African colony, Russwurm always regarded the conduct of his office as a test of the ability of the Negro. His governorship was regarded by the Society as highly successful.

If the four above-mentioned pan-Negro nationalists owed much of their ideas about the future of Africa to humanitarian and missionary propaganda, they added their own contribution by asserting or implying that the Negro race had a worthy past, and that undoubtedly a great future awaited black Africa. Although the status of free American Negroes continuously deteriorated, no other American champion of the pan-Negro cause succeeded those strong and ambitious men before the half century had run its course; but as if by way of compensation for the lapse, a new champion came on the scene, the most vigorous, dedicated and greatest of them all—Edward Wilmot Blyden.

[14] See William M. Brewer, 'John B. Russwurm', *Journal of Negro History*, XIII, Oct. 1928, 413–22. Russwurm was a graduate of Bowdoin University, Brunswick, Maine.

2. Liberia and Pan-Negro Plans
1850-62

Because Blyden believed that Liberia had to play the central role in any attempt to elevate the Negro race, it is pertinent to examine briefly the republic's history and society. A strong sense of mission had informed the activities of the earliest emigrants to Liberia. They had emigrated, they felt, for the purpose of laying the foundation of a nation which would reflect credit on the Negro race, and up to the 1830's visitors to Liberia commented favourably on its progress.[1] But from 1827 the Negroes sent out by the Society were generally of a poor quality: the majority of them were slaves who had been set free expressly for emigration, and only because they had become a financial burden rather than an economic asset to their owners. Blyden himself was to protest strongly against the practice of slave-holders who 'desiring to be lauded for humanity and benevolence' foisted upon Liberia 'a set of worn-out, miserable wrecks of humanity who immediately upon their arrival are thrown upon the charity of the community'.[2]

It is, then, not surprising that the promising progress which Liberia had made in its early history was not sustained.[3] Among the factors retarding the progress of Liberia was the existence, as in America, of social stratifications based on colour—the mulattoes considering themselves superior to the black emigrants, while the colonists, generally speaking, believed the indigenous peoples inferior to them.[4] There was, too, very little economic development: there were, it is true, some thriving plantations on the St. Paul's River, but the most intelligent, industrious and enterprising Liberians tended to neglect agriculture for trading, which

[1] F. H. Rankin, *The White Man's Grave*, London 1836, Vol. I, 36–40; MacGregor Laird and R. A. K. Oldfield, *Narrative of an Expedition into the Interior of Africa*, London 1837, 41–3.

[2] Edward W. Blyden, *A Voice from Bleeding Africa*, Monrovia 1856, 26.

[3] Johnston, *op. cit.*, 149, 182–4.

[4] Abayomi Karnga, *History of Liberia*, Liverpool 1926, 25.

brought quick profits; these were unfortunately spent on con-
spicuous consumption and in a non-productive way.[5]

Until its independence, the American Colonization Society
constituted the supreme authority of the colony. Independence
came from the desire on the part of some Liberians for the
sovereign power necessary to deal with recalcitrant European
traders who flouted the commercial regulations of the colony.[6] And
so, on 26 July 1847, Liberia became a sovereign nation with a
constitution modelled on that of the United States. Ironically, its
sovereignty was quickly recognized by all the major nations,
except the United States, where the influence of the slave states
prevented recognition of a nation that had been comprised, to a
large extent, of ex-slaves; it was not until April 1862—during the
course of the American Civil War—that the United States formally recognized Liberia's independence.

The Liberian constitution contained provisions which later
kept the young nation in a chaotic, political condition: the
President, the House of Representatives, and half of the Senators
were to be elected every two years. The franchise was confined
almost exclusively to American colonists. Nevertheless after its
independence, there were some signs that Liberia might make
rapid progress. Its political sovereignty invested it with a new
significance in the eyes of New World Negroes. Congratulations
to the new Republic had come from several parts of the Negro
World and many hoped with John B. Hepburn of Port-au-Prince,
Haiti, that Liberia's course was now 'onward to empire and to
fame'.[7] Among American Negroes the new interest in Liberia
reflected itself in a substantial increase in the number of emigrants. The number rose dramatically from 51 in 1847 to
441 in 1848—the year after Liberia's independence—and this
new rate of emigration was maintained for more than a decade.[8]
Also important was the fact that the majority of these emigrants
were from the free Negro community and were people of some
property and education.

At the time of Blyden's arrival, Liberia was a country of roughly

[5] George Brown, *The Economic History of Liberia*, Washington 1941, 141.

[6] Johnston, *op. cit.*, 187–95; Ernest Jerome Yancy, *Historical Lights of Liberia's
Yesterday and Today*, Ohio 1934, 49.

[7] *Maryland Colonization Journal*, IV, 1848, 213.

[8] American Colonization Society, *Fifty-Second Annual Report*, Washington 1869;
see inside back cover.

13,000 square miles, with a coastline of approximately 300 miles. Its emigrant population, depleted by a high mortality rate, was just over 6,000, living mainly in small and scattered settlements. Monrovia, the capital built on Cape Mesurado peninsula, was easily the largest settlement with a population of 1,300, and gave the appearance of a quiet village.[9] Modelled on Washington, D.C., it was ambitiously laid out with wide, unpaved streets, covered with grass and periodically with huge obtruding boulders. One entered it via 'miserable fishing huts', mangrove swamps and across a 'rickety bridge'.[10] The houses in the town were of wooden frames built on elevated stone or brick foundations. Altogether, Monrovia was not an attractive showcase for the new Negro Republic.

When Blyden arrived in Monrovia, he seemed to have had no firm plans. He noted regretfully, that there was no opportunity to practise his skill as a tailor because all clothing was imported readymade.[11] But he had been provided with contacts. After a short stay in the capital, he went to Bexley, a village on the left bank of the St. John's River eight miles from the coast, as the guest of a Mr. Charles Gray.[12] After a stay here, he went to the near-by coastal trading settlement of Grand Bassa, as the guest and probably the clerical assistant of Stephen A. Benson, a prosperous trader, who was to succeed J. J. Roberts in 1856 as the second President of Liberia. At Benson's home, Blyden was gratified to find evidence of Liberian loyalty to the Negro race: on a wall was a signed portrait of the militant American Negro leader, Henry Highland Garnet, with his motto: 'Better die free men than live to be slaves.'[13]

By mid-August 1851, Blyden was back in Monrovia where,

[9] W. Winwood Reade, *The African Sketch-Book*, London 1873, Vol. II, 249; also W. Winwood Reade, *Savage Africa*, London 1863, 29.

[10] J. A. B. Horton, *West African Countries and Peoples* . . . , London 1868, 270: Horton, a champion of his race and one of the earliest West African nationalists, was disappointed at the appearance of Monrovia when he visited the town early in 1866. He had added that 'The entrance to Monrovia . . . reminds one of the entrance to a purely native town where the light of civilization has never reached, and it gives to the casual observer the idea of a want of firm government, a want of revenue, a want of developmental powers, and the existence of great inertia in the municipal authority. . . .'

[11] Blyden to Lowrie, Feb. 1851, *P.B.F.M. Papers*, Vol. 3.

[12] *African Repository*, XXVII, Sept. 1851, 107.

[13] *Monrovia Observer*, V, 12 Jan. 1882. Blyden recalled this incident on 4 Jan. 1882 at a reception for Garnet as the new U.S. Minister to Liberia.

although suffering from 'acclimating sickness', he earned his
board as a part-time clerk for a merchant, and resumed his studies
at Alexander High School, a new Presbyterian institution under
the principalship of the Rev. D. A. Wilson, a graduate of Princeton Theological Seminary. The school had about a dozen students
and was badly housed and ill-equipped in a small dark rented
lower storey, formerly used as a grocery store. Here Blyden began
his part-time study of theology, the classics, geography and
mathematics. So impressed was Wilson with his exceptional
ability and exemplary character that he wished Blyden to devote
himself fully to study.[14] Wilson was able to persuade Knox and
his congregation in St. Thomas jointly with the Presbyterian
Board of Foreign Missions to pay for his upkeep so as to permit
him to become a full-time student. Blyden devoted most of his
spare time to a study of Hebrew (with which he had made his first
acquaintance as a boy living in a Jewish neighbourhood) so that
he could read passages in the Bible purporting to relate to the
Negro.[15]

Blyden made rapid progress. In 1853 he became a lay preacher,
and in 1854, a tutor at his High School, and acted as Principal
during Wilson's frequent absences through illness. In 1858 he was
ordained a Presbyterian minister, and at the same time succeeded
Wilson as Principal of Alexander High School where he worked
with rare devotion under unfavourable conditions. He wanted to
make the High School a model institution. He pleaded, unsuccessfully, with the Presbyterian Board to have the school more
attractively housed, and provided with adequate facilities for a
much larger number of students than the fifteen with whom he
began his principalship. He begged constantly, and sometimes
successfully, for books and journals from America and England.[16]

[14] D. A. Wilson to J. L. Wilson, 1 Oct. 1851, *P.B.F.M. Papers*, Vol. 3; D. A.
Wilson to J. P. Knox, 23 Jan. 1852, in Edith Holden, *The Story of Blyden*,
1940.

[15] Edward W. Blyden, 'The Negro in Ancient History', *The Peoples of Africa*,
New York 1871, 1; Blyden, *The Jewish Question*, 7: Blyden sought help from Dr.
Isidor Kalisch, the distinguished Jewish American scholar who sent him 'a Hebrew
Grammar with the Key and his commentaries on Exodus and Genesis'.

[16] Blyden to W. E. Gladstone, 20 April 1860, *British Museum Add. Mss.*, 44393/
271; Blyden to Gladstone, 25 April 1861, *ibid.*, 44395/223; Blyden to John
L. Wilson, 2 Feb. 1859, *P.B.F.M. Papers*, Vol. 5; Blyden to John L. Wilson,
8 Dec. 1859, *ibid.*, Vol. 6; Blyden to Lord Brougham, 5 Sept. 1863, *Brougham
Papers*.

However, he carried on, uncritically, his predecessor's concentration on the teaching of classics.

He wished to prepare himself thoroughly for leadership, and unlike other Liberians, believed that the prerequisite for this was intense intellectual training. In a country where all ambitious young men became traders, he disdained 'commerce, manufactures, or any of the other money-making pursuits'.[17] He kept up with current affairs outside Liberia by reading available British and American newspapers and journals. So great was his conception of the duties involved as a leader in Liberia, that despite his exemplary industry, he continued to feel that his knowledge and training were too limited. It is typical of him that in March 1858, one month before he was due to be ordained as a Presbyterian Minister, he wrote to the Presbyterian Board of Foreign Missions appealing for assistance to study for a further two years at one of the theological colleges in the United States. 'I feel', he wrote, 'that to start out just now as I am upon the duties of life, particularly duties of so high a character would be to invite failure.'[18]

Unsuccessful in this plea, he sought to widen his education by seeking interesting correspondents in England. The first of these, significantly, was an ex-teacher and clergyman, Rev. Henry Melvill, a former Principal of East India College, Haileybury, and at the time Canon of St. Paul's.[19] But his most important correspondent in this period was W. E. Gladstone, the British Chancellor of the Exchequer, to whom he had been attracted because of their mutual interest in classical literature, and because Gladstone's free trade views coincided with his. Blyden first wrote to the British minister on 20 April 1860, and after apologizing profusely for 'intruding upon the time and patience of one so distinguished', went on to ask for study advice in his pursuit of classical languages and literature, and for the gift of a small library composed of twelve major works in the field.[20] As justification for this request, he acquainted Gladstone with his views of Liberia's role in Africa: 'This little Republic . . . is no doubt destined . . . to revolutionize for good this whole part of Africa. But we need, in order to carry out the great work . . . men of

[17] Blyden to J. L. Wilson, 20 Mar. 1859, *P.B.F.M. Papers*, Vol. 5.
[18] Blyden to J. L. Wilson, 5 Mar. 1859, *ibid*.
[19] Blyden to J. L. Wilson, 2 Feb. 1859, *ibid*. I have been unable to trace this correspondence.
[20] Blyden to Gladstone, 20 April 1860, *op. cit.*

enlightened minds, of enlarged views, of high-toned character.'
To the responsive British minister, Blyden further emphasized
that his request for help was not a selfish one: 'My desire to en-
large my education arises from the interest I feel in the Negro
race, and my great anxiety is to labour with increased efficiency
to promote and accelerate that progress.'[21]

But even during this 'period of preparation' for leadership,
Blyden was no ivory-tower scholar. He participated actively in
public life and won the admiration of the leading men. A year
after arriving in the Negro Republic, it was reported of him that
'It is such men that, above all others, are pressingly needed
here. . . Here is one willing to devote himself to the cause of Negro
elevation.'[22] Soon after settling, he became a correspondent of the
Liberia Herald, an organ of the government and the only newspaper in Liberia, and was appointed by President Roberts as its
editor for a year in 1855-6. He played his part, too, in the
defence of the Republic. In January 1852, the Liberians sent an
expedition against the Kru people; he was unable to accompany
it but kept guard at night. In 1853, he was part of a Liberian
expedition against a recalcitrant Vai chief, King Boombo.

These two military experiences are instructive in showing
Blyden's attitude to Africans. The Krumen had been defeated and
Blyden's reaction was that of a typical Liberian emigrant. He
reported to a friend that the 'enemy' had been 'subdued' and
added, 'Surely, God is on our side.'[23] But his attitude to Africans
was soon to change. His journey to Boombo's town at Cape
Mount was his first major contact with indigenous Africans, and
he came away impressed. He found King Boombo's town 'remark-
ably fortified', and saw this as evidence of 'the inventive genius
of the natives', and proof of 'the unfairness of those who represent the native Africans as naturally indolent, and living in a state
of ease and supineness'.[24] Henceforth, Blyden was to berate
Liberians for making a distinction between themselves and the
native Africans, and urged that they should be encouraged to
participate in the life of the Republic.

[21] Blyden to Gladstone, 7 Sept. 1860, *British Museum Add. Mss.* 44394/102.
[22] D. A. Wilson to J. P. Knox, 23 Jan. 1852, in Holden, *The Story of Blyden*; also
African Repository, Sept. 1851, 266.
[23] Blyden to J. P. Knox, Feb. 1852, cited in Holden, *op. cit.*
[24] *New York Colonization Journal*, 111, July 1853.

Blyden became, too, a propagandist for the pan-Negro cause. His writing appeared in the *African Repository*, the journal of the American Colonization Society, the *Journals of the New York and Maryland Colonization Societies*, and as privately published pamphlets, and were characterized by advocacy of American Negro emigration to Liberia, defence of the Negro Republic from the unsympathetic attacks of foreigners, criticisms of its short-comings, patriotic admonitions to his fellow-citizens, and an attempt to vindicate the ability of the Negro. His first letter to the United States described his rapture and pride at being on African soil. 'You can easily imagine the delight with which I gazed upon the land ... of *my* forefathers', he wrote. He assured that 'the land here is teeming with everything necessary for the subsistence of man'; he advised the sceptics to come and see for them-selves.

An opportunity for him to act as defender and champion of Liberia came in 1852 when Gerrit Smith, a United States Senator from New York and a former supporter of Negro colonization who had become one of its severest critics, in opposing a proposed scheme to send New York Negroes to Liberia, dubbed the American Colonization Society 'the deadliest enemy of the Negro race' and Liberia 'a frightful graveyard'.[25] Blyden argued that Smith was well-meaning but was 'doing ... considerable harm ... by blinding the minds of colored men to their true interests'. Colonization in Africa, he contended, was 'the only means of delivering the colored man from oppression and of raising him up to respectability'. He was contemptuous of the advice of Smith and other abolitionists that, if necessary, free Negroes should retire to Canada to await the outcome of the issue of slavery. Admitting that the mortality rate in Liberia was high, Blyden claimed that this was a temporary condition, common to all pioneer communities: it was an unimportant consideration in view of the high purpose for which Liberia existed.[26] This passion-ate rebuke of a famous philanthropic figure made Blyden at twenty, the foremost champion of Liberia.

While Blyden was reproving Senator Smith, Martin R. Delany,

[25] See Howard H. Bell, 'The Negro Emigration Movement: A Phase of Negro Nationalism', *Phylon*, XX, Nov. 1959, 136.
[26] *Liberia Herald*, III, 7 July 1852; also *Maryland Colonization Journal*, VI, Nov. 1852, 277–80.

a Harvard-trained doctor, and a former newspaper editor and abolitionist, was devising a chimerical scheme for a Negro empire in the Caribbean and South and Central America.[27] He too, had, after the passage of the Fugitive Slave Bill, despaired of American Negroes ever enjoying the full rights of citizenship. But although from his youth he was interested in Africa, he refused to support American Negro emigration to Liberia. Like most American Negro leaders, he had viewed the American Colonization Society as a tool of slave-holders, and was severely critical of Liberia's continued dependence on it.

Delany's attack on the American Colonization Society and Liberia was Blyden's cue for another spirited defence of both.[28] He regarded Delany's plans as a diversionary measure that was doomed to failure. It was only in Africa, he felt, that Negroes could establish an 'empire' of their own.

Meanwhile sentiment for emigration was growing among American Negroes, and in August 1854, the emigrationists, led by Delany, James M. Whitfield, a poet, and James T. Holly, an accomplished episcopalian clergyman, met in conference in Cleveland, Ohio. It was, according to Delany, the most widely representative Negro conference ever convened.[29] Shortly before it met the passage of the Kansas-Nebraska Act (1854) which stipulated that the question of slavery in the western states should be decided by their own legislatures, had provided another triumph for the supporters of slavery. Understandably, the mood of the conference was militant. Here Delany repeated his call for the urgent need of a Negro empire in the New World.[30] A National Emigration Board was set up, and at another conference in August 1856, again held in Cleveland, the delegates reaffirmed their commitment to emigration, and the leaders were authorized to begin negotiations with the various governments of South and Central America and Haiti.

[27] See Martin R. Delany, *The Condition, Elevation and Destiny of the Colored People of the United States, Politically Considered*, Philadelphia 1852.

[28] *Liberia Herald*, III, 6 Oct. 1852.

[29] Martin R. Delany, *Official Report of the Niger Valley Exploring Party*, New York, 1861, 6.

[30] Martin R. Delany, 'The Political Destiny of the Colored Race of the American Continent', Appendix No. 3: *Report of the Select Committee on Emancipation and Colonization*, Washington 1862, 37–59.

Blyden strongly felt that the emigrationists were mis-directing their energies. He wanted all tides of emigration from the United States to flow to Liberia. It is perhaps no coincidence that his first pamphlet was published just before the 1856 Emigration Conference was due to meet. In it he appealed to 'colored men of every rank and station, in every clime and country' to support emigration to Liberia. He told his readers that 'the object of Liberia was the redemption of Africa and the disenthralment and elevation of the African race, objects worthy of every colored man. . . .'[31]

Blyden realized that to give Negroes confidence, self-respect and pride—indispensable attributes for effective race action in Africa—it was necessary to refute charges of Negro inferiority and provide proof of Negro ability. Even as a very young man he had become curious about this history of his race but found that the available material was limited and written mainly by white men whose interpretations were highly prejudiced.[32] He was determined to correct misrepresentations of the Negro. His first letter to the United States from Liberia demonstrates his striving to recall what was worthy in the African past when he claimed Africa as 'the land of Cyprian and Tertullian, ancient fathers in the Christian Church; of Hannibal and Henry Diaz, renowned generals'.[33] Writing in 1856, he asserted that 'the African has no superior among the races and is in advance of some'. He went on to give a list of twenty-seven distinguished Negroes including two eighteenth-century African-born scholars, J. E. J. Capitein, who studied at the University of Leyden and became an author, linguist and theologian, and A. W. Amo, the classical scholar and philosopher who was educated at the University of Wittenberg; the American Negroes, James Derham, a distinguished physician, and Benjamin Banneker, a mathematician and astronomer; Toussaint L'Ouverture, the celebrated general and liberator of Haiti; and Francis William, a Cambridge-educated Jamaican. The majority of slave-holders, 'ordinary white men', could not match the 'intellectual and moral greatness' of many outstanding Negroes, he asserted.[34]

---

[31] Blyden, *Voice from Bleeding Africa*, 27.

[32] Edward W. Blyden, *Christianity, Islam and the Negro Race*, London 1888, see preface.

[33] Blyden to Lowrie, Feb. 1851, *P.B.F.M. Papers*, Vol. 3; *African Repository*, XVII Sept. 1851, 266.

[34] Blyden, *Voice from Bleeding Africa*, 21.

In 1857 Blyden made his first attempt designed specifically to vindicate the Negro race.[35] He examined and rebutted with cogency the theories which purported to prove Negro inferiority. He went to the extent of carefully examining the original Hebrew of verses 25, 26, and 27 of Chapter nine of the Book of Genesis which were commonly cited to prove that Negroes—the offspring of Ham—were under a divine curse and that their enslavement was preordained, and offered elaborate proof that there was no evidence to support the assertion. Indeed, Blyden convincingly argued that all assertions of inherent Negro inferiority were nothing but unfounded propaganda by Anglo-Saxons to justify their atrocities against the Negro. They had unfairly overlooked outstanding Negroes, and taken as typical of the race the most degenerate physical and mental specimens. But he admitted that slavery had had a demoralising effect on American Negroes and urged their leaders to 'use every means' to crush servility because it was 'fearfully injurious' to 'general progress of the race'.[36]

It was because Blyden believed that the Negro was at least potentially the equal of other races, that he was so anxious that Liberia should succeed. And so at twenty, Blyden, a youth of quiet demeanour, frail 'of medium height and physically unprepossessing', found himself giving admonitions usually associated with persons of greater robustness or of more advanced age: he called 'most solemnly upon the young men and women of Liberia to apply themselves to study . . . so as to secure the success of Liberia and the perpetuity of her institutions'.[37] He called, too, upon older Liberians to play their part before they became incapacitated by age.

Blyden was especially disturbed that there were few signs of the emergence of a young and vigorous leadership in Liberia. Thus, when in 1854, both Hilary Teage and Samuel Benedict, two outstanding leaders, died, Blyden felt compelled to issue further criticisms and admonitions:

How painful is the reflection that there are but few of the young men of Liberia who seem to give the future of their country a moment's thought. . . ! O young men and women of Liberia, arise from your lethargy, shake off your puerile notions and practices! It is high time to bestir yourself to be men and women. Let the brave achievements

---

[35] Edward W. Blyden, *A Vindication of the Negro Race*, Monrovia 1857.
[36] *Ibid.*, 64.   [37] *Liberia Herald*, III, 6 Oct. 1852.

and noble deeds of your fathers arouse you to effort. Let the future
glory that awaits your country kindle within you an honourable
ambition and urge you onward.[38]

He wanted to see 'the young men of Liberia like the youth among
the ancient Spartans exercise themselves vigorously in all things
which pertain to the country's welfare!'[39]

Similarly, five years later, the death of the Rev. John Day, a
patriotic Liberian, caused Blyden to deliver a masterly sermon
holding up Day's life as an example to Liberians.[40] John Day was
born free in North Carolina in 1797, grew up under comparatively
favourable circumstances, and became a prosperous member of
the free Negro community. But then, said Blyden, he 'caught the
flame of liberty and independence' and in 1830 emigrated to
Liberia. With unostentatious dedication he played a variety of
roles as missionary, teacher and founder of schools, politician, and
finally Chief Justice of Liberia. 'There was never a time in the
history of Liberia', Blyden pleaded 'when the necessity seemed
greater to hold up to our view whatever was virtuous and
exemplary in the character of our fathers ... ' In an oblique
criticism of Liberian leaders he commented that men like Day
'had no gold and silver to lavish upon improvements; but mark
their superior self-abnegation and heroism, they gave themselves'.

On another occasion—his address in 1857 at the annual celebration of Liberia's independence—he frankly exposed the
deficiences and weaknesses of Liberia. He deprecated the moral
decadence of Liberians, their preoccupation with the material to
the exclusion of the literary or the cultural, their predilection for
the foreign and exotic rather than the native, and their dependence on foreign philanthropy. He warned his countrymen that
'a state of dependence is entirely incongruous with liberty', and
tried to bring them to a sense of their responsibility: 'Liberia is no
place for base inactivity and repose. No: it is the scene of a
struggle; a race down-trodden and oppressed, struggles for a place
among the nations of the earth. In this struggle to be unfaithful
is criminal, to slumber is dangerous, to cease to act is to die.'[41]

[38] *New York Colonization Journal*, IV, Aug. 1854.
[39] *African Repository*, XXXI, April 1855, 18.
[40] Edward W. Blyden, *A Eulogy of Rev. John Day*, Monrovia, 1859.
[41] Edward W. Blyden, *Liberia as She is, and the Present Duty of her Citizens*, Monrovia, 1857, 17.

Blyden's castigation of Liberian life had brought a storm of protest from the ruling class. But, far from being repentant, he was 'glad of the excited feelings of the community on the subject'; it meant that his address had provoked thought and he hoped that this would lead to improvement. Nor was he without support. The Hon. Daniel B. Warner, Secretary of State, fully endorsed Blyden's views. He maintained that such criticisms as Blyden's should have been made much earlier in Liberia, and recommended his address to be read 'from one end of the Republic to the other'.[42]

But it was not Blyden's intention to create dissension. On the contrary, he was always anxious to promote unity. That was why he was so keenly disappointed when the retirement of President Roberts in 1855, brought a fiercely contested presidential election between Stephen Allen Benson and Edward James Roye. Blyden sought to be peacemaker. He deprecated 'partyism' and criticized the holding of biennial presidential elections.[43] He implied that Liberia should be ruled by a meritocracy, but did not elaborate on this, perhaps because it was not clear even in his own mind. At Benson's inauguration, Blyden again called for unity because there was 'a great work to be done . . . high and lofty duties to be executed'.[44] He himself was closely associated with the new President to whom he dedicated his first pamphlet 'as a humble tribute to lofty patriotism, distinguished talents and sincere piety'.[45]

If Blyden did not say explicitly what form of government he thought best for Liberia, he stated cogently what the Republic's 'responsibilities and duties' were:

Liberia occupies a two-fold relation of the deepest interest first, to the aboriginal inhabitants; and secondly, to the descendants of Africa in American thraldom. By the first, we are placed under the obligation to do all we can by effort and example to rescue the heathen around us from moral debasement.

By the second relation, it is incumbent upon us to exert ourselves to the utmost to hasten the disenthralment and elevation of our exiled brethren . . . Here we have the opportunity of compelling the

[42] *Ibid.*, Introduction.
[43] *African Repository*, XXXI, June 1855, 186.
[44] Edward W. Blyden (ed.), *A Brief Account of the Proceedings of the Retirement of President J. J. Roberts and of the Inauguration of Hon. S. A. Benson*, Monrovia 1856, 35.
[45] Blyden, *Voice from Bleeding Africa*, see dedication.

world to an audience. Standing upon the soil of freedom in the land of our forefathers, and employing the powerful lever furnished by the combination of Religion, Literature, Science and Arts, we have a fulcrum and a lever wherewith we can move the world on behalf of our race.[46]

If he called for reform within Liberia, he was equally critical of external influences which threatened to retard its progress. Such a threat existed in the late 1850's with the attempt of the French Government to recruit 'voluntary labour' from West Africa for her West Indian colonies. In fact, ruse and coercion were sometimes used to secure recruits, creating 'jealousies and unrest' among the Liberian tribes. Blyden saw it as his duty to expose an operation 'so disastrous' to Liberia's welfare.[47]

Blyden had proved to be a reformer and an idealist. Such a man in any society is bound to be part of a small minority, and yet he fervently wished all Liberians to share his dedication to country and race. Many of the aspects of Liberian life he criticized, for example the preoccupation with achieving material success and the lack of cultural and intellectual interests, are common failings in all new frontier societies. The demands which Blyden made of Liberians were such that more advanced and sophisticated societies would find hard to meet. But to view it thus is to look at it through ordinary rational eyes. And Blyden was a visionary determined that Liberia should do the impossible, if needs be, to elevate the Negro race. Only such a man would write 'Let me forever be discarded by the black race, and let me be condemned by the white, if I strive not with all my powers, if I put not forth all my energies' to bring respect and dignity to the Negro race.[48]

It is interesting to note that his despair over Liberia always alternated with hope for a successful future. Writing to an American friend in December 1858, he expressed the opinion that Liberia was having a healthy influence on indigenous Africans, adding hopefully: 'The native mind is undergoing a complete revolution. There exists among them the belief that some great day is approaching for Africa—some year of golden harvest.'[49]

[46] Blyden, *Liberia . . . and the . . . Duty of her Citizens*, 9–10.
[47] Blyden, 'A Chapter in the History of the Slave Trade', *Liberia's Offering*, 151–66.
[48] Blyden to J. L. Wilson, 9 June 1860, *P.B.F.M. Papers*, Vol. 6.
[49] Blyden to Wilson, 8 Dec. 1859, *ibid*.

Likewise, he was optimistic that Liberians were 'doubtless the forerunners of a powerful exodus ... the pioneers of a large empire'. He saw 'visions of a mighty Christian influence being exerted over the length and breadth of Africa', and that continent 'rising on the wings of a Christian civilization, the last ... of time's empire and the noblest'.[50]

The major justification for Blyden's grand vision was his knowledge that there was an ever-increasing feeling for emigration on the part of American Negroes as a result of further discriminatory measures taken against them. In 1857, American Negroes received a rude shock by the Dred Scott Decision in which the Supreme Court laid down two principles: that slaves were property, and could not bring a suit in the federal courts, and secondly, that residence of a slave in a free state did not make him a free man. In effect, the highest court of the land had given legal sanction to slavery.[51] In addition, the founding of the avowedly anti-slavery Republican Party and the abortive attempt led by John Brown, the fiery abolitionist, to seize the Federal arsenal at Harper's ferry in 1859, had served further to exacerbate feelings against the Negro, and consequently to give impetus to the emigration movement.

By 1858, the geographical bases for a pan-Negro programme had been more realistically narrowed to Haiti and West Africa. Delany had given up his fanciful scheme for a New World Negro empire, and had decided to explore the Niger Valley in search of a base for building a Negro nation. He had come to this decision through reading 'the interesting and intelligent account' of Yorubaland, in a book published in 1857 by the American missionary and explorer, Thomas J. Bowen.[52] Robert Campbell, a young Jamaican chemist, agreed to be Delany's assistant on the expedition. At the third National Emigration Conference which met in Chatham, Ontario, Canada, in August 1858, Delany's new plans were endorsed. In 1858, too, the African Civilization Society was founded, with Henry Highland Garnet as President 'to establish in West Africa a grand center of Negro nationality from which shall flow the streams of commercial, intellectual and

---

[50] Blyden, *Liberia ... and the ... Duty of her Citizens*, 35.

[51] John Hope Franklin, *From Slavery to Freedom*, New York 1956, 264.

[52] Delany, *Official Report of the Niger Valley Exploring Party*, 10; Thomas J. Bowen, *Central Africa: Adventures and Missionary Labors in the Interior of Africa, 1849–1856*, Charleston 1857.

political power which shall make colored people everywhere respected.'[53] Garnet also supported American Negro emigration to Haiti.

Since 1804, when the former Negro slaves of Haiti, led by Toussaint L'Ouverture, wrung independence from the reluctant hands of France, many New World Negroes hoped that it would provide a convincing answer to assertions of Negro inferiority by its progress. But, consumed with internal conflict, Haiti failed to fulfill its early promise. Yet it remained potentially an asylum for New World Negroes, and indeed had over the years attracted a trickle of New World Negroes. In the late 1850's James T. Holly and other American Negro leaders began advocating large-scale emigration to Haiti.[54] This emigration movement received a fillip in 1859 when the Haitian Government itself gave official sanction to it.[55] But Blyden continued to maintain that only Africa could suffice as the scene of future Negro greatness.

Meanwhile, Campbell and Delany had travelled separately to West Africa. Campbell landed at Sierra Leone on 12 July 1859, and after a few days here made further short stops at Cape Palmas and Cape Coast before arriving at Lagos on 21 July.[56] While waiting for Delany to join him, he travelled as far as Abeokuta. Delany sailed from New York aboard the Liberian vessel *Mendi* on 24 May, arriving in Monrovia in early July. Blyden was ecstatic at the visit of the Negro leader, and was prominent among those who welcomed him. At a large public meeting in Monrovia, Delany was thunderously applauded when he reported that 'the desire for African nationality has brought me to these shores'.[57] And Blyden, glad of the new attention which Delany paid to Liberia, referred to him as 'the far-famed champion of the elevation of colored men', and the 'Moses' who would 'lead the exodus of his people from the house of bondage'.[58] At a private meeting at Grand Bassa Blyden and other 'eminent Liberians' approved

[53] *Weekly Anglo-African*, I, 3 Sept. 1859.

[54] See James T. Holly, *A Vindication of the Capacity of the Negro Race for Self-Government, and Civilized Progress, as Demonstrated by Historical Events of the Haitian Revolution; and the Subsequent Acts of the People since their National Independence*, New Haven 1857.

[55] James Redpath, (ed.) *A Guide to Hayti*, Boston 1861, 97–9; *New York Colonization Journal*, X, July 1860.

[56] Robert Campbell, *A Pilgrimage to My Motherland*, New York 1861, 11.

[57] *Weekly Anglo-African*, I, 1 Oct. 1859.

[58] *New York Colonization Journal*, IX, Oct. 1859.

Delany's 'mission and policy'.[59] On 26 July Delany participated in the celebration of the twelfth year of Liberia's independence. On 1 August Delany and Blyden both spoke at the twenty-fifth anniversary of the emancipation of West Indian Negroes. Altogether, Delany spent ten weeks in Liberia and was especially impressed with the vicinity of the St. Paul's River—its beautiful location, its thriving sugar and coffee plantations, its 'livestock of all kinds' and its neat brick buildings.[60] Although still wishing to see the Negro Republic more self-reliant, he was now able to recommend it to the 'intelligent of the race'.[61]

From Liberia, Delany travelled to Lagos where he spent five weeks during which he won the confidence of King Docemo. From Lagos he journeyed to Abeokuta where he joined Campbell, and together they spent six weeks touring the principal towns of Yorubaland. On their return to Abeokuta, they held palavers with the Oba and Chiefs, and on 27 December signed a treaty which assigned to them as 'Commissioners on behalf of the African race in America, the right and privilege of settling in common with the Egba people, on any part of the territory belonging to Abeokuta, not otherwise occupied.'[62] Samuel Crowther the famous African Missionary and his son, Samuel Jr. witnessed the signing of the treaty. Delany felt that he had taken the first step in his goal of building a progressive nation in West Africa. And Blyden envisaged the time when all of West Africa would be one vast Negro nation.

Liberia had benefited from the widespread feeling for emigration among American Negroes. In the decade ending 1860, the Negro Republic had settled the unprecedented total of 5,029 emigrants—almost as many as had been settled in the previous thirty years.[63] Stimulated by this steady flow of emigrants, other prominent Liberians joined Blyden in making appeals to American Negroes to come in large numbers. Late in 1860 the Rev. James Payne, a Presbyterian minister, made such a plea in a series of articles in the *Liberian Herald*. About the same time, D. B. Warner, now Vice-President of the Republic, pleaded with

[59] Delany, *Official Report of the Niger Valley Exploring Party*, 23.

[60] *Weekly Anglo-African*, I, 24 Sept. 1859.

[61] *New York Colonization Journal*, IX, Oct. 1859.

[62] Delany, *Official Report of the Niger Valley Exploring Party*, 27.

[63] American Colonization Society, *Fifty-Second Annual Report*, Washington 1869, see inside back cover.

American Negroes to 're-establish themselves in this our fatherland'.[64] In September 1860, Alexander Crummell, a Negro
graduate of Queens' College, Cambridge (1853) and an intellectual episcopalian clergyman, and teacher, who was a close
associate of Blyden, wrote an open letter to American Negroes
urging them to support any scheme, be it emigration or establishment of missionary activities or trade links, which would benefit
Africa and the Negro race.[65] In the early summer of 1861 Blyden
and Crummell on a visit to the United States were to make
personal pleas.

In March 1861 both men were commissioned by the Liberian
Government to interest British and American philanthropists in
Liberian education. In London, Blyden made the personal
acquaintance of, among others, his old correspondents, Gladstone
and Melvill, as well as Lord Brougham, Dr. Thomas Hodgkin,
and Samuel Gurney, all well-known humanitarians.[66] He was able
successfully to raise funds for the purpose of constructing a girls'
school in Liberia. In Edinburgh, the young Liberian spoke
eloquently before the United Presbyterian Synod about Liberia
and its struggles on behalf of the Negro race, and was instrumental in arranging scholarships to the University of Edinburgh
for two of his students.[67]

Blyden himself had received an offer of support at a British
University from Gladstone, together with the Bishop of Oxford
and Lord Brougham. But he declined the generous offer. He
explained that although it had been his 'earnest and all-controlling
desire to obtain a thorough education', the duties to be performed
on behalf of his race were too pressing to permit him to take years
off for further full-time study.[68] Instead, he sought to get the
British statesman to be of service to Liberia. The British Consul-
ship there had been closed as an economy measure. Blyden saw
this as a blow to Liberia's prestige and pressed Gladstone to use
his influence to have a Consul reappointed. But in this he was

[64] African Repository, XXXVI, Jan. 1861, 87.
[65] Alexander Crummell, The Relations and Duties of the Free Colored Men in America
to Africa, Hartford 1861, 27.
[66] Blyden, Liberia's Offering, see introduction; Blyden to J. L. Wilson, 8 June
1861, P.B.F.M. Papers, Vol. 6.
[67] New York Colonization Journal, XI, June 1861.
[68] Blyden to Gladstone, 23 Mar. 1861, British Museum Add. Mss., 444395/
23.

unsuccessful; private philanthropy came easier to Gladstone than public expenditure.

Crummell had preceded Blyden to the United States and the latter joined him there in June 1861 via Toronto. Two months earlier Civil War had erupted between the Union and the Confederacy, but this seemed to make no difference to the plans of the emigrationists. In May, the National Emigration combined with the African Civilization Society in an attempt to raise adequate funds to promote colonization to the Niger Valley.[69]

Blyden and Crummell were as much interested in the emigration movement as in collecting books and raising funds for Liberian schools, and they joined the forces of the emigrationists. Blyden himself welcomed the Civil War as 'the purifier of a demoralized American conscience', and as a possible means of bringing slavery to an end, but he saw no reason why it should delay plans for American Negro emigration to Africa. He told his Negro audiences, hopefully, that Africa was about to take a progressive forward leap, and they were to participate in these 'events . . . of transcendent importance to the race'.[70]

When Blyden and Crummell returned to Liberia in the fall of 1861, they reported that American Negroes were anxious to emigrate. The Liberian government decided to act. The legislature passed an act authorizing the appointment of commissioners 'to present the cause of Liberia to the descendants of Africa in that country, and to lay before them the claims that Africa has upon their sympathies, and the paramount advantage that would accrue to them, their children and their race by their return to the fatherland'.[71] On 18 March 1862, President Benson appointed Blyden, Crummell and J. D. Johnson, a wealthy merchant, as commissioners.

Before leaving again for the United States, Blyden and Crummell had been appointed Professors at Liberia College—the first secular English-speaking institution of higher learning in tropical Africa.[72] Both felt that this was an added reason why American

[69] *Constitution of the African Civilization Society*, New Haven 1861, 4.

[70] E. W. Blyden, *A Hope for Africa*, New York 1861, 17.

[71] *African Repository*, XXXVI, Jan. 1861, 87.

[72] Fourah Bay College was founded in Freetown in 1827 by the C.M.S. for the purpose of training teachers, catechists and missionaries, and it was not until 1864 that the first secular students were admitted. In 1876 it achieved University status by affiliating with Durham University; see chap. 5.

Negroes should support Liberia. Giving the inaugural address at the opening of the College on 23 January 1862, Blyden was optimistic that it would attract Negro scholars and students from all parts and 'draw towards us the attention and respect of the civilized world'.[73] Translating his wish into prophecy, he hailed the institution as 'the precursor of incalculable blessing to this benighted land—as the harbinger of a bright and happy future for science, literature, and art, for the noblest interest of the African'.[74]

The Liberian commissioners left late in March for England and the United States. In England Blyden spent much of his time disseminating information about Liberia. He also visited some English educational institutions, including Cambridge University, as part of his preparation for his 'novel and responsible position' as Professor of Classics at Liberia College.[75]

The commissioners arrived in New York late in May, and Blyden immediately headed South for Washington and was to experience new aspects of American segregation and discrimination. In Philadelphia, he was shocked to find that 'no colored person was allowed to ride in the street-cars of which the city is so full'.[76] From Philadelphia to Washington he was forced to travel in a smoking car 'with all sorts of ruffians and vagabonds, spitting and swearing, and doing everything but what is agreeable to a gentleman'. His pride hurt, his dignity ruffled, his comprehension baffled that American Negroes could submit to such indignities, he poured forth a torrent of flaming anger in a letter to the *Liberia Herald*:[77]

All the way to Washington a feeling of degradation held possession of me. I felt that I would rather be a citizen of Marmora's town[78] with all its attendant disadvantages, than be compelled, as a black man, to live in this country; that I would rather go naked and wander among the natives of the interior than occupy the position of some of the 'respectable colored people' I see here. For then I should feel that I was in a country of my own—untrammelled by the prejudice of 'white thrash' to which many of these intelligent and

[73] Blyden, 'Address at the Inauguration of Liberia College', *Liberia's Offering*, 96.
[74] *Ibid.*, 123.
[75] Blyden to Gladstone, 16 April 1862, *British Museum Add. Mss.*, 44398/183; *New York Colonization Journal*, XII, July 1862.
[76] *New York Colonization Journal*, XII, Nov. 1862.   [77] Reprinted in *ibid.*
[78] The town of an African King—Marmora—in the hinterland of Liberia.

respectable colored people so willingly submit, fondly hoping for the day when things will be better for them.

I thought how sad it was that so many colored people seem disposed to cling to this land—fearing to go to Liberia lest they die of fever. But are they *living* in this country? Their color is the sign of every insult and contumely! Everybody and everything is preferred to them. Afraid of dying! Would it not be much better for the whole five million of them to leave this country, if everyone died in the process of acclimation . . . than to remain in servitude at the base of society? A whole race in degradation! The idea is horrible. If they all went and died it would be a noble sacrifice to liberty.

Blyden suffered further humiliation in Washington. Although Congress had recently recognized Liberia as a sovereign nation, he was debarred from entering the House of Representatives because he was a Negro. And although slaves in the District of Columbia had been freed by an Act of Congress of 16 April 1862, Blyden reported that the Fugitive Slave Law still operated there; and he himself had to get a white man to vouch that he was a free man, before the Provost-Marshall of Washington gave him a written 'permishun' to leave that city.[79] For the next five weeks a bitter and angry Blyden toured the 'principal cities of the North' extending the Liberian invitation to American Negroes. Great was his chagrin when he found the feeling for emigration among American Negroes had perceptibly cooled. He began to berate his audiences for a lack of pride in Africa and a want of feeling of duty towards it. He castigated Negroes for merely expressing 'an indolent and unmeaning sympathy which put forth no effort, made no sacrifices for the sake of advancing African interests' and with 'having no faith in negro ability to stand alone'.[80] He sought to persuade them that it was part of 'a grand Providential design' that they should return and help in the civilizing of Africa; they were to do so before it was 'usurped' by Europeans.[81]

To this transcendental argument, Blyden added a plea based on racial pride:

An African nationality is our great need. . . We shall never receive the respect of other races until we establish a powerful nationality.

[79] Blyden to Gladstone, 16 June 1862, *British Museum Add. Mss.*, 44398/301. Blyden claimed that 'permishun' was the spelling used by the Provost-Marshall.
[80] Blyden, 'The Call of Providence to the Descendants of Africa in America', *Liberia's Offering*, 69.
[81] *Ibid.*, 75.

We should not content ourselves living among other races, simply by their permission or their endurance... We must build up negro states; we must establish and maintain the various institutions; we must make and administer laws, erect and preserve churches ... we must have governments; we must have legislation of our own: we must build ships and navigate them; we must ply the trades, instruct the schools, control the press and thus aid in shaping mankind. Nationality is an ordinance of Nature. The heart of every true Negro yearns after a distinct and separate nationality.

Liberia was offering such:

Liberia, with outstretched arms earnestly invites all to come. We call them forth out of all nations; we bid them to take up their all and leave the country of their exile... We summon them from the States, from the Canadas, from the West Indies, from everywhere, to come and take part with us in our great work.[82]

But the stirring pleas of Blyden and the other Liberian commissioners were to no avail. For, appearances to the contrary, the outbreak of the Civil War was the signal for dropping schemes for Negro emigration. The emigrationists, who had at first regarded the war as irrelevant to their plans, were unable to act because of lack of funds. Negroes saw it as their duty to help the Union defeat the Confederacy. In this way they hoped to bring slavery to an end and win the rights and privileges of American citizenship. Indeed, when in the summer of 1862, Lincoln decided to put into effect his scheme of gradual Negro emancipation with colonization he got no support from American Negro leaders.[83] Among the few consolations Blyden derived from that summer's stay in the United States were extended conversations with Charles Sumner, the ebullient and liberal Senator from Massachusetts and with Oliver Wendell Holmes, the famed American litterateur of Boston.[84]

Blyden had proved that he was a man unsparingly dedicated to his race and his country. He probably made an earlier and more active start than any other prominent nationalist of the nineteenth century. But he was more of a visionary and a man of ideas than a practical man of affairs. Indeed, his visions of the

---

[82] *Ibid.*, 76.

[83] Walter H. Fleming, 'Historic Attempts to Solve the Race Problem in America by Deportation', *Journal of American History*, IV, 1910, 202–4.

[84] *New York Colonization Journal*, XII, Nov. 1862.

future of the race, influenced to some extent by the romantic humanitarian picture of a regenerated Africa, were so splendidly grand as to bear no relation as to what was probable. He never seemed to have thought out the practical implications of his ideas. He gave little thought to the problems of the organization of the mass exodus for which he so devoutly wished, the settlement of emigrants, and of the conflicts physical and cultural, that any massive emigration to an already peopled area would bring. But his commitment to promoting the advancement of his race was complete and he unflaggingly continued his efforts as best he knew.

3. The Pan-Negro Goal, Class and Colour Conflict in Liberia 1862-71

Despite the halt of American Negro emigration to Liberia during the Civil War, Blyden maintained the vision of an expanding and improving Negro Republic. This vision was based on his conviction that although the War had brought the emancipation of American Negroes, they would never be treated as equals in American society, and the realization of this would cause them to seek refuge in Liberia. Blyden was to be disappointed that this anticipated exodus never took place. Further, he was one of the main protagonists in the mulatto-Negro conflict which raged in Liberia in the 1860's retarding the progress of the Republic, and finally causing him to flee in 1871. During these years Blyden was Professor of Classics at Liberia College, and also acted as Secretary of State between 1864-6.

When, in the late summer of 1862, Blyden realized that American Negroes had given up plans for emigration, he turned his attention instead to West Indian Negroes. Ever since their emancipation, West Indian Negroes, particularly those in Jamaica and Barbados, had shown a marked interest in Africa.[1] But because of the lack of adequate financial resources among them, or aid from any quarter, no major emigration scheme was organized. However, it was on the urging of West Indian Negroes that both the British Baptist and the United Scottish Presbyterian Societies began missionary work in West Africa in the 1840's. West Indians played an important role in their work as well as in that of the Basel and Wesleyan missions. And in the 1850's the West Indian Church Association, manned and financed almost wholly by West Indians, began missionary work in the Rio Pongo area in West Africa. During this period, too, West Indian artisans and pro-

[1] A. E. Payne, *Freedom in Jamaica*, London 1946, 73-4; C. P. Groves, *The Planting of Christianity in Africa*, London 1954, Vol. II, 23–44; *A General Account of the West Indian Church Association for the furtherance of the Gospel in West Africa*, London 1853; A. Barrow, *Fifty Years in Western Africa: Being a Record of the West Indian Church on the Banks of the Rio Pongo*, London 1900, passim.

fessionals emigrated to West Africa, particularly Sierra Leone, because of better economic opportunities there.[2]

Blyden sought to keep alive West Indian Negro interest in Africa until a scheme for regular emigration could be implemented.[3] He revisited St. Thomas in November 1862 and persuaded 'the most prominent Negroes' of the island to found the St. Thomas-Liberia Association to encourage emigration to the Negro Republic. On a visit to Bermuda he found 'intelligent and hard-working Negroes' who were anxious to emigrate. From the two islands he despatched circulars to other West Indian islands, extending the invitation of the Liberian Government to Negroes there. Next he visited eastern Canada and exhorted the Negro communities of Halifax and Windsor, Nova Scotia; and St. John's, New Brunswick, to emigrate to Liberia.

Blyden returned to Liberia in February 1863, and took up his appointment as Professor of Greek and Latin at Liberia College. But, in a country where there was a shortage of skilled or educated men, he found it difficult to confine himself to one job. When his friend and colleague, Daniel B. Warner, became President in 1864, Blyden accepted an appointment as Secretary of State, the most important position in the cabinet. In this capacity he continued his efforts to promote West Indian emigration to Liberia. His circular to the West Indian islands had fallen on fertile soil. A West Indian missionary reported that Negroes in British Guiana and St. Kitts had 'fallen in with Blyden's circular';[4] and some in Barbados had founded the 'Fatherland Union Society', and the 'Barbados Company for Liberia'.[5] To further stimulate the feeling for emigration among West Indian Negroes, President Warner issued a proclamation in February 1864 to the 'Brethren of the Antilles . . . of all classes and pursuits' to come to Liberia to 'build up an African Nationality . . . and thus aid in restoring to this ancient cradle of civilization her pristine glory.'[6] The Legislature voted the sum of $4000 for the emigration

[2] Abioseh Nicol, 'West Indians in West Africa', *Sierra Leone Studies*, New series, No. 13, June 1960, 14–23.
[3] Blyden, *Liberia's Offering*, see introduction; Blyden, *The Jewish Question*, 6.
[4] L. M. McKenzie to Alexander Crummell, 13 Sept. 1864, *A.C.S. Papers*, Vol. 13.
[5] John McLain to Blyden, 1 April 1865, *ibid.*
[6] 'A Proclamation To the Descendants of Africa Throughout the West Indian Islands', *A.C.S. Papers*, Vol. 13, No. 10.

scheme, and as an added inducement, offered twenty-five acres of land to the head of each family compared to ten hitherto granted.

The sum voted by the Liberian legislature was far from enough to cover the expenses of one batch of emigrants from the West Indies to Liberia, but Blyden was able to persuade the American Colonization Society to appropriate a sum of $10,000 for use towards this end.[7] Strictly speaking, its constitution permitted the Society to colonize only American Negroes, but because it had money in its coffers and no American Negro volunteers, its executive members had decided to act in a generous spirit. The Society appointed its treasurer, the Rev. John McLain, to go to Barbados to select the emigrants. Out of a large number of volunteers, 346 were carefully selected. The brig *Cora* was chartered for this voyage, and the British Governor, having satisfied himself that 'the Queen's subjects were provided for', the expedition left on 6 April 1865 for Liberia.[8]

The Barbadian emigrants, the most select and highly-skilled group ever to emigrate to Liberia, arrived without loss of life on 10 May, and were eventually settled at Careysburg in the vicinity of the St. Paul's River.[9] They were the first major emigrant group since 1860 and their arrival was regarded as a special event. Among the emigrants was the talented Barclay family, of whom, Arthur, then a boy, was later to have a distinguished public career culminating with his occupancy of the presidency for eight years (1904–12). Blyden and Crummell welcomed the Barbadians 'to a common burden of duty and obligations in this infant state'.[10] But despite this promising start, West Indian emigration to Liberia came to an abrupt end for want of financial resources.

Blyden once again turned his attention to American Negroes hoping that they would resume emigration. He had closely watched the course of the American Civil War and the fortunes of the American Negro. In a letter to Gladstone in June 1864, he condemned the North for not taking a strong moral stand on the

[7] Blyden to J. B. Pinney, 8 Mar. 1864, *ibid.*; Blyden to the Sec. of the American Colonization Society, 10 Mar. 1864, *ibid.*

[8] The American Colonization Society, *Forty-Ninth Annual Report*, Washington 1866, 7–8.

[9] Dr. Laing to McLain, 18 May 1865, *A.C.S. Papers*, Vol. 13.

[10] Alexander Crummell, *Africa and America*, Springfield, Mass., 1891, 429.

war, and the South for its reactionary adherence to the idea of Negro slavery.[11]

If American Negroes shared Blyden's views of both the North and the South, they did not show it in a desire to emigrate. Both Coppinger and McLain reported to Blyden in 1864 that emigration to Liberia was not immediately likely because American Negroes were optimistic of exercising their rights as citizens, but they both added that they believed this optimism was ill-founded and that there might yet be 'a grand exodus of these people to Liberia as their only refuge'.[12] The American Negro mood of hopefulness was reflected at the National Conference of Coloured Men held in Syracuse, New York, in October 1864.[13] The Conference recorded the commitment of Negroes to staying in America and their determination to struggle for rights still denied them; Garnet was alone in arguing that continuing discrimination still justified plans for Negro emigration to Africa.

The substantial contribution of American Negroes to the success of the Union in the Civil War[14] had further heightened their optimism for acceptance as citizens. Negroes had performed so unstintingly and so valiantly as to win the respect even of their former detractors. Blyden noted that 'the heroic martial deeds and ... valorous demeanour' of American Negroes during the war had brought them an improved social status, but he warned that this was bound to be temporary, and insisted that Negroes would never achieve equality with whites in the United States. He expressed the opinion that 'half the time and energy that will be spent by them in struggles against caste ... if devoted to the building up of a home and nationality of their own would produce results immeasurably more useful and satisfactory'.[15]

Blyden's admonition was timely, his prediction turned out to be true. For the humbled South was in no mood to be generous to the Negro. No sooner had the war ended than the white legislatures in the former rebel states enacted 'black codes' which

[11] Blyden to Gladstone, 16 June 1864, *British Museum Add. Mss.*, 44398/301.

[12] Coppinger to Blyden, 7 May 1864, Coppinger Letter-Book, Vol. 1; cf. McLain to Blyden, 7 Sept. 1864, *A.C.S. Papers*, Vol. 13.

[13] *Proceedings of the National Convention of Colored Men ...*, Syracuse, New York 1864.

[14] See Benjamin Quarles, *The Negro in the Civil War*, Boston 1953.

[15] Edward J. Blyden, *Our Origin, Danger and Duties, The Annual Address before the Mayor and Common Council of the City of Monrovia, 26 July 1865*, 36.

restricted the rights and movements of freedmen. Indeed, the end of the war was the signal for a reign of white terror in many parts of the South: hundreds of unarmed freedmen were massacred, and Negro men, women, and children were persecuted in every conceivable way.[16] Also, by February 1866, it was clear that Southern Negroes were not going to receive the 'Forty Acres and a Mule' which the humane Thaddeus Stevens had led them to expect, and which could have provided the economic basis from which they could work to attain real equality.

Under these circumstances, it was not surprising that the thought of emigration should again spring to the minds of many Negroes. On 22 April 1866, Coppinger wrote informing Blyden that so great 'a spirit of emigration to Africa had sprung up among the freedmen' that the Society found itself without the means to send out most of the applicants.[17] In that year the Society sent out 621 emigrants, and 643 and 443 respectively in the following two years.

As in previous years, the feeling for emigration was a true barometer of the pressure being exerted on Negroes. The fall in the number of emigrants was due partly, as Coppinger pointed out to Blyden, to the fact that 'the temper of the country was hostile to colonization',[18] and therefore funds for this purpose could not be easily raised, partly because the start of Radical Reconstruction in the South had again raised the hopes of Negroes. The violent vindictiveness of the South had brought its own nemesis: the North, goaded by the liberal-minded Charles Sumner and Thaddeus Stevens, gave the Negro his civil and political rights and treated white southerners as vanquished traitors. On 2 March 1867, Congress passed the first of a series of Reconstruction Acts which divided the former Confederate states into five military districts under the command of Northern generals. The fourteenth amendment to the Constitution passed on 28 July 1868, gave civil rights to Negroes while disenfranchising the majority of white Southerners. The fifteenth amendment passed on 30 March 1870 was meant to ensure the political rights of Negroes.

[16] Lerone Bennett, *Before the Mayflower*, Chicago 1962, 193. Bennett quotes from the report of General Carl Schurz who made a special investigation of post-war conditions in the South for President Ulysses S. Grant.

[17] Coppinger to Blyden, 22 April 1866, *Coppinger Letter-Book*, Vol. 3.

[18] Coppinger to Blyden, 27 April 1868, *ibid*.

Southern Negroes did not hesitate to use their new-won rights. They filled practically the whole range of state political offices, and to the amazement of sceptics, showed ability comparable to their white counterparts. But Blyden remained unimpressed with these gains. He continued to maintain that American Negroes were too optimistic about their future in the United States. In 1867 he wrote:

They are now . . . carried away by the fascinating and absorbing speculations about the rights and privileges they are to enjoy in that land. Numerous politicians are endeavouring to advance their own ambitious purposes by agitating questions of the black man's future in the United States. But unless they can succeed in altering the estimation of the negro entertained by the masses of white men in that country; unless they can effectively remove the predominant, if not instinctive feeling, that he is, in some way, an alien and inferior being; unless they can succeed in bringing to pass a general and honourable amalgamation, so as to render the social and domestic interest of the two people identical—they will contribute nothing to the solution of the black man's difficulties.[19]

Indeed, Blyden feared that miscegenation would obliterate the Negro type in the United States. And this he regarded as undesirable, because he believed that Africa needed the service of every 'genuine' American Negro.

In 1869, Blyden was still finding it 'difficult . . . to understand how, with the history of the past accessible and the facts of the present before their eyes', Negroes could hope for 'any distinct, appreciable influence' in the United States.[20] He believed that the large European emigration which was then taking place would make it even more difficult for Negroes to make progress. And so he continued to repeat 'with undiminished earnestness the wish . . . that the eyes of the blacks may be opened to discern their true mission and destiny that, making their escape from the house of bondage, they may betake themselves to their ancestral home, and assist in constructing a Christian empire',[21] but to no avail. Yet if in 1871 the lot of the American Negro seemed immeasurably better than it had ever been, as we shall see in Chapter Six, Blyden's prognostication that the Negro would never be accepted

[19] Quoted in American Colonization Society, *Fiftieth Annual Report*, Washington 1867, 15.
[20] Blyden, 'The Negro in Ancient History', *op. cit.*, 32.   [21] *Ibid.*, 34.

by white Americans as an equal was amply justified by events in his own life time.

In Liberia itself much of Blyden's energies were consumed in a conflict between educated blacks and the mulatto ruling class. For the colour problem of America had reproduced itself in Liberia as a dividing and disrupting influence: here near-white replaced white as the badge of the social elite, and mulattoes considered themselves superior to the blacks, took it for granted that they were to be the rulers, and although numerically weak, were able to maintain themselves in positions of power because of their superior economic strength.[22] This division became institutionalized socially in masonic clubs, and politically, into two parties, the Whig being that of the blacks, and the Republican that of the mulattoes.[23] Blyden himself disapproved of masonic clubs and deprecated party politics on the ground that the one fostered unhealthy cliques and the other was for Liberia a harmful luxury. But it would be an over-simplification to suggest that the division between mulattoes and blacks were clear-cut. Exceptional black men were allowed in mulatto circles provided they did not seriously seek to challenge their power. Blyden himself had in 1856 married a mulatto—Sarah Yates—the niece of B. P. Yates, a wealthy merchant who was at that time the Vice-

[22] This aspect of Liberian history has been commented on by several contemporary writers: see Reade, *African Sketch-Book*, 257–8, where he wrote: 'There are no real parties in Liberia. . . . The real parties consist of mulattoes and negroes'; a correspondent of the *African Times* (23 June 1871) wrote that 'There has been for a long time a great division amongst the black population and half-caste. The mulattoes look down on the blacks as inferior, and claim the right to govern, and want to have always a mulatto or half-caste as President.' See also John H. Smyth, U.S. Minister to Liberia, to U.S. Secretary of State, 26 April 1879, *Papers Relating to the Foreign Relations of the United States* (Washington 1879), No. 321, 712–17, who reported: 'This hybrid class the unwritten history of Liberia declared to be superior in intellectual development . . . to the native or emigrant negro. . . . The government was formed with the aboriginal freeman the base, the general structure the emigrant negro, the superstructure the hybrid.'

[23] The factions which existed in the colonial era shortly after independence organized themselves into two political parties: the True Liberian Party—that of the mulattoes, and the Old Whigs—that of the blacks. Between 1865 and 1867 both parties reorganized, the True Liberian Party changing its name to the Republican Party (after the party by that name in the United States), the Old Whigs renaming itself the True Whig Party. See Abayomi Karnga, *A History of Liberia*, Liverpool 1926, 45; Blyden to C. T. O. King, etc., Feb. 1887 (*A.C.S. Papers*, Vol. 18), in which in declining the nomination of the Republican Party for the Presidency, Blyden briefly reviewed the history of party politics in Liberia. He gave 1851 as the date of the founding of the Whig Party.

President of Liberia. Their relationship turned out to be un-congenial, and Blyden claimed that this was because her loyalty to the mulatto clique took precedence over her loyalty to him as her husband; but at least part of the explanation must lie in the fact that his wife was semi-literate and did not share his intel-lectual interest, and that Blyden who became an itinerant with-out a regular income was not a good family provider and far from an ideal husband. At any rate, he became a fanatical opponent of mulattoes because he believed that although they wielded power, they did nothing to promote the interest of Liberia and that of the Negro race. He came to believe that their very presence was an insult to the Negro Republic: in 1888 he wrote to a friend: 'The appearance of the people of Monrovia is enough to disgust any man who came to Africa with the idea of coming to a Negro Republic.'[24]

Symptomatic of the 'colour struggle' was mulatto opposition to Blyden's scheme for promoting the emigration of skilled and intelligent West Indian blacks to Liberia. The mulattoes regarded this as an attempt by Blyden to build up a personal following and a threat to their continued wielding of power. J. J. Roberts, the leader of the mulattoes, and himself with only the slightest trace of Negro blood, and almost indistinguishable from a white man,[25] sought to discourage further West Indian emigration by arguing that West Indians were better suited for living in Sierra Leone 'where the manners and morals of the people are more English, and . . . more adapted to their early habits'.[26] With greater justifi-cation, mulattoes protested against the fact that the land grants were raised from ten to twenty-five acres for the head of each emigrant family especially to facilitate the West Indians; so sharp a cleavage arose over the issue that the Act authorizing the larger land grant had to be repealed.

One of the earliest examples of Blyden's alienation of the mulatto leaders was in 1857 when his Independence Day address obliquely criticized them as being shallow and decadent.[27] A year

[24] Blyden to Coppinger, 29 June 1888, *A.C.S. Papers*, Vol. 30.

[25] Johnston, *op. cit.*, 185, 236; A. Doris Banks Henries, *The Life of Joseph Jenkins Roberts*, London 1964, 76. Roberts was one of the most outstanding early leaders of Liberia and its first President, 1848–56.

[26] Roberts to Coppinger, 15 May 1865, *A.C.S. Papers*, Vol. 13; cf. Reade, *African Sketch-Book*, 258–9.

[27] Blyden, *Liberia . . . and the . . . Duty of her Citizens*, 12–14.

later, latent antagonism between the blacks and the mulattoes crystallized around the choice of a site for Liberia College. The College was being made possible through New England philanthropy: in March 1850 the Trustees of Donation for Education in Liberia was incorporated by an Act of the legislature of Massachusetts, and permitted to hold real estate to the value of $100,000, the income from which was to be used for the promotion of higher education in Liberia.[28] The Boston trustees constituted the ultimate authority of the College, but also associated with it was the New York Colonization Society which set up a special fund for paying the salary of one Professor and providing a limited number of scholarships to deserving students. In December 1851, the Liberian legislature passed an Act incorporating the College and appointing a local Board of Trustees, but partly because of disagreement over the site, it was not until January 1858 that the cornerstone was laid. The blacks, led by Blyden, Crummell and Benson favoured a site in the interior, which, they argued, would be more healthful, and less distracting than on the coast, and would make the College more easily accessible to native students. The mulattoes favoured a site in Monrovia. They had their wish and to the further disappointment of the blacks, Roberts was appointed by the American Trustees as the first President of the College.

The struggle between the two opposing factions continued. Joining Blyden and Crummell on the staff of the College in November 1864 as Professor of Mathematics and Natural Philosophy was another race-proud black, Martin H. Freeman, a graduate of Middlebury College and an experienced teacher; he had also been a close associate of Delany and an executive member of the National Emigration Board.[29] Blyden had become Secretary of State without relinquishing his position as Professor at the College, but during his attempt to promote West Indian emigration to Liberia, Roberts forced him to relinquish his political appointment on the grounds that it was incompatible with the holding of his Professorship.[30] Yet four months later, when the West Indian emigration scheme was dropped, and the

[28] Gardner W. Allen, *The Trustees of Donations for Education in Liberia: A Story of Philanthropic Endeavour, 1850–1923*, Boston 1923, 1–2.

[29] *African Repository*, XXXVIII, Nov. 1863, 322; Delany, *Report of the Niger Valley Party.* 7, 13.

[30] Allen, *op. cit.*, 26.

position of Secretary of State was still unfilled, Blyden was again allowed to assume that office.

The antagonism between the two groups grew increasingly intense. Blyden charged that Roberts refused admission into the College to Negro youths, while 'ample provision was made by beneficiary funds for mulattoes, boys and girls'; he charged further that mulattoes 'hated the very word "Negro"'.[31] And Crummell reported to Coppinger in March 1864 that 'Never have I in all my life seen such bitterness, hate and malice displayed as has been exhibited by the two factions of the state.'[32] Later Crummell explicitly charged that 'the difficulty' in Liberia was due to 'the constant enmity and opposition' of mulattoes. He wrote to Coppinger that 'it is the saddest of all things to come here to Africa, and find one's black face a disgrace both in his ecclesiastical and social relations with half-caste people. For this, after all, is our difficulty; and has been the difficulty for years'.[33] Crummell further charged that mulattoes did not want educated blacks in Liberia and did everything to 'degrade' them. In 1865 the black Professors tried to get a bill passed in the Liberian legislature modifying the charter in such a way as to give them greater protection against 'a hostile President and Board of Trustees', but failed.[34]

In retaliation Roberts wrote to the American Board of Trustees charging Blyden and Crummell with being delinquent and intractable. On 11 July 1866, at a regular quarterly meeting the Boston trustees decided to dismiss Crummell. Because Blyden's salary was paid by the New York Colonization Society, the Boston Board could take no action against him. Moreover, he was fortunate that both J. B. Pinney and William Tracy, two influential members of the New York Board, thought well of his ability and character. Indeed, even Roberts admitted that Blyden was 'unquestionably the best linguist in the country and a good teacher of languages'.[35]

Appointed to replace Crummell was Hilary W. Johnson, son of the illustrious Liberian pioneer, Elijah Johnson; before long he, too, was involved in a controversy with Roberts and resigned his

[31] Blyden to Coppinger, 4 July 1866, A.C.S. Papers, Vol. 13.
[32] Crummell to Coppinger, 26 March 1864, ibid.
[33] Crummell to Coppinger, 4 July 1866, ibid.
[34] Blyden to Crummell, 14 April 1866, John E. Bruce Papers.
[35] Allen, op. cit., 28.

Professorship.[36] Freeman, too, was resentful of Roberts' super-
cilious attitude towards his Professors and his inept conduct of
the College, but seemed to have been less openly rebellious than
the other Professors.

Another issue causing conflict between the leading blacks and
mulattoes was the latter's opposition to the extension of Liberia's
jurisdiction into its hinterland for fear that this would diffuse the
trade with the interior which was largely in their hands and
would eventually lead to a lessening of their political influence,
while Blyden, Benson and Crummell were keen on pushing
Liberia's boundaries interiorwards.[37] But their attempts met with
mulatto opposition. Indeed, Crummell stated that Benson's death
in March 1865 had been hastened by 'bitter mulatto persecution'.[38]

Benson's death and the dismissal of Crummell from his College
post were the turning points after which Blyden 'fixed himself on
the side of truth':[39] he now felt with unshakeable conviction that
the greatest single barrier to Liberia's progress was the powerful
mulatto group which was unsympathetic to any aspirations of
Liberia on behalf of the Negro race. Crummell himself returned
to settle in the United States in 1873.

In this atmosphere of class and colour conflict, Blyden, nonetheless, attempted to carry out conscientiously his duties on behalf
of the Republic. As Secretary of State, he was anxious to settle the
dispute over Liberia's north-west boundary which had arisen

[36] *Ibid.*, 31.
[37] In 1856 President Benson despatched the first expedition into the hinterland
of Liberia; it travelled about 280 miles inland probably as far as the Mandinka
kingdom of Kwaña. The next important expedition was in 1868 under Benjamin
Anderson, and it was Blyden who made this possible by persuading two New York
bankers to finance it. See Johnston, *op. cit.*, 238–9, 250–3; and Benjamin Anderson,
Narrative of a Journey to Musardu, the capital of the Western Mandingoes, New York
1870, 5.
[38] This is probably a reference to the fact that Benson was charged with mis-
appropriation of public funds. See *Report of the Special Committee of the House of
Representatives on the Public Accounts*, adopted 19 Feb. 1864, cited in Raymond L.
Buell, *The Native Problem in Africa*, New York 1928, Vol. II, 795. Crummell, Blyden and other educated blacks believed that the charge against Benson was part of
the 'mulatto persecution' and indeed they maintained that Benson was a great
President: *African Times*, 23 June 1871, also Blyden to Coppinger, 28 April 1888,
A.C.S. Papers, Vol. 25, where he wrote that 'Benson was one of the most brilliant
rulers West Africa has ever seen'.
[39] Blyden to Coppinger, 19 May 1879, *A.C.S. Papers*, Vol. 19.

between the Republic and the British Government at Sierra Leone. The root cause of the dispute was the competition between Liberians and Europeans for trade with the Africans along the coastline claimed by the Liberian Government. As has already been noted, one of the main reasons for Liberia's declaration of independence was to achieve the sovereignty necessary to deal with Europeans who flouted its commercial regulations. But much of the territory which the Liberians claimed was not effectively settled by them, and the European traders encouraged African chiefs to disown treaties made with the Liberian Government, and continued to trade with the Africans in disregard of the Liberian authorities.

The immediate background to the dispute can be traced from 1860 when John Myer Harris, an English trader, took advantage of the lack of effective Liberian occupation west of Cape Mount to establish himself between the rivers Sulima and Mano.[40] The Liberian Government sought to assert its jurisdiction over the area, but found that Harris was supported by the Government of Sierra Leone. On the protest of Liberia, the British Foreign Office pointed to treaties it had entered into with the African chiefs pledging to safeguard their territories from 'aggressors'.[41] In fact, these treaties were signed in 1862 after the dispute had begun, and were specifically for the purpose of eradicating the slave trade in that area; it did not invalidate the prior treaty arrangements made between the Liberian Government and the chiefs of the area in the years 1850 to 1856.[42] Yet the British Foreign Office, in condescending fashion, advised the Liberian Government to concentrate on developing that part of its territory which was not in dispute, 'rather than seeking to extend Liberian jurisdiction over tribes and races who are unwilling to come under Liberian rule', and suggested that if Liberia were 'wisely governed and the country civilized and prosperous, the neighbouring people will be glad to be annexed to the Republic'.[43]

Blyden was distressed by the attitude of the Foreign Office. In his first despatch on the subject of the boundary dispute he correctly pointed out that in denying the political sovereignty of

[40] Johnston, op. cit., 242–5.
[41] F.O. 403/7, Layard to Ralston, 12 Nov. 1863; *Confidential Prints, Correspondence Respecting the Boundaries of the Republic of Liberia.*
[42] Johnston, op. cit., 241.
[43] Layard to Ralston, 12 Nov. 1863, op. cit.

Liberia, the African chiefs had been influenced 'by mercenary motives' which had been incited by 'unscrupulous foreign traders'. He pleaded that unless the British recognized the lawful claims of Liberia 'an interminable series of difficulties' would arise: 'It is impossible not to see that if it should become generally known to the tribes within our borders that Her Majesty's Government sanction the repudiation by native chiefs of claims possessed in their territory by the Liberian Government, it would be a comparatively easy matter ... for unprincipled foreigners to present complaints to the Foreign Office, denying Liberian jurisdiction,'[44] he wrote. Blyden also took the opportunity of again urging the British Government to reappoint a Consul in Monrovia so as to facilitate the settling of disputes between Liberia and British subjects, and in the hope of the Republic maintaining a harmonious relationship with Sierra Leone.

In reply, the Foreign Office 'saw no reason to alter its decision' with regard to the Liberian claims; nor did it make any reference to Blyden's plea for a British consul.[45] It is characteristic of Blyden that although Liberia's claim was legally strong, he sought to win the sympathy of the British Government by claiming for Liberia a 'peculiar relation with the natives', and by painting an optimistic picture of the Negro Republic. He assured the British Government that

Our relation to the Aborigines is no mere commercial relation like that generally of the Europeans who reside upon the coast; ours is a fraternal connection. They are our kith and kin; and thus far we have proved that our influence in civilizing them to Christian law, had been fully as successful as the influence of the oldest and most powerful colony in West Africa.

Liberia is the only portion of Africa which her civilized descendants returning from a painful exile of centuries occupy; the only spot on this vast continent ... where any portion of the race can be said to hold an intelligent rule. To this bright spot thoughtful Africans everywhere are looking with the deepest interest ... it would be sad that this mere speck on the Continent of our fathers, should be circumscribed. ... [46]

[44] F.O. 403/6, Blyden to Ralston, 5 Feb. 1864, enc. in Ralston to Russell, 23 March 1864.
[45] F.O. 403/7, Layard to Ralston, 2 June 1864.
[46] Blyden to Ralston, 5 Feb 1864, op. cit.

Blyden was attempting to revive the active sympathy shown for Liberia by the British Government during the Palmerstonian era[47] but without success: no constructive step was taken during his term as Secretary of State towards settling the dispute, and indeed it was almost another three decades before it was finally settled.

If he attempted to settle Liberia's major external problem, he also remained concerned about its internal ones. Blyden had correctly seen that the frequency of elections and the exhibition of a 'violent party spirit' retarded Liberia's development. In 1864–5, he led a campaign to have the constitution amended: he proposed that the President should be elected for a term of six to eight years, and should not be immediately eligible for re-election; that the big time gap between the election of the President in May and his inauguration in January should be closed; that the powers of the President to appoint and dismiss Government employees should be rescinded, and that an independent Civil Service recruited on merit and free from political interference be established.[48] None of these sensible and progressive suggestions were implemented.

But Blyden continued his role as critic and exhorter. His Independence Day address of 1865, 'Our Origin, Dangers and Duties,' was typical, his admonitions characteristic: 'We must, as a holy and solemn duty, labour to benefit our country. . . . We must cultivate pride of race . . . we must have faith in the Negro race.'[49] In the same address Blyden pointed to the spirit of nationalism which was abroad and was proving an incentive to unity among such peoples as the Italians, the Germans and the Slavs. He was anxious that this spirit should not pass the Negro by: he wished Liberia to regard itself as the nucleus of a West African state and work towards that goal.

Although Liberia possessed a small, quite well-educated, intelligent elite, it suffered another drawback in the fact that its population was largely illiterate, and the majority of its clergymen and teachers were only semi-literate. This was why Blyden devoted most of his time and energies to teaching, but he also believed that an enlightened ministry was an indispensable agency in preparing Liberia for its pan-Negro role. Thus, in a brilliant sermon preached on the occasion of the installation of a young

[47] Johnston, *op. cit.*, 224–7.
[48] Horton, *op. cit.*, 18–19; Blyden, *Our Origins, Dangers and Duties*, 21.
[49] *Ibid.*, 33.

Presbyterian as a minister, Blyden demanded of Liberian clergymen qualifications which were unusually high even for such men
in longer established and more literate nations. Blyden would
have the Liberian clergyman not only 'spiritually enlightened'
but 'intellectually, the ... equal if not the superior to the most
enlightened of his congregation'; at all times must he be the best
informed man of his community.[50] He would have him be a
scholar 'who would not be content to take at second hand the
views of the meaning of passages; but he should repair to the
fountain head'. He noted that in both England and America
many of the names eminent in literature and science were those of
clergymen; and that they influenced to a great extent 'the thought
and tendency of their age'. He thought idealistically that it ought
to be so in Liberia. He would enjoin the following precepts on the
Liberian clergyman:

He should never forget his duties and privileges as a citizen. He
should labour ... for the upbuilding of his country... He should
constantly inculcate the duty of choosing wise and righteous rulers. . .
He should always be in sympathy with the better social and political
movements of the times, though not subservient to them. While he
should stand forth as a Reformer, he should not allow himself to
serve by his sermons any party or administration, nor suffer himself
to become an advocate or a tool for any political sect. He should
carefully avoid all cliqueships, even in the best cause, as tending to
fossilize opinions, to foster prejudice more than encourage truth. But
he must conscientiously preach his own views of such reforms in
social and political relations as he may deem necessary... [51]

Finally, Blyden would have Liberian pastors themselves undertake
the instruction of the young in their congregations so as to ensure
their proper training and the future success of Liberia.

This sermon again illustrates Blyden's intense racial patriotism
and the idealism and romanticism in his character: it is true that
he himself had successfully met the high demands he required of
Liberian clergymen, but with his exception, such demands were
utterly divorced from what was likely or possible in the Liberian
context.

To help in the 'proper training' of youth, apart from his teach-

[50] Edward W. Blyden, 'The Pastor's Work': *A Sermon Preached on the Installation
of the Rev. Thomas A. Amos*, London 1866, 9.
[51] *Ibid.*, 15-16.

ing and preaching duties, Blyden, together with Crummell, founded in Monrovia in 1864 the Athenaeum Club where young men could meet and through lectures, debates and discussions, better prepare themselves for making a significant contribution to Liberian life. The two Negro patriots hopefully regarded the Athenaeum as 'one of the grand means of moral reformation among our youth'.[52]

Blyden remained anxious that Liberia should have regular intercourse with the Muslim states of the interior with the aim eventually of incorporating them into the Negro Republic. To facilitate this, he decided to learn Arabic and teach it to students at Liberia College whom he hoped would act as emissaries to the Mohammedan chiefs of the interior. On 11 May 1886, he left Liberia for Lebanon, and spent three months at the Syrian Protestant College furthering his study of Arabic.

He had travelled to Syria via England, Gibraltar, Malta and Egypt. In Egypt he made one of those gestures which bespoke his pathological concern that Liberia should succeed, and his anxiety lest it might not: at the entrance to the pyramids, he engraved the word 'Liberia' with his name and the date 11 July 1866, immediately under it; he had done this to ensure 'that the name at least of that Republic will go down to posterity'.[53]

Characteristically, in Lebanon Blyden regarded himself as Liberia's ambassador. He was the first Liberian to visit Lebanon and the fact that he was the only one there did not deter him from arranging for the celebration of the anniversary of Liberia's independence. He had to tell American missionaries and citizens in Lebanon of 'Liberia: Past, Present and Future'. As usual, his picture of Liberia for foreigners was more like what he wished it to be than what it really was:

Most wonderful have been the changes which, within a few years, the moral and religious aspects of that portion of Africa have undergone. Where, a few years ago stood virgin forests or impenetrable jungles, we now behold churches erected to the living God; we hear the sound of the church-bells, and regular Sabbath ministrations are enjoyed. If you could see Liberia as she now is with her six hundred miles of coast snatched from the abomination of the slave-trade, her

[52] Crummell to Coppinger, 5 Sept. 1864, A.C.S. Papers, Vol. 13.
[53] Edward W. Blyden, From West Africa to Palestine, Freetown, Manchester and London 1873, 112.

thriving towns and villages, her spacious streets and fine houses, her happy homes with their varied delights, her churches and Sabbath schools and their solemn and delightful services; could you contemplate all the diversified means of improvement and enjoyment and indication on every hand of ease and happiness and plodding industry of her population without those feverish and distracting pursuits and rivalries which make large cities so unpleasant; could you behold these things and contrast the state of things now with what it was forty years ago, when eighty-eight pilgrims first landed on these shores, where the primeval forests stood around with their awful, unbroken solitude... you would exclaim what God hath wrought! You would acknowledge that the spirit of Christianity and civilization has moved upon the face of these turbid waters, and that beauty and order have emerged out of material rude and unpromising; you would recognize on that coast a germ of moral renovation which shall at length burst into glorious efflorescence all over the land; the wilderness and desert shall bloom and blossom as a rose.[54]

On his return, Blyden introduced the study of Arabic into Liberia College even though Roberts as President 'did all he could to discourage it'.[55] In a further effort to open the interior to Liberian influence, Blyden persuaded two New Yorkers, Henry M. Schieffelin and Caleb Swan, to finance an expedition into the interior under the Liberian explorer, Benjamin Anderson.[56] Anderson's expedition which set out on 14 February 1868, and occupied thirteen months, was one of major significance in the exploration of West Africa. It took him through the forest belt across a country of parkland into one of open grass land and as far as the Muslim kingdom of Musardu. Anderson made treaties of friendship and alliance with the King of Musardu and several of the Mandinka chiefs. In 1869, Blyden himself began preparatory work for a 'manual-labour school' at Vonswah, a Muslim town in the interior of Liberia, after he had received an offer of £500 from Robert Arthington, a wealthy and philanthropic cotton manufacturer of Leeds, for that purpose.[57] But before he could start effective work in the interior he was forced to flee Liberia.

[54] Edward W. Blyden, *Liberia: Past, Present and Future*, Washington 1869, 13.
[55] Blyden to Coppinger, 5 July 1879, *A.C.S. Papers*, Vol. 19.
[56] Anderson, *op. cit.*, 5.
[57] Blyden to Coppinger, 4 Oct. 1872, *A.C.S. Papers*, Vol. 16; American Colonization Society, *Annual Report*, Washington 1869, 7.

The events leading to Blyden's forcible departure from Liberia originated with the accession to the presidency in 1870 of Edward James Roye, 'a pure descendant of the Ibo tribe', who had won the presidency from its incumbent, James Sprigg Payne, a mulatto, after one of the most fiercely contested elections in Liberian history.[58] An American College graduate, Roye had emigrated to Liberia in 1846, and as a shrewd trader and ship-owner, had become one of the wealthiest men in the Negro Republic. In his public career, he had been a journalist, a member of the Liberian House of Representatives, and a government official in several capacities, including that of Chief Justice from 1865 to 1868.[59] Blyden was optimistic that Roye's presidency would greatly benefit Liberia. They had been close friends; both were resentful of mulatto influence, and believed that Liberia's future lay in making the indigenous Africans active members of the nation. The programme which Roye outlined in his inaugural address was an ambitious and comprehensive one: it included 'a thorough financial reconstruction and the establishment of a national banking system, the general education of the masses, the introduction of railroads, the improvement and incorporation of the native tribes contiguous to Liberia, and the formation of a friendly alliance with distant and powerful tribes'.[60] Roye intended to pay special attention to education: he planned to establish a 'practical common school system' throughout the country and early in his presidency set up a committee of education to inaugurate and direct this comprehensive education scheme. Blyden was closely identified with these grandiose plans for Liberia.

To finance such an ambitious programme, and 'to redeem the currency of the country, and . . . furnish the people with a circulating medium which they had not had for years', Roye decided to negotiate for a British loan and received the consent of the Liberian legislature. A loan of £100,000 was finally arranged in the summer of 1871 through David Chinery, the Consul-General for Liberia in Britain, assisted by two Liberian commissioners,

[58] Blyden to the Committee of the Republican Party, Feb. 1887, *A.C.S. Papers*, Vol. 24.

[59] For the best biographical sketch see A. Doris Banks Henries, *Presidents of the First African Republic*, London 1963, 48–56.

[60] Quoted in the American Colonization Society, *Fifty-fourth Annual Report*, Washington 1871, 21.

William S. Anderson, Speaker of the House of Representatives, and Henry W. Johnson, Secretary of the Interior, from a British banking firm of which Chinery was an agent. Despite the offer of future custom receipts as security, the loan was obtained on 'unconscionable terms': £30,000 as discount and advance interest was retained by the bankers; and the entire loan was to be repaid in fifteen years at seven per cent interest. Roye, himself, who had gone to England in an attempt to settle Liberia's north-west boundary dispute with Sierra Leone, did not take part in the negotiations but sanctioned the terms of the loan.[61] In doing so, Roye made himself vulnerable to the attacks of his political opponents who were opposed to the President's acceptance of the loan the more so as the interest to be paid on it was exorbitantly high.

The two factions also disagreed violently on whether the length of Roye's term of office was two or four years. In 1869 the Liberian legislature had agreed to hold a referendum at the same time as the presidential election on a proposal to extend the presidential term to four years. This seems to have been a manoeuvre on the part of the mulattoes to keep Payne in office for an extended period; but although the overwhelming majority in a small poll voted for the amendment to the Constitution, it was Roye and not Payne who won the elections.[62] The House of Representatives declared the Constitution amended but the mulatto-dominated Senate refused to sanction the amendment. Finally it was agreed to have the proposal resubmitted to the electorate and in May 1870 another referendum was held. The Legislature, apparently without counting the electoral votes, and without the necessary two-thirds majority declared that the Constitution was not amended.[63] Thus thwarted, Roye issued a Proclamation in November 1870 declaring the Constitution amended on the results of the 1869 special election, and hence the

[61] Brown, op. cit., 143; Johnston, op. cit., 259; Charles S. Huberich, The Political and Legislative History of Liberia, New York 1947, Vol. II, 1134; Raymond L. Buell, The Native Problem in Africa, New York 1928, Vol. II, 796.

[62] J. M. Turner, U.S. Minister to Liberia, to Hamilton Fish, U.S. Secretary of State, 30 Oct. 1871, Papers Relating to the Foreign Relations of the United States, Washington 1873, 325. Turner gave the count as 350 to 2 in favour of amendment.

[63] Ibid. Turner wrote: 'Subsequent to the second submission, it seemed to have been impossible to procure the necessary two-thirds vote of both houses for the determination of the count of the vote. The speaker of the house and the president of the senate was deposed, and thus a vote declaring the constitution not amended was secured.'

presidential term extended to four years. However, Roye's opponent maintained that his proclamation was unconstitutional and therefore that the constitution was not amended.[64] The controversy developed into a minor crisis. A correspondent of the *African Times* in a letter from Monrovia in December 1870 wrote: 'Matters stand in a very serious condition here. The country is in a great uproar. . . . Every man seems to have the law in his hands.'[65]

The situation was to worsen. J. J. Roberts returned to active political life and declared himself a presidential candidate for election in May 1871. Roye, who clung to the view that his was a four year term, issued a proclamation forbidding the holding of elections at that time. But undaunted, Roberts stood for the Presidency without opposition and got himself 'elected'. Shortly thereafter he left for England. On 22 October Roberts returned to a demonstrative welcome. On that same evening violence broke out in Monrovia: cannon shots were fired into Roye's home.[66] In the following days there were skirmishes between the two factions; Roye's followers were overpowered and he himself was caught and imprisoned. On 26 October, the Senate and the House of Representatives met, and in an 'extra-legal action' declared Roye deposed.[67] Before he could be tried, Roye escaped from prison and was killed.[68] While the struggle lasted there had been

[64] See Roberts' Inaugural Address for 1872: Bank Henries, *J. J. Roberts*, 132–4.

[65] *African Times*, X, 23 June 1871.

[66] According to Turner, *op. cit.*, it was the Roberts faction which started the violence. However, Winwood Reade, *African Sketch-Book*, 249, who was not in Liberia at the time of the incidents, told the implausible story that 'Mr. Roye made war on the town, and, going into the street, flung hand grenades in every direction. The people, in return, loaded a cannon and fired a ball into his mansion.' Johnston, *op. cit.*, 261, and other writers on Liberian history have repeated the story.

[67] Huberich, *op. cit.*, 1134.

[68] The usual story is that Roye with a bag of specie—part of the loan—tied about his body was drowned while attempting to board an English steamer. Again, Winwood Reade, *African Sketch-Book*, 250, seems to have been the source of this story. However, Blyden claimed that when Roye 'escaped from prison and was waiting for a boat, a mulatto shot him and published he got drowned': Blyden to Coppinger, 22 Oct. 1887, *A.C.S. Papers*, Vol. 24. No evidence has been found to support either of the two assertions, but it might be questioned whether Roye did escape with any part of the loan: it would seem physically impossible to swim any distance carrying a bag of specie; moreover, it was unlikely that the new Government would have allowed him to retain any part of the loan. But Roye had most of his money in British banks and had he escaped from Liberia could have lived comfortably abroad.

several political murders and chaos continued even after Roye's deposition. In a letter of 6 November 1871, H. W. Erskine, the Superintendent of the Presbyterian Mission in Liberia, wrote:

We are in a state of anarchy and confusion out here—one hardly knows when he lies down at night whether he will not be murdered before morning. Thousands would gladly return to America if they had the means to do so. Military arrests are the usual sights nowadays. Men are arrested and imprisoned for no other cause than they differ from the dominant party who deposed President Roye . . . [69]

It is ironic that the man who conceived the most grandiose plans for the development of Liberia should have occasioned the Republic one of its greatest drawbacks: the inability to repay the Roye loan and its accumulated interests was to be for long a serious embarrassment to the Negro state. And yet, indubitably, the beginning of the Roye administration had created a new, hopeful and expansive mood among his followers. Years later Blyden commented that he 'was refreshed when he looked back to that year and felt its impulse'.[70] It was symptomatic of the new mood that, shortly after Roye's inauguration as President, Blyden undertook a mission of friendship to King Marmora of Boporo, whose kingdom was 75 miles from the coast. With the consent of the Muslim king, Blyden opened a school and left a Liberian teacher in charge.[71] This he had regarded as a first step in a new effort by Liberia to extend its influence interiorwards.

Ironically, too, Roye himself was partly responsible for Blyden's flight from Liberia five months before he was deposed. One of the reasons why Blyden had held Roye in high esteem was that he was one of the very few successful black men who had taken a 'pure' Negro woman as wife. Indeed, Blyden claimed that Mrs. Roye was the first black (as opposed to mulatto) woman to occupy the presidential mansion. Understandably, Blyden was much friendlier to her than he had been to any of her predecessors. But this gave his opponents the pretext of charging that he had committed adultery with Roye's wife while the President was abroad.[72] At this time Blyden was more unpopular than ever with the

---

[69] H. W. Erskine to J. C. Lowrie, 6 Nov. 1871, *P.B.F.M. Papers*, Vol. 9.

[70] Blyden to Coppinger, 28 April 1888, *A.C.S. Papers*, Vol. 25.

[71] *The Peoples of Africa*, 103; also Reade, who accompanied Blyden, *African Sketch-Book*, 253.

[72] Blyden was declared innocent of the charge by the Presbytery of West Africa who investigated it: Blyden to Coppinger, 7 Jan. 1873, *A.C.S. Papers*, Vol. 16.

mulattoes because he had made uncomplimentary references to them to an American friend which were published as a short article on 'The Mixed Races in Liberia', copies of which had found their way back to the Negro Republic. By the use of statistics, Blyden had proved that although mulattoes occupied privileged positions in Liberia, the death rate among them was significantly higher than among Negro emigrants. Blyden claimed that American trust funds were spent on educating mulatto instead of Negro students and that that was money wasted as many of the mulattoes died young. He asserted that 'decadent mulattoes in important positions accounted in part for Liberia's want of enterprise and progress'.[73] Under the guise of moral outrage at his alleged adultery, and apparently with the connivance of Roye who seemed to have thought that he could lessen mulatto opposition to himself,[74] a 'mulatto-incited' mob of 'forty poverty-stricken and ignorant blacks' on 5 May dragged him through the streets with a rope around his neck and would have lynched him but for the timely intervention of his influential friend, D. B. Warner.[75] Rescued, Blyden fled to Sierra Leone.

For Blyden, his own forcible departure from Liberia and the deposition and death of Roye were signal triumphs for the mulattoes and great blows to the Negro Republic. Of his twenty years' residence in Liberia up to the time of his flight he wrote truthfully that he had 'striven by night and day for the advancement of the people and the country. I gave myself no leisure or repose. It was with me a passion as well as a principle to labour for the upbuilding of Liberia.'[76] But despite his efforts and wishes, Liberia failed to progress: lack of trained manpower, lack of money for economic development, and the virulent conflict between Negroes and mulattoes had all militated against its success. But for all its disabilities, it remained the focus of Blyden's pan-Negro thinking, and he was to return to it after a sojourn away.

[73] Edward W. Blyden, 'Mixed Races in Liberia', *Smithsonian Institute Annual Report*, Washington 1870, 386–8. This material was not intended for publication. It was a letter to a member of the New York Colonization Board. This letter was sent to Professor Joseph Henry, the first President of the Smithsonian Institute, who considered it 'scientific' enough for publication.

[74] Blyden to Coppinger, 2 Aug. 1871, *A.C.S. Papers*, Vol. 204; Blyden to Coppinger, 1 Oct. and 4 Oct. 1871, *A.C.S. Papers*, Vol. 16.

[75] Blyden to Col. J. C. Hemphill, 8 July 1909, *Hemphill Papers*.

[76] Blyden to Coppinger, 2 Aug. 1871, *A.C.S. Papers*, Vol. 204.

4. Vindicator of the Negro Race

Because Blyden was one of a few Negroes to make a significant impact on the English-speaking literary and scholastic world in the nineteenth century,[1] it is pertinent to devote a chapter to the main themes in his writings. Such an examination is useful at this point as a background against which to view his later activities. We have already noted his early writings which appeared mainly in the colonization journals of America and as privately published pamphlets. As early as 1862, a half a dozen of his essays and lectures were considered of enough general interest to be published commercially.[2] But it was not until the 1870's, when his ideas had reached maturity that he made a notable impact on the literary scene. Basically, his writings were designed to vindicate the Negro race. His major themes were: that the Negro race did have past achievements of which it could be proud; that it had special inherent attributes which it should strive to project in a distinctive 'African Personality';[3] that African culture—its cus-

[1] The major works in English were those (a) of the American Negroes: William Wells Brown, *The Black Man*, New York 1863, and *The Negro in the American Revolution*, Boston 1867; Robert Campbell, *A Pilgrimage to my Motherland*, New York 1861; Alexander Crummell, *The Relations and Duties of the Free Colored Men to Africa*, Hartford 1861, and *Africa and America*, Springfield, Mass., 1891; Martin R. Delany, *Official Report of the Niger Valley Exploring Party*, New York 1861, and *Principia of Ethnology: The Origin of Races and Color*, Philadelphia, 1879; Frederick Douglass, *The Life and Times of Frederick Douglass*, Hartford 1881; William C. Nell, *The Colored Patriots of the American Revolution*, Boston 1855; William Still, *The Underground Railroad*, Philadelphia 1879; and George Washington Williams, *History of the Negro Race in America, 1619–1880*, New York 1880, 2 vols.; and *A History of the Negro Troops in the War of the Rebellion*, New York 1888; and (b) of West Africans: S. A. Crowther, *Journal of an Expedition Up the Niger*, London 1843; Frederick Alexander Durham, *The Lone Star: Being the Outcome of Reflections on Our Own People*, London 1892; James A. B. Horton, *West African Countries and Peoples*, London 1868, and *Letters on the Political Condition of the Gold Coast*, London 1870; C. C. Reindorf, *History of the Gold Coast and the Asante*, Basel 1895; A. B. C. Sibthorpe, *The History and Geography of Sierra Leone*—which was first published in London in 1868 and went through several subsequent editions; and James Mensah Sarbah, *Fanti Customary Laws*, London 1897.

[2] *Liberia's Offering, op. cit.*

[3] In his writings Blyden frequently referred to the character of the Negro race, but he used the phrase 'African personality' for the first time in a lecture entitled

toms and institutions—were basically wholesome and should be preserved; and finally, that Christianity had a retarding influence upon the Negro, while that of Islam had been salutary—his most controversial theme, and one on which he wrote at length.

It is significant that he made his first notable literary success in an article in which he sought to prove that Negroes had played a prominent part in one of the world's earliest flourishing civilizations—that of Egypt. The article entitled 'The Negro in Ancient History', appeared in the first issue for 1869 of the *Methodist Quarterly Review*, one of America's outstanding literary journals, published in New York, and edited by Daniel E. Whedon, a controversial clergyman, and a former University Professor of classical languages and literature. Blyden's article was the first by a Negro to appear in a literary quarterly, and was also the most serious attempt made by a member of the Negro race to reconstruct aspects of early Negro history.[4]

Blyden had been long and careful in the preparation of the article. It was undoubtedly his search for evidence of distinguished Negro achievements in the earliest times which induced him to visit Egypt in 1866. His observations here, together with his own readings, convinced him that Negroes did play an important part in the early civilization of that country. He concluded then that the Pyramids were the works of Negroes, and told vividly of the stirring emotions which the sight of them aroused in him:

This, thought I, was the work of my African progenitors. . . . Feelings came over me far different from those I have ever felt when looking at the mighty works of European genius. I felt that I had a peculiar heritage in the Great Pyramid built . . . by the enterprising sons of Ham, from which I descended. The blood seemed to flow faster through my veins. I seemed to hear the echo of those illustrious Africans. I seemed to feel the impulse from those stirring characters who sent civilization to Greece. . . . I felt lifted out of the commonplace grandeur of modern times; and, could my voice have reached every African in the world, I would have earnestly addressed him . . . : 'Retake your Fame.'[5]

'Race and Study', delivered in Freetown on 19 May 1893, see *Sierra Leone Times*, 27 May 1893. This phrase was subsequently used by him occasionally.
[4] Edward W. Blyden, 'The Negro in Ancient History', *Methodist Quarterly Review*, LI, Jan. 1869, fn. 1; Blyden to W. E. Gladstone, 11 May 1869, *British Museum Add. Mss.*, 44420/255.
[5] Edward W. Blyden, *From West Africa to Palestine*, Freetown, Manchester and London 1873, 112.

Inspired by his findings in Egypt, he longed to present to the world his conclusions about early Negro achievement there. But before doing so, he wished to document his thesis as carefully as possible. Towards this end, for instance, he wrote in 1867 to Gladstone, a classical scholar, asking for 'sources of information on the Ancient Ethiopians'.[6] In the following year he wrote up the results of his research.

In part Blyden's article had expressly set out to refute the Anglo-Saxon charge as expressed by the American, Commander A. H. Foote that

if all the Negroes of all generations have ever done were to be obliterated from recollection forever, the whole world would lose no great truth, no profitable arts, no exemplary form of life. The loss of all that is African would offer no memorable deduction from anything but the black catalogue of crime.[7]

His article showed that he was fully familiar with the literature containing arguments for and against Negro participation in early Egyptian history. For proof that Negroes played an important part in the early history of Egypt, Blyden depended on the historical evidence provided by the tenth chapter of Genesis, using the original Hebrew version of the Bible, on evidence from the works of Herodotus and Homer, as well as that from comparative philology. As active participators in the world's first great civilization, Blyden argued ingeniously, Negroes had been partly responsible for passing to posterity 'the germs of all the arts and sciences'. While this is still a contentious issue recent research on the subject, and particularly archaeological evidence has tended to support Blyden's thesis.[8]

Blyden also argued that the Negroes of West Africa were the descendants of those who helped in the building of the great Egyptian civilization. He claimed that they made 'extensive migrations' spreading 'westward and southward', so that as early as the time of Homer, 'they had not only occupied the northern provinces of Africa, but had crossed the great desert, penetrated into Soudan, and made their way to the West Coast'.[9] Most

[6] Blyden to Gladstone, 13 April 1867, *British Museum Add. Mss.*, 44412/207.

[7] Quoted in 'The Negro in Ancient History', 71; cf. A. H. Foote, *Africa and the American Flag*, New York 1854, 207.

[8] The major work arguing this thesis is Cheik Anta Diop, *Nations Nègres et Culture*, Paris 1954.

[9] Blyden, 'The Negro in Ancient History', 77.

West African peoples do claim original descent from 'the east' but this subject of their actual origins is still debated by scholars.

Later in his writings, Blyden referred to the Ethiopians—a Negroid people who lived far to the South of Egypt—as the 'most creditable of the ancient peoples'. Again using as his sources, the Bible, Herodotus and Homer, Blyden claimed that they represented 'the highest rank of knowledge and civilization'. He wrote:

In the earliest traditions of nearly all the more civilized nations of antiquity, the name of this distant people is found. The annals of the Egyptian priests were full of them; the nations of inner Asia, on the Euphrates and Tigris . . . [have written about them]. When the Greeks scarcely knew Italy and Sicily by names, the Ethiopians were celebrated in verses of their poets as . . . 'the most just of men', 'the favourites of the gods'.[10]

In other references to early African history, Blyden claimed with some truth, that although Christianity and Islam had had their origins elsewhere, 'North Africa was the cradle which cherished their helpless infancy'. He further pointed out, correctly, that it was the 'African' Church Fathers—Tertullian, Cyprian and St. Augustine, who largely shaped early Christian theological thought.[11] He also saw it as being to Africa's credit that Egypt had provided 'refuge' for the infant Jesus when his life was threatened.[12]

Nor was he not reticent about New World Negro contribution to civilization. In a lecture entitled 'Africa's Service to the World' delivered in the United States in 1880, Blyden eloquently but with sound historical judgement, assessed that contribution thus:

He who writes the history of modern civilization will be culpably negligent if he omits to observe and to describe the black stream of humanity which has poured forth into America from the heart of the Soudan. That stream has fertilized half the Western continent. It has affected commerce and influenced its progress. It has affected culture and morality . . . and has been the means of transforming European colonies into a great nationality. Nor can it be denied that the material development of England was aided by means of the same dark stream. By means of Negro labour, sugar and tobacco

[10] *African Repository*, LX, Jan. 1884, 52.
[11] Edward W. Blyden, *Christianity, Islam and the Negro Race*, London 1887, 131–4; Edward W. Blyden, *Hope for Africa*, New York 1862, 5.
[12] *African Repository*, LX, Jan. 1884, 50.

were produced: by means of increased commerce the arts of culture and refinement were developed. The rapid growth and unparalleled prosperity of Lancashire are, in part, owing to the cotton supply of the Southern States, which would not have risen to such importance without the labour of the African.

Perhaps as a corrective to the prevailing view that the Negro contribution to New World civilization was minimal, he added the hyperbolical statement that 'The political history of the United States is the history of the Negro. The commercial and agricultural history of nearly the whole of the Americas is the history of the Negro.'[13]

By recounting Negro achievements both in Africa and the New World, Blyden wished to show how nonsensical was the use by white men of such derogatory terms as 'the despised race' and the 'dark continent' in describing the Negro race and Africa.[14] But more than this, it was intended to spur the race to future greatness. If Negroes had in the past made outstanding contributions to civilization, there was no reason why they should not be able to do so in the future; indeed, Blyden went further, and extrapolated that they were destined to perform distinguished deeds.

BLYDEN'S CONCEPT OF RACE

To understand the nature of the contribution which Blyden expected Negroes to make to civilization, it is necessary to examine his concept of race. This was not fully formulated until the early 1870's. Before this he had accepted the prevailing American view of the Negro as any person with an admixture of Negro blood, no matter how small. But the bitter conflict in Liberia between blacks and mulattoes in which he was involved, his knowledge of Haitian history with its perennial Negro-mulatto conflict, and his own observations in the United States that mulattoes were regarded as socially superior to blacks, prompted him to come to the conclusion that the mulatto no more belonged to the Negro race than he did to the Caucasoid or Mongoloid races. Although from about the late 1860's onwards, Blyden continuously expressed the view that mulattoes were not Negroes, and were, in fact, a hindrance to the Negro race, this point of view appeared

[13] Blyden, *Christianity, Islam and the Negro Race*, 136–7.
[14] *Ibid.*, 160, 314.

in print only twice, mainly because it was regarded as an unpopular and a highly explosive one politically, both in the United States and Liberia. In fact his first published uncomplimentary reference to mulattoes was not intended to appear in print.[15] Blyden's only other published opinion on this subject was in an article entitled 'Africa and the Africans' which appeared in the British Quarterly, *Fraser's Magazine* of August 1878. This article contained one of his most significant statements on race and his opinion on mulattoes is worth quoting in part:

> One of the melancholy results of the enslavement of the Africans by the European is the introduction on a very large scale of the blood of the oppressors among their victims, which even when largely preponderant over or even balanced with the Negro blood, is still reckoned, by what rule of fairness or on what principle of ethnology we cannot understand, as Negro blood. . . . If this difference between the Negro and the mulatto is understood hereafter, it will much simplify the Negro problem, and the race will be called upon to bear its own sins only, and not the sins also of a 'mixed multitude'.[16]

Blyden's argument that there was no good ethnological reason why a hybrid person with as much or more Caucasoid or Mongoloid as Negroid physical characteristics should be deemed a Negro was a reasonable one. Moreover he found confirmation for his derogatory opinion of mulattoes in contemporary writings on race. Ironically, his own concept of race was strongly influenced by the anti-Negro contemporary currents of ideas on race as enunciated by the American colonizationists and upholders of slavery; by the English school of anthropology led by James Hunt and Richard Burton; and by the writings of the Frenchman, Count Arthur de Gobineau, whose *Essay on the Inequality of the Races*, has been regarded as the classical nineteenth-century statement on the subject. The main ideas in these writings on race can be summed up as follows: there was a hierarchy of races with the Negro at or near the bottom; there were 'innate and permanent differences in the moral and mental endowments' of races: each race had its own 'talents', 'instincts' and 'energy', and that race rather than environmental or circumstantial factors 'held the key

---

[15] See chapter three, p. 53, fn. 73.

[16] Edward W. Blyden, 'Africa and the Africans', *Fraser's Magazine*, XVIII, Aug. 1878, 188; the passage relating to mulattoes was excised from the article when it appeared as part of *Christianity, Islam and the Negro Race*.

to the history' of a people; that there existed 'an instinctive antipathy among races', and that homogeneity of race was necessary
for successful nation building; that miscegenation was 'un-
natural', and that mulattoes were 'immoral' and weak people
with 'confused race instincts'.[17] Although these views were being
vociferously promulgated it is certain that at the time they represented a minority opinion. And it is almost superfluous to point
out that the concept of a 'pure race' is now regarded as scientifically untenable; that culture is learned rather than instinctive or
innate, that a people's history is largely determined by environmental and circumstantial factors, and that homogeneity of race
is not at all essential for the creation of a nation.

Yet, interestingly, Blyden subscribed completely to all but two
of the above mentioned ideas on race. He denied that there was
any 'absolute or essential superiority . . . or inferiority' among
races: 'each race was equal but distinct; it was a question of
difference of endowment and difference of destiny'.[18] In addition,
he maintained that environmental and circumstantial factors did,
to some extent, influence the history of a people. His own concept
of race demonstrated his skill in drawing on the main current of
ideas and synthesizing them in such a way to suit his own purpose.
His acceptance of the theory of 'mutual antipathy among races',
and that homogeneity was necessary for the successful creation of
a nation, provided theoretical justification for the 'repatriation of
genuine Negroes' to Africa, while debarring mulattoes; just as his
recognition (despite his affirmation that race largely held the key
to history) that environmental and adventitious factors helped to
shape a people's history permitted him to show the circumstances
which prevented the Negro race from fully developing and
demonstrating its special talents.

Blyden seemed also to have been profoundly influenced by the
writings of such European philosophers and nationalists as Herder,
Fichte, Hegel and Mazzini, who advocated racial and national
unity and averred that every people had its special mission to
fulfil. Ideologically, Blyden seemed to have been influenced most
of all by Herder. If we substitute Herder's 'Nationality' for

[17] See James Hunt, *On the Negro's Place in History*, London 1863; and Count
Arthur de Gobineau, *Essai sur l'inégalité des races humaines*, 2 vols., 2nd ed. Paris 1884,
earlier published in the United States, Philadelphia 1856, as *The Moral and Intellectual Diversity of Races.*
[18] Blyden, 'Africa and the Africans', 191.

Blyden's 'Race', we find a striking similarity in their ideas. Theirs was a humanitarian nationalism which disavowed conquest or domination of other people. Herder did not believe in the inherent superiority of one nation over another, just as Blyden did not believe that one race was inherently superior to another. They both believed that the ultimate goal of a nation or race was to serve humanity at large, and that the individual could fulfil himself best through unselfish, dedicated service to nation or race. One of the best expressions of Blyden's view that each race had its own 'personality' and 'mission' was made in a lecture delivered in Freetown Sierra Leone in 1895 on 'Race and Study', and is worth quoting in part:

For everyone of you—for everyone of us—there is a special work to be done—a work of tremendous necessity and tremendous importance—a work for the Race to which we belong ... there is a responsibility which our personality, which our membership in the Race involves ... the duty of every man, of every race is to contend for its individuality—to keep and develop it. . . . Therefore, honour and love your Race. Be yourselves. . . . If you are not yourself, if you surrender your personality, you have nothing left to give the world. You have no pleasure, no use, nothing which will attract and charm men, for by the suppression of your individuality, you lose your distinctive character. . . . You will see, then, that to give up our personality, would be to give up the peculiar work and glory to which we are called. It would really be to give up the divine idea—to give up God—to sacrifice the divine individuality; and this is the worst of suicides.[19]

But what, in Blyden's view, were the distinctive attributes of the Negro race, what the special contribution it could make to civilization? In so far as he attempted to determine this, Blyden was obviously influenced by the historical circumstances of the Negro race, as well as by certain aspects of contemporary nationalist ideas. Blyden portrayed his African as the antithesis of the European, and serving to counteract the worst aspects of the influence of the latter. The European character, according to Blyden, was harsh, individualistic, competitive and combative; European society was highly materialistic: the worship of science and industry was replacing that of God. In the character of the African, averred Blyden, was to be found 'the softer aspects of

[19] *Sierra Leone Times*, 27 May 1893.

human nature': cheerfulness, sympathy, willingness to serve, were some of its marked attributes. The special contribution of the African to civilization would be a spiritual one. Africa did not need to participate in the mad and headlong rush for scientific and industrial progress which had left Europe little time or inclination to cultivate the spiritual side of life, which was ultimately the most important one. Blyden's African would 'pursue the calling of a man in his perfect state': he would cultivate agriculture which was 'the basis at once of life and religion'. Blyden did not anticipate for Africa industrialism or 'any large and densely crowded cities'—which for him was merely man's 'marring of God's handiwork'—the rural landscape. He defined the future relations of the African with the European as follows:

The Northern races will take the raw material from Africa and bring them back in such forms as will contribute to the comfort and even elegance of life in that country; while the African in the simplicity and purity of rural enterprises will be able to cultivate those spiritual elements in humanity which are suppressed, silent and inactive under the pressure and exigencies of material progress.[20]

As the 'spiritual conservatory of the world', Africa would act as peace-maker among the ever-warring European nations, and as 'consoler' when the destructive scientific inventions of white men led to a crisis in their civilization.[21]

Blyden's 'natural African man' is strikingly similar to Rousseau's 'noble savage' living in a 'perfect state of nature'—a state which they both claimed was the necessary prerequisite for the development of the spiritual resources of mankind. Herder had adopted and repeated Rousseau's romantic notions. But it is probable that in the conception both of his ideal African, and of the role he was to play in civilization, Blyden was again directly influenced by contemporary nationalist thought. Such Russian nationalists as Karamazin and Dostoevsky had, in their reaction to European technological and cultural superiority, idealized the rural Slav as 'perfect man', and had extravagantly prognosticated that Russia would be the 'founder of a new civilization and the bearer of universal salvation'.[22] Similarly, Mazzini had claimed

[20] Blyden, *Christianity, Islam and the Negro Race*, 126.
[21] *Ibid.*, 143; also Blyden, *The Jewish Question*, 8.
[22] Hans Kohn, *Prophets and Peoples: Studies in Nineteenth-century Nationalism*, New York, 1961, chap. 5; see also John H. Hallowell, *Main Currents in Political Thought*, New York 1957, chap. 6: 'Nationalism'.

that Italy would assume the moral leadership in the regeneration of mankind. Blyden followed in this romantic tradition. In each case the idealization of the *status quo*, and the promulgation of wishful expectations, was intended to dispel a feeling of inferiority, and to act as a spur to united, concerted action.

Yet it is also true that Blyden was genuinely concerned that European civilization by its concentration on material and scientific progress, and its combativeness, would bring about its moral decay or physical destruction. This humanitarian and philosophical approach raises his writings above the level of mere racial propaganda, and places him among the thoughtful men of his age who recognized the problems which European civilization faced, and who attempted to suggest a solution; Blyden's was that of moral regeneration by putting into practice the essence of Christian teaching. Two quotations from Blyden's writings would serve to illustrate this point. In 1898 he wrote: 'Science for all the really higher purposes of humanity is a dead organism of latent forces unless it is taken up by the moral nature, unless it is animated by earnest purpose and inspired by a great spiritual idea.'[23] In 1907, he wrote 'Science is not the last word for humanity. It cannot be. It is continually threatening the existence of the mighty offspring to which it gives birth. It keeps itself armed to the teeth against its neighbour. Its most popular and lucrative inventions are machinery for the destruction of life. It multiplies its armies and increases its navies; and men wonder when all this would end and where it will lead.'[24] Blyden's concern that the moral development of European man did not keep pace with his scientific inventions, and that he was likely to become a victim of the latter, was fully justified by the fact that war on an unprecedented scale broke out a little more than two years after his own death.

If, in fact, Blyden was aware of the claims of the Slav and Italian nationalists to the spiritual and moral leadership of civilization, he was not prepared to concede these. But he did not claim for the Negro a monopoly of the spiritual role; he was prepared that his race should share this with the Jews. He saw a parallel in the history of the Negro and the Jew: each had a

[23] Blyden, *The Jewish Question*, 22.
[24] *Proceedings on the Occasion of a Banquet Given at Holborn Restaurant . . . to Ed. W. Blyden, LL.D., by West Africans*, London 1907, 35.

history of intense suffering, and this, he argued, had served to develop the spiritual side of their natures, and fitted them to be the spiritual leaders of the world. This viewpoint was most fully developed in a pamphlet entitled *The Jewish Question*, published in 1898 in Liverpool and dedicated to Louis Solomon, a Jew, who had for many years participated in the West African trade. Blyden viewed the booklet as a 'record of the views held by an African of the work and destiny of a people with whom his own race is closely allied both by Divine declaration and by a history almost identical of sorrow and oppression'.[25] He recounted his early connections with Jews and his life-long interest in the study of their language, literature and history. He had visited Jerusalem in 1866. His article showed that he was highly conversant with contemporary Jewish thought. He had of course shown a very keen interest 'in that marvellous movement called Zionism', which can be said to date effectively from the publication of Theodor Herzl's *Judenstaat* in 1896, which called for the creation of an internationally recognized state preferably in Palestine. Naturally, Blyden saw a parallel between the Jewish desire to return to their homeland and that of 'thousands of the descendants of Africa in America anxious to return to the land of their fathers', and not surprisingly, strongly championed the right of the Jews to return to Palestine. He asserted with hyperbole:

There is hardly a man in the civilized world—Christian, Mohammedan, or Jew—who does not recognize the claim and right of the Jew to the Holy Land; and there are few who, if the conditions were favourable, would not be glad to see them return in a body and take their place in the land of their fathers as a great—a leading—secular power.[26]

But desirable though the establishment of such a state was, Blyden advised Jews against aiming at political aggrandisement; the primary contribution of Jews and Negroes to world civilization must be to provide the spiritual element to a world 'immersed in materialism'. They were, he asserted, providentially appointed to this task by the fact of their long suffering and lack of political status; he rationalized that 'none of the spiritual saviours or regenerators of humanity have had, at least at the beginning of their career, either as individuals or communities any political force'.[27]

[25] Blyden, *The Jewish Question*, see dedication.   [26] *Ibid.*, 8.   [27] *Ibid.*, 11.

He urged that, because the world tasks of Jews were similar if not identical to that of Negroes, they were to regard Africa as an important field for their activities; it was an invitation, so to speak, by the ablest spokesman of the Negro race to share the African fatherland with a 'kindred' people who were practically without a homeland of their own. He asserted that the Jews 'in their early history, and in their impressionable condition, were more closely related to Africa, and to the Negro race, than to any other country or people': Africa had given succour and comfort to Jesus and his parents; in Africa was born 'the great prophet and legislator who delivered Israel from the House of Bondage— Moses'; Africa had acted as a cradle and nourisher of Judaism in its early critical history.

In view of his strong detestation of miscegenation, it must be assumed that in inviting Jews to Africa, he expected them to found separate and autonomous societies; and he might have felt that their strong group spirit would have enabled them to interact culturally with Africans without much danger of inter-breeding. It is interesting to note that Blyden's good-will gesture (it was no more than this as he had no political authority to make it) pre-dates by five years the offer made by the British Government (1903) to the Zionist movement, of 6,000 square miles on the uninhabited Guas Ngishu plateau of Uganda for the establish-ment of an autonomous settlement, an offer which Herzl himself was disposed to accept, but which was turned down because of the opposition of orthodox Zionists who regarded Palestine as the only homeland.[28] Blyden's invitation to Jews once again illustrates his romantic and idealistic nature; his belief that Jews in Africa would act primarily as 'spiritual agents' and avoid becoming exploiters of Africa's material resources, was highly unrealistic. Once again his theory of race had led him to take stands which appear naïve, and in some ways incongruous: he strenuously struggled to keep mulattoes out of Africa, and yet was prepared to give easy entry to Jews on a permanent basis.

If Blyden had suggested some of the attributes of the Negro race, he also maintained that there were others yet to be dis-covered. He admitted that of the 'personalities' of the major races, that of the Negro, mainly through adverse historical

[28] See Julian Amery, *Life of Joseph Chamberlain, 1901–3*, Vol. 4, London 1951 chap. XXII.

circumstances, had been the least developed; and asserted that its
full development would reveal new and fascinating facets.[29] The
'personality' of the race could be developed, he suggested, through
emulation of the outstanding Negro personalities of the past, and
even more significantly, through the careful study and appreciation of African customs and institutions in which were to be
found the 'soul' of the race. With regard to the first method, a
typical advice of Blyden to Negroes was as follows: 'History
furnishes example for your inspiration and guidance from among
your own race.... You ought to prefer the "Life of Toussaint
L' Ouverture", the greatest Negro produced in the western world,
over "the Life of Napoleon", or the "Life of Admiral Lord
Nelson."'[30] Thus he believed that Negro admiration for the heroes
of other races was a distraction which his race could ill afford.

From early in his writings Blyden assumed the role of defender
of African culture. He clearly saw that the impact of European
culture on Africa might result in the destruction of wholesome
African customs and institutions, and repeatedly he warned
Europeans that if they were to be useful in Africa, they would
have to lay aside their arrogant assumption of the superiority of
European culture, recognize that African culture was, on the
whole, best suited to the circumstances of the African people, and
carefully study African society so as not to destroy any customs
and institutions which were important and humane elements of
African culture. Blyden believed that African society could benefit
from contact with European culture by absorbing the most wholesome aspects of the latter. It was the task of properly educated Africans, he believed, to guide this selective and additive
process.

If before the partition of Africa, Blyden made frequent if only
passing references to the need both for Europeans and Africans to
preserve the basic wholesome fabric of African society, after the
partition, when the danger of the disruption of African society
was greater, Blyden wrote explicitly and insistently on the theme,
his most ambitious work on this being *African Life and Customs*,
published in 1908.[31] In it he was concerned to show that there
existed 'an African Social and Economic System most carefully

[29] *Christianity, Islam and the Negro Race*, 164, 192.
[30] *Liberia Bulletin*, No. 23, Nov. 1903, 29.
[31] Edward W. Blyden, *African Life and Customs*, London 1908.

and elaborately organized, venerable, impregnable, indispensable'. He pointed out that the African social system was socialistic, co-operative and equitable—an ideal for which Europe was desperately striving as the answer to ills created by individualism and unscrupulous competitiveness; the European system bred 'poverty, criminality and insanity', while 'under the African system of communal property and co-operative effort, every member of a community has a home and a sufficiency of food and clothing and other resources of life and for life'. Many of the institutions condemned by Europeans, and especially by missionaries, he argued, were important and integral parts of the African social system; polygamy, for instance, 'operated to protect from abuse the functional work of sex, and to provide that all women shall share normally in this work with a view to healthy posterity and an unfailing supply of population'; likewise, African secret societies had important educative functions. The African was a pantheist and the most religious of men, and even his reputedly barbaric customs had a religious basis.

As a vindicator of the Negro race, Blyden was concerned to discuss those influences operating most powerfully to influence the Negro race, and it is therefore not surprising that he discussed at some length the impact of Islam and Christianity on the Negro race. This was the aspect of his writings which established his literary and scholarly reputation. In four articles written between 1871 and 1876, three of which appeared in *Fraser's Magazine*, a leading British Quarterly, Blyden expounded the controversial thesis that Christianity had stifled and thwarted the development of the Negro, had disparaged African customs, and disrupted African society. On the other hand, Islam had helped to develop the 'African Personality', had purged African custom of its grosser elements, had kept intact most African customs and institutions and had acted as a unifying factor by transcending tribal divisions.

As a pan-Negro nationalist, Blyden could not be indifferent to Islam, which beginning from the late eighteenth century spread rapidly through a series of jihads as well as by peaceful penetration, throughout West Africa, and brought to those areas under its influence marked changes in their social and political organizations. This Islamic movement constituted an important intellectual and religious as well as social and political revolu-

tion.[32] But the European view of Islam, except for a few Orienta-
lists, was largely disparaging and derogatory; Islam, it was
generally believed, barely represented an advance over pagan
superstition.[33] Through his personal contact with Islam in West
Africa, Blyden knew that the popular conception of Islam,
fostered by missionary propaganda, was an erroneous one, and
he set out to help dispel prejudices against Islam.

Although Blyden seriously began his study of Islam and Arabic
in the early 1860's, significantly, it was only after a visit to Boporo,
a Muslim town in the interior of Liberia that he wrote his first
article on the subject. Blyden had discovered that Boporo was an
important centre of Muslim learning. Here he found 'extensive
manuscripts in poetry and prose', many of them the works of
Negro Muslims themselves, and even then correctly speculated
that 'some valuable manuscripts may yet be found in the heart of
Africa'. He conversed with *ulamas* or learned teachers who could
not only 'reproduce from memory any chapter of the Koran, with
its vowels, and dots and grammatical marks', but could also
learnedly discourse on many of the classical works of Islam.
Blyden reported that those Muslim youths who aspired to be
ulamas had to go through a long and rigorous intellectual training.[34] It was these findings which inspired Blyden to write an
article on 'Mohammedanism in West Africa' which appeared in
the Methodist Quarterly Review of January 1871.[35] In it he
claimed that Islam had a salutary influence on West African
Negroes for the following reasons: 'as an eliminatory or subver-
sive agency, it had displaced or unsettled nothing as good as
itself'; it had 'established a vast Total Abstinence Society throughout Central Africa'; it was 'the most important if not the sole
preservative against the desolation of the slave trade'; it had
given rise to a corpus of Muslim Negro scholars and was responsible for whatever learning and scholarship there was in West
Central Africa; it was a unifying factor 'binding tribes together in
one strong religious fraternity'; it was a system which fostered
egalitarianism; finally, it encouraged industry which reflected

[32] H. F. C. Smith, 'A Neglected Theme in West African History: The Islamic
Revolutions in the 19th century', *Journal of the Historical Society of Nigeria*, 11 Dec.
1961, 169.
[33] See below a brief discussion of the reaction to R. B. Smith's work on Islam.
[34] Edward W. Blyden, 'Mohammedanism in Western Africa', *Methodist Quarterly Review*, LIII, Jan. 1871, 68–9.   [35] *Ibid.*, 62–78.

itself in large towns and cities. Blyden's article was a necessary
corrective against the popular view of Islam in West Africa, but
his unqualified praise did not always accord with the realities of
the situation there. It is certain, for instance, that some Muslim
leaders, under the pretext of making war against non-believers
pursued largely political and economic goals, and that their warlike exploits helped in ravaging West Africa and contributed
largely to the trans-Saharan slave trade.[36] One can point, too, to
his contradictory position in claiming that he did not wish Africa
to be urbanized, and yet praising Islam for creating large towns
and cities through its industry.

Four years elapsed before Blyden's next article entitled
'Mohammedanism and the Negro Race', appeared.[37] In the
interim he had conducted two expeditions into the interior from
Sierra Leone, in 1872, and 1873, which had taken him through
much Muslim territory. Again he was impressed with the intellectual activities, the industry, the dignity and the diplomacy of
the Muslim Negro. By this time, Blyden's writings and interests
were well-known among a small group of literary friends in
England, and this article was actually the result of a request to
review a series of public lectures on 'Mohammed and the
Mohammedans', which had been delivered by R. Bosworth Smith,
a master at Harrow, and which was subsequently published as a
book. Smith's views on Islam were strikingly similar to those of
Blyden's. Having come to the conclusion that most Christian
writers had sought to 'villify and misrepresent' Islam, Smith set
out to give an honest and sympathetic picture of that religion,
pointing out that there was much in common between it and
Christianity, and that Islam had been a powerful agency for good
among 'the less progressive races'. Those European reviewers who
took notice of the book violently assailed it.[38]

Blyden, on the other hand, enthusiastically endorsed most of
Smith's views, the editor being careful to point out that the author

[36] On his expedition to Falaba, Blyden himself described the Houbous, a Muslim
people, as waging war and committing 'acts of brigandage under the dexterous
euphemism of war against the enemies of Islam': C.M.S., CA1/07, Blyden to
Kendall 5 Feb. 1872; cf. J. Spencer Trimingham, *A History of Islam in West Africa*,
London 1962, *passim*.

[37] Edward W. Blyden, 'Mohammedanism and the Negro Race', *Fraser's Magazine*, XII, Nov. 1875, 598–615.

[38] R. B. Smith, *Mohammed and the Mohammedans*, London 1874; Lady Ellinore
Grogan, *Reginald Bosworth Smith: A Memoir*, London 1909, 137.

of the article was 'a Negro of the purest blood'. Much of the
material in this article had already appeared in his former article
on 'Mohammedanism'. But, in addition, he effectively contrasted
the influence of Islam and Christianity on the Negro race. Again
he emphasized that Islam had 'strengthened and hastened . . .
tendencies to independence and self-reliance' among West African
Negroes:

There are numerous Negro communities and states in Africa which
are self-reliant, productive, independent. . . . In Sierra Leone, the
Mohammedans, without aid from the Government—or any contribution from Mecca or Constantinople, erect their own mosques, keep
up religious services, conduct their schools.

He was careful to point out that the impact of Islam on West
African society had resulted in 'improved' social and political
organizations without disrupting the society.

Local institutions were not destroyed by the Arab influence. . . . They
only assumed new forms, and adapted themselves to the new teaching. In all thriving Mohammedan communities in West and Central
Africa . . . the Arab superstructure has been superimposed on a
permanent indigenous substructure; so that what really took place
when the Arab met the Negro in his own home, was a healthy
amalgamation, and not an absorption or an undue repression.

Thus, he argued, the Negro had put his own impress upon Islam
in West Africa. But he emphatically denied that Islam had, 'as is
too generally supposed', degradingly compromised itself with
pagan superstitions: what had occurred, Blyden argued ingeniously, was a healthy synthesis.

Further, the egalitarian influence of Islam, and its discouragement of racial prejudice had given Negroes the opportunity to
rise to positions of distinction not only in West Africa but in Arab
countries as well. He pointed out that in the *Biographies* of the
Arab historian, Ibn Khallikan, there were many sketches of distinguished West African Negroes.[39]

Finally, Blyden praised highly the two outstanding nineteenth-
century leaders of the *jihads* in West Africa—Usuman dan Fodio
and Sheik Al Hajj Omar—as scholars, warriors and statesmen,
who had stimulated an intellectual and religious renaissance in
West Africa, and extended the sway of Islam over large areas.

[39] Blyden, 'Mohammedanism and the Negro Race', 70; cf. Ibn Khallikan,
Biographical Dictionary, tr. de Slane, 4 vols., London and Paris 1843–71.

Christianity, Blyden convincingly argued, had had no such salutary effect upon the Negroes. Negroes first became Christians in significant numbers, he pointed out, as 'slaves or at least a subject race in a foreign land', and from the Christian teaching, 'they received lessons of utter and permanent inferiority and subordination to their instructors, to whom they stood in the relation of chattels'. Unlike the Muslim convert, 'no amount of allegiance to the Gospel relieved the Christian Negro from the degradation of wearing the chain which he received with it, or rescued him from . . . political or ecclesiastical proscription'. Both 'Aryan art' and literature had been employed to make the Negro submissive and servile. Indeed, he asserted, 'it is not too much to say that the popular literature of the Christian world since the discovery of America, or at least for the last two hundred years, has been anti-Negro'. He deprecated 'the singular anxiety' on the part of Christian writers 'to disparage and depress the character of Mohammedan influence'. 'A Mohammedan writer', he wrote, 'taking the same superficial view of Christianity might say "Christianity has consecrated drunkenness; it has consecrated slavery; it has consecrated war . . ."'

If Blyden was in agreement with many of Smith's views, he nonetheless chided the English scholar for using 'Negro'—a term used 'to designate one of the great families of man'—with a common 'n'; subsequently he continued to insist that the term Negro denoted a scientific racial idea and that the 'N' in it should be capitalized.[40] In addition, while Smith believed that Islam was better suited to the 'less progressive' races, Blyden contended that Christianity in its essence was the highest form of religion to which any people could subscribe; indeed, he still insisted that Islam in West Africa was 'preliminatory and preparatory' to Christianity.

Blyden's article had proved that he was a highly knowledgeable scholar of Islam. He had shown an easy acquaintance with its literature in English, French, German, as well as Arabic, and had demonstrated the advantage of first hand acquaintance with its operation in West Africa. It was the work of an original and independent mind; it was well-written, ingeniously argued, and controversial.

[40] Blyden, 'Mohammedanism and the Negro Race', 604; cf. *African Repository*, LXIV, Oct. 1888, 107–9; Blyden to Coppinger, 16 May 1888, *A.C.S. Papers*, Vol. 25; *Sierra Leone Weekly News*, V, 8 Dec. 1888; *Lagos Weekly News*, IV, 30 June 1894.

So impressed was the editor of *Fraser's Magazine*, with this article, that he invited the Negro scholar to contribute others. His next, 'Christianity and the Negro Race' was foreshadowed in his previous article, and in it he continued his indictment of Christianity.[41] He repeated his charge that Christianity had been used to condition the Negro into accepting himself as inferior, and to destroy his racial pride. He wrote:

From the lesson he every day receives, the Negro unconsciously imbibes the conviction that to be a great man, he must be like the white man. He is not brought up—however he may desire it—to be the companion, the equal, the comrade of the white man, but his imitator, his ape, his parasite. To be himself in a country where everything ridicules him is to be nothing. To be as like the white man as possible—to copy his outward appearance, his peculiarities, his manners, the arrangement of his toilet, that is the aim of the Christian Negro—this is his inspiration. The only virtues which under such circumstances he develops are, of course, parasitical ones.

Blyden here pin-pointed the incongruity of the position of the New World Negro: that he was forced to accept as his ideal the values of the very people who despised him.

But Blyden did make a distinction between the influence of Roman Catholicism and Protestantism on New World Negroes to the advantage of the former:

The only Christians who have had the power successfully to throw off oppression, and maintain their positions as freemen, were Roman Catholic Negroes—the Haitians; and the greatest Negro the world has yet produced is a Roman Catholic—Toussaint L'Ouverture. At Rome, the name of Negroes, males and females, who have been distinguished for piety and good works are found in the calendar under the designation 'saints'. The Negro under Protestant rule is kept in a state of tutelage and irresponsibility as can scarcely fail to make him constantly dependent and useless whenever, thrown upon himself, he has to meet an emergency.

The yardstick which Blyden used to measure the efficacy of a religion was that expected of a race patriot: the extent to which it encouraged Negroes to assert themselves, and its willingness to recognize Negro merit.

Blyden's next article, 'Christian Missions in West Africa', which appeared in October 1876, contended that missionary work

[41] Blyden, 'Christianity and the Negro Race', *Fraser's Magazine*, XIII, May 1876, 554–68.

in this area had been a failure.[42] This conclusion was the opposite
of the typically European point of view which Blyden had as a
young man accepted, that 'the missionary's work is constructive
rather than destructive; he has nothing to demolish; he has only
to arrange his materials and proceed to build'.[43] But from about
1860 he began to criticize the operations of missionary work in
Africa on the grounds that its sectarianism, and, at times, fierce
competitiveness, its disrespect of Africans and disregard for their
customs and institutions, had produced deleterious results.[44] However, his article was his first major published statement on the
subject. In it he pointed out that despite so many years of effort
and so vast a sacrifice of life and money, Christian missionary
work in West Africa had made no substantial progress. This he
ascribed to the arrogant belief of European missionaries in their
own superiority, 'the pernicious influence' of European traders on
the Coast, and the unhealthiness of the coast itself. He urged
European missionaries to push into the interior but also emphasized that they ought to make 'a special and constant study' of
the customs and institutions of the Africans among whom they
worked. He chided European missionaries for regarding 'the
African mind . . . as blank or worse than blank, filled with everything dark and horrible and repulsive'. Taking the 'sanguinary
customs' of the King of Dahomey as an example of European
disparagement of African customs without attempting to understand them, he correctly pointed out that

the account often circulated of the large numbers killed are gross
exaggerations, and the customs, far from being the result of a wanton
desire to destroy human life, are a practice founded on a pure
religious basis, designed as a sincere manifestation of the King's filial
piety, sanctioned by long usage, upheld by a powerful priesthood,
and believed to be closely bound up with the existence of Dahomey
itself. It is not in the power of the king to abrogate the customs. Its
gradual extinction must be the result of the increasing intelligence
of the people.

In 1887 a miscellaneous collection of Blyden's articles was
published as a book and took its title, *Christianity, Islam and the*

[42] Blyden, 'Christian Missions in West Africa', *Fraser's Magazine*, XIV, Oct.
1876, 504–22.
[43] Blyden, *Hope for Africa*, 15.
[44] For example, *From West Africa to Palestine*, 1866, 25–67; *Correspondence between
E. W. Blyden and His Excellency J. Pope-Hennessy.*

Negro Race, from one of the major themes in it. All Blyden's published articles on this theme were republished. In addition, Blyden wrote two more articles on Islam, 'Islam and Race Distinctions', and 'The Mohammedans of Nigritia', for special inclusion in the book.[45] In the former, Blyden further developed his thesis that 'Islam extinguishes all distinctions founded upon race, colour or nationality.' The latter was partly a repetition of claims already made for the beneficial results of Islam in West Africa, but, in addition, brought up to date the progress of the *jihad*. He wrote of the exploits of the great warrior, Samori, a Mandinka from the Konia country east of Liberia, who since the early 1870's had conquered a wide area around the upper Niger and had imposed Islam on his conquests. As a result of Samori's efforts, Blyden wrote, 'large and powerful states which . . . were practising all the irrational and debasing superstition of a hoary Paganism are now under the influence of schools and teachers and the regular administration of law'.

The publication of his book, with an introduction by the most distinguished lawyer of Sierra Leone, Sir Samuel Lewis, repre-sented the high water mark of Blyden's literary career. As a collection of miscellaneous essays, the book had no genuine unity, but the articles had been extremely well-written, the ideas in them challenging and stimulating. Partly because of the topical nature of the themes—the influence of Christianity and Islam on the Negro, the character and achievements of the Negro race, and the role past and future of westernized Negroes in Africa—a first edition of 500 copies quickly sold out, necessitating the printing of a second edition.

In England the reaction of critics not personally acquainted with Blyden was one of astonishment or disbelief that a book of such undoubted literary and scholarly merits, could have been written by a Negro,[46] and one, moreover, as Lewis had pointed out in his introduction, whose formal education had not gone beyond High School. The reviewer in the *Athenaeum* noted that 'the most immediately noteworthy fact about this volume . . . is that its author is a Negro'; the *C.M.S. Intelligencer* stated that if Blyden's formal education stopped at High School, then 'the

[45] Blyden, *Christianity, Islam and the Negro Race*, 277–97 and 350–82 respectively.

[46] See Athenaeum, No. 3122, 27 Aug. 1887, 277; *C.M.S. Intelligencer*, Nov. 1887, 650; *Notes and Queries*, IV, 1887, 429; *Nation*, 9 Feb. 1880, 123.

teacher as well as the pupil could have been no ordinary man';
it regretted that Lewis had not given more details about Blyden's
youth. Finally, a correspondent of *Notes and Queries* questioned
Blyden's assertion that he was a 'full-blooded Negro'; the name
Blyden suggested that he had at least 'a strain of pure European
blood'. It is an indication of the widespread view of the inferiority
of the Negro, particularly if he were not partly of European stock,
that the critics had been sceptical.

But without exception, the critics conceded that the essays were
of high merit. The reviewer in the *Athenaeum* thought it remarkable that the author could write so 'clearly and feelingly' yet
'without bitterness'. The Rev. J. Stephen Barras, a correspondent
in *The Times*, thought Blyden's book 'may yet prove the greatest
contribution of the age on the gigantic subject of Christian
missions'.[47] The most enthusiastic review of Blyden's book came
from his friend R. B. Smith, who wrote in part:

I regard . . . *Christianity, Islam and the Negro Race* . . . as one of the
most remarkable books I have ever met. . . . Hitherto, no light has
shone, no voice has come, audible at all events to the outer world,
from Africa itself. It is in the pages of Mr. Blyden's book that the
great, dumb, dark continent, has at last begun to speak, and in tones
which . . . even those who most differ from his conclusions will be
glad to listen to and wise to ponder. . . . In their pathos and passion,
their patriotic enthusiasm and their philosophic calm, their range of
sympathy and genuine reserve of power, they will . . . arrest the
attention of even the most casual reader. If ever anyone spoke on his
subject with a right to be heard, it is Mr. Blyden, and, for this simple
reason, that his whole life has been a preparation for it. . . .[48]

Not unexpectedly, the most extended and the most vitriolic review
of Blyden's book appeared in the *Church Missionary Intelligencer*.
Although admitting that 'the essays hold their own well with the
contributions usually supplied to our best English periodicals',
the reviewer took violent exception to Blyden's high praise of
Islam, his criticisms of Christianity in practice, and his contention
that Roman Catholicism was less of an evil influence on Negroes
than Protestantism; he further berated Blyden for 'hymning the
praise of Liberia', and 'running amuck of all that made him what

[47] *The Times*, London, 8 Oct. 1887.
[48] R. Bosworth Smith, 'Mohammedanism in Africa', *Nineteenth Century*, XXXI,
Dec. 1887, 793.

he is'. While it is undoubtedly true that Blyden's picture of Islam had too rosy a hue, the C.M.S. reviewer adopted the traditional Christian attitude of contempt for Islam and made no attempt to understand why that religion should be so attractive to a highly intelligent Negro. To the further chagrin of the C.M.S., Blyden's point of view on Islam was 'produced indiscriminately, sometimes almost verbatim' by Canon Isaac Taylor at an Anglican Church Conference held at Wolverhampton in November 1887.[49] This wholehearted endorsement of Blyden's views on Islam by 'a respectable beneficed clergyman of the Church of England' raised 'a storm which raged in the Church pages, *The Times* and the *Reviews* for weeks and even months'[50] giving Blyden's book invaluable publicity.

In the preface to the second edition, Blyden took the opportunity of expressing his regret that the C.M.S. reviewer had spent much of his review bringing charges against Islam 'when the necessity was so pressing for a careful consideration of the elements in the methods of foreign Christian workers in Africa which prevent wider and more permanent results'. And if he had hymned the praise of Liberia it was because

That Republic represented two principles for which, in common with all intelligent Christian Negroes, he should contend: First, the return of the exiled African from the house of bondage; and Christian Negro autonomy in Church and State on African soil.

Blyden's book was well-received in the American press; the Negro press was particularly enthusiastic: the highly influential *A.M.E. Church Review* wrote of Blyden as 'The one Negro of standing in the English world of recognized scholarship';[51] the *Southern Recorder*, Atlanta, Georgia, praised it to the point of exaggeration:

We pronounce the work not only the most learned production that ever emanated from a black man, but one of the most learned in the English language. . . . It is a book for the leaders of the race, and such others who desire to see the true inwardness of the Negro and his country. The work will be an authority in the higher literary circles for ages to come.[52]

[49] *C.M.S. Intelligencer*, Nov. 1887, 655.   [50] Grogan, *op. cit.*, 151.
[51] *A.M.E. Church Review*, Oct. 1887, 216.
[52] *The Southern Recorder*, 4 Dec. 1887.

The white press, too, was impressed without being extravagant in their praise. Typical was the review which appeared in *The Nation*, New York, an influential weekly:

That he is not deficient in the rarer qualities of thorough and patient study, some of the papers in the book . . . give abundant testimony. They show broad reading, minute investigation, a surprising mental alertness. . . . [53]

Blyden's book was also acclaimed in the Muslim world; the journals and newspapers of Damascus, Constantinople and Beirut, carried highly complimentary reviews of it, and gleefully reported the controversy which the book had generated in the British press.[54]

Perhaps of peculiar interest is the recorded reaction to Blyden's book of John X. Merriman, a prominent, contemporary South African politician. Merriman's comment comes from an entry in his diary dated 5 February 1891 and is worth quoting extensively:

Read *Christianity, Islam and the Negro Race* by Blyden, a Negro. Extremely well-written from the Negro point of view, which is indeed seldom presented. The writer feels all the contumely and indignities that are the lot of the race because they are black, and tries to persuade himself and us that the Negro has a future of equality. He is more successful in pointing out the advantage that Islam has over Christianity from the Negro standpoint, and how much more effective the teaching of Mohammed is in enforcing the Christian Commandment 'Love one another.' The account of 'Nigritia', as he calls the region about Lake Chad and the upper Niger, and which is subjected to negro Mohammedans, is interesting. *If one thought that the cultivated writer represented any aspirations or ideas of a considerable section of black people, it would give one an uncomfortable feeling*, but he is as much a *rara avis* in his way as Toussaint L'Ouverture was in his. . . . Blyden is . . . successful in pointing out the failure of European enterprise to touch more than the fringe of the Continent and showing how climate enforces his demand of 'Africa for the Africans.' The book is a clever *tour de force* but it is questionable whether it gets at the bottom of the true black view of the white.[55]

[53] *The Nation*, 9 Feb. 1888, 123–4.

[54] *C.M.S. Intelligencer and Record*, April 1888, 269.

[55] Quoted from Phyllis Lewsen, ed., *Selections from the Correspondence of John X. Merriman, 1890–98*, Cape Town 1963, 30. The italics are that of Merriman. I am indebted to Mrs. Shula Marks, lecturer in South African History, School of Oriental and African Studies, London, for bringing this extract to my attention.

Merriman although reputedly liberal, was a supporter of apartheid, and to such as him who believed in the inferiority of Negroes, the achievements of men like Blyden were always embarrassing.

Finally, it is worthy of note that Blyden's book found its way into at least one Royal Library: in 1892 as Liberian ambassador to the Court of St. James, Blyden offered Queen Victoria a copy of his book at an audience with Her Majesty, and it was 'thankfully received'.[56]

Blyden was, of course, delighted that his book commanded so much attention. 'The United States was much older than Liberia when it was asked with a sneer: "who reads an American book",[57] he boasted to an American friend. But for him, the most important result of 'the generous reception' given to his book was 'that it would convince the intelligent Negro youth, first that in the Republic of letters . . . there is no such thing as caste; and secondly, that if any man, whatever his race, has anything worth listening to, men of all race will give him a respectful hearing'.[58]

After 1887 most of Blyden's writings were devoted to explaining African customs and institutions to an European audience, and in insisting more than ever that there was much in traditional African culture that was worth retaining; he also urged educated Africans to play the lead in explaining African society to foreigners so that they would come to understand and respect it. Indeed, his most significant work after *Christianity, Islam and the Negro Race* was *African Life and Customs*, 1908, the first important attempt at a sociological analysis of African society as a whole. In fact, in the last years of his life he laid emphasis on a highly conservative cultural nationalism which sought to stem the advance of European culture by seeking to retain as much as possible of traditional African culture including such customs as polygamy and secret societies. But his attempts to educate both Europeans and Africans about the merits of traditional African society will be more fully discussed in Chapters eight and nine.

It is very much to be regretted that two major books on which Blyden had long worked—*A History of Liberia*, and *Comparative Theology* were never completed, or at least never appeared in

[56] *Sierra Leone Weekly News*, VIII, 11 June 1892.
[57] Blyden to Coppinger, 13 Oct. 1887, *A.C.S. Papers*, Vol. 24.
[58] *Christianity, Islam and the Negro Race*, preface to second edition.

print, and (as in the case of his voluminous personal papers) have so far not been located. It is perhaps a pity, too, that despite the promptings of friends, white and black, to write his autobiography, he declined to do so. In the very last days of his life he seemed to have begun dictating an autobiography to J. S. Davies,[59] Postmaster-General of Sierra Leone, and one of his few close friends, but these jottings, too, have so far not been located. Blyden had also begun research for a history of Sierra Leone but did not seem to have proceeded far on this.

It is all the more lamentable that Blyden did not complete and publish his *History of Liberia*, because he had made it plain that he was not going to aim at 'bloodless objectivity' in such a history. He had planned a didactic, 'patriotic and loyal history', which was intended 'at once as a record of the labors and triumphs of the Africa Colonization and an illustration of the capacity of the race'; it would also have given 'in no offensive way the credit of all the really progressive efforts in Liberia to the men to whom it belongs'.[60] If Blyden's history would obviously have been a biassed one, if mulattoes would have been given less than fair treatment, it would, nonetheless, have been interesting and well-written literature and would doubtless have been a valuable document for the reconstruction of nineteenth century Liberian history.

But even without Blyden's *History of Liberia*, it is clear from his other writings what his philosophy of history was: the inscrutable working of a Divine Providence for the ultimate good of the Negro Race. Such a view stemmed partly from his deeply religious nature and was partly a convenient rationale for the unhappy lot of his race. It possessed the supreme advantage of being able, theoretically at least, to salve the suffering and humiliation of the race in the past and in the present, while holding out to it the promise of a bright future. But while theocratic determinism—really no more than an act of Faith—had its advantages, it led to contradictions in Blyden's whole scheme of thought and caused him to maintain ridiculous positions. He had, for instance, consistently argued that it was part of the Providential design that

[59] J. E. Casely Hayford, *The Truth about the West African Land Question*, London 1913, 113, where the author quotes an extract of a letter from Blyden dated 10 July 1910, in which he stated that 'Professor' Davies had been making 'daily notes on the story of my life'.

[60] Blyden to Coppinger, 23 Aug. 1865, *A.C.S. Papers*, Vol. 13; cf. Blyden to Coppinger, 23 Jan., 28 April and 10 Nov. 1888, *A.C.S. Papers*, Vol. 25.

Negroes should be taken to the New World so that they could acquire Christianity and other elements of western culture and civilization with the ultimate destiny of returning to christianize and civilize Africa. Thus as late as 1900 when the prospect of American Negro return to Africa was almost nil, Blyden could still write:

To those who have lived any time in West Africa, three things are indisputably clear; first, that it was absolutely necessary that large numbers of the people should be taken into exile for discipline and training under a more advanced race; second, that they should be kept separate from the dominant race; third, that chosen spirits from among the exiles should in course of time return and settle among their brethren in the fatherland to guide them into the path of civilization.[61]

This statement of 1900 represented a modification of his earlier viewpoint that an entire Negro exodus was inevitable. But by taking a transcendental view of history, Blyden, in effect, gave divine sanction to the slave trade, absolved those who had taken part in it, and nullified his argument that Christianity had stunted the 'growth of manhood' among New World Negroes. Of course, the main difficulty in subscribing to theocratic determinism as a philosophy of history lies with the interpretation of the Divine Plan. And if Blyden, being merely human, had wrongly predicted that the Negro exodus would take place in his own lifetime, he could later essay the interpretation that the scheme of repatriation had been deferred by Providence because mulattoes had complicated the issue, and it was God's wish that Africa should be reserved only for Negroes. To Blyden, every reverse, every disaster, every set-back was merely God's inscrutable unfolding of the divine plan. He expressed this view with eloquence and pathos in a sermon delivered in Boston in 1882:

They (Negroes) were to remember that if they were despised and scorned, a far greater than themselves had had a similar experience. Christ was to be held up to the suffering African ... as a blessed illustration of the glorious fact that persecution and suffering and contempt are no proof that God is not the loving father of a people— but may be rather an evidence of nearness to God seeing that they have been chosen to tread in the footsteps of the first born of the creation, suffering for the welfare of others. . . . All the advancement

[61] *Liberia Bulletin*, No. 16, Feb. 1900, 93.

made to a better future, by individuals or race, has been made through paths marked by suffering. This great law is written not only in the Bible, but upon all history.[62]

But just as in the case of Marxism, workers were expected to be activists in bringing about the 'inevitable' classless society, even so, Blyden expected Negroes to take concerted action to help accelerate 'the divine plan' of bringing glory to the Negro race.

Blyden was an original and provocative thinker, if not a systematic one. His writings were a curious blend of propaganda and scholarship, of the messianic, the mystical and metaphysical with the historical and sociological. The abstract part of his writings—his theory of race, his philosophy of history—was often contradictory, illogical or unclear. But this is a criticism that is true of all contemporary European nationalists who, like Blyden, were primarily concerned with promoting the goal of national or racial greatness, and so were not primarily concerned with logic or consistency. On the other hand, a substantial portion of Blyden's historical and sociological writings can bear the scrutiny of exact academic standards. His interpretation of Negro achievements both in the New World and Africa was sound and reasonable. Moreover, Blyden was one of the first serious advocates and pioneers of the sociological, anthropological and historical study of Africa.

More than any other Negro in the nineteenth century, Blyden's writings and scholarship had won him widespread recognition and respect in the English-speaking literary world, as well as acclaim in the Muslim world. His outstanding literary reputation, his vast learning and catholicity of interests, his charm and sophistication, his brilliance in conversation, and eloquence as a speaker, combined to create a great demand for him as a lecturer, contributor to learned journals, or as the honoured guest of litterateurs on his visits to Britain and America, particularly after the publication of *Christianity, Islam and the Negro Race* in 1887. His literary achievements won him many academic awards and rare honours. He received the degrees of Doctor of Laws (1874) and Divinity (1880) from Lincoln University. He was elected to honorary membership in several learned societies or distinguished organizations: in 1878 he was elected an honorary member of the Athenaeum, one of the most exclusive gentlemen's clubs of

[62] *African Repository*, LX, Jan. 1884, 11.

London; in 1880, Fellow of the American Philological Association; in 1882, honorary member of the Society of Science and
Letters of Bengal; in 1884, Vice-President of the American
Colonization Society; in 1890, honorary member of the American
Society of Comparative Religion; in 1898, Corresponding Member of the newly-founded American Negro Academy; in 1901
founding member and a Vice-President of the African Society.

Blyden had two books by English authors dedicated to him.
The first was by James John Garth Wilkinson, a disciple and
biographer of Emanuel Swedenborg, the eighteenth-century
Swedish religious mystic, and was entitled *The African and the
True Christian Religion*, published in 1892. This was an attempt
to interpret Swedenborg's views on religion as it could relate to
the needs of Negroes in the late nineteenth century. Blyden himself was keenly interested in the views of Swedenborg who had
conceived of Africans as the people potentially most capable of
religious perfection. In his dedication, Wilkinson expressed his
indebtedness to Blyden's 'powerful work', *Christianity, Islam and
the Negro Race* of which he made 'large use' in his own work.
In 1896, J. P. Mansel Heale, a distinguished author and traveller,
dedicated his book *A Chapter of Genesis* to Blyden 'as a token of
admiration for one of the "blameless Ethiopians", a worthy
representative of a much misunderstood and ancient people'.

He was also the recipient of honours from several governments.
He was made Knight Commander of the Liberian Humane Order
of African Redemption; received the Grand Band of the Order of
the Green Dragon of Annam from the French Government; the
Order of the Medijidieh from the Sultan of Turkey, and a similar
Order from the Bey of Tunis. He was awarded a Coronation
Medal by King Edward VII and Queen Alexandra; and in the
last few years of his life was given a small pension by the British
Government 'in recognition of his literary services'.

Blyden's impact in the world of ideas was greater than that of
any of his Negro contemporaries. American Negroes produced
their men of learning, among them W. S. Scarborough, a noted
linguist and classical scholar; George Washington Williams, the
outstanding historian of the Negro in the nineteenth century,
Alexander Crummell, the sophisticated episcopalian divine,
Francis Grimké, theologian and prolific writer on social problems,
Frederick Douglass and Booker T. Washington, primarily men of

action, but also competent with the pen. But among these and others were no peers of Blyden; his nearest equal was the brilliant American Negro, William E. B. Du Bois,[63] who in Blyden's last years had already begun to make a profound mark in the world of scholarship and ideas; but they were barely contemporaries— almost two generations separated them; Blyden properly belongs to the nineteenth century; Du Bois to the twentieth century. Among West Africans he was the only author who was primarily a man of letters. As a nineteenth century figure, Blyden, because of the scope and breadth of his learning, the topicality of his subjects, the originality of his thought, and the felicity of his style, made an impact in the world of ideas far beyond that of any of his Negro contemporaries. As one of the important thinkers of the century, he undoubtedly did much to vindicate his race, and dispel the myth of inherent Negro inferiority.

[63] There is no evidence that the two men met personally, but Du Bois was certainly acquainted with Blyden's writings and admired him. In *Crisis*, Jan. 1912, Du Bois described him as 'the leading representative of his race in West Africa' and the March issue of *Crisis* carried an obituary of Blyden, 'the "Grand Old Man of West Africa" ... [who] had had many honors bestowed upon him'.

5. Race Work in Sierra Leone 1871-3

Driven from Liberia in 1871, Blyden continued his work on behalf
of the Negro race for two and a half years in Sierra Leone. For his
task as he conceived it, Sierra Leone was, after Liberia, the logical
choice of venue. Education had taken root earlier here than elsewhere in West Africa and its schools attracted privileged students
from other West African territories.[1] Moreover, from the late
1830's links between Sierra Leone and various parts of West
Africa, particularly Lagos and Yorubaland, were made by
liberated Africans trading along the coast or returning to their
homeland, and these movements made of Sierra Leone the centre
of an emerging British controlled or influenced West African
community.[2] Sierra Leone, too, was the first European West
African colony to manifest an incipient nationalism. Between
1855 and the time of Blyden's arrival seven newspapers were
published by West Indian emigrants, and these attacked government abuses and called for elected political representation.[3] But
they also fostered sectionalism in their abusive assaults on individuals or various elements of the society comprised primarily of
New World Settlers, liberated and indigenous Africans of various
tribes, and Muslim Negroes, among whom was mutual antagonism,[4] a factor which, as Blyden was to find, militated against
united, effective action for advancing the interest of his race.

In Sierra Leone, Blyden attempted to put into practice his ideas
on race, and as a result inspired among a small group of educated
Africans an ethnocentric movement which was characterized by a
revolt against attempts at Europeanization of Africans, by an
emphasis on racial differences, and by the assertion that there was

[1] Colin G. Wise, *A History of Education in British West Africa*, London 1956, 18-19,
100; F. H. Hilliard, *A Short History of Education in British West Africa*, London 1957,
20-30.
[2] See Jean H. Kopytoff, *A Preface to Modern Nigeria: The 'Sierra Leoneans' in
Yoruba, 1830-1890*, Madison 1965.
[3] C. H. Fyfe, 'The Sierra Leone Press in the Nineteenth Century', *Sierra Leone
Studies*, New series, No. 8, June 1957, 229-31.
[4] Fyfe, *History of Sierra Leone*, 383.

need to develop 'the special attributes of the Negro race' and to maintain a distinctive African culture. But this was not an attempt to rid West Africa of Europeans. Indeed, it was one of Blyden's major goals to seek to persuade the British to extend their influence and jurisdiction in West Africa and thereby help to pacify, unite and develop this vast territory—an imperial role that Liberia had been unable to play.

The existing condition which favoured Blyden's fostering of ethnocentrism was the tension which had existed between the African pastors and the European missionaries of the Church Missionary Society over the control and management of the native pastorate, and the rampant sectarian rivalry in the colony. Under the stimulus of Blyden, this tension within the C.M.S. erupted into an open controversy and assumed a wider significance when some lay Africans joined the issue on the side of the clerics. The Africans charged the European missionaries with creating unnecessary sectarian divisions among them, with showing contempt for African customs and institutions, and with destroying the wholesome base of African society. They claimed that these evils created by European influence could be eliminated by setting up an independent, non-sectarian African church, and a secular University, run by Negroes themselves.

Blyden's actions and influence in Sierra Leone can best be understood against the background of two pertinent decisions taken in England: the first was in the forward-looking plan of Henry Venn,[5] the honorary secretary of the C.M.S. from 1841 until his death in 1873, for the creation of 'self-governing, self-supporting, self-propagating native churches'; the other in the Report of the Select Parliamentary Committee of 1865 which recommended that future British policy in West Africa should be directed towards 'encouraging in the natives the exercise of those qualities which may render it possible for us more and more to transfer to them the administration of all the Government. . . .'[6] Under Venn's plan, C.M.S. missionaries were to found nuclei of

---

[5] For this, see Venn's own four papers, three on 'The Native Pastorate and Organization of Native Churches', and the other, 'On Nationality', in William Knight, *Memoir of H. Venn*, London 1880, 305–21, and 282–92 respectively. The quotations from Venn which follow are taken from these sources. See also J. F. A. Ajayi, 'Henry Venn and the Policy of Development', *Journal of the Historical Society of Nigeria*, No. 4, 1959, 331–42.

[6] Report of Select Committee on West Africa, *Parliamentary Papers*, V, 1865, 3.

Christian communities, provide them with African leadership, and then withdraw to repeat the process elsewhere, while continuing to exercise a moral influence *ab extra*. To carry out this delicate and difficult task Venn gave 'practical instructions' to his missionaries, the salient ones of which are worth noting: they were 'to study the national character of the people' among whom they worked, and 'show the utmost respect for national peculiarities'; Venn, like Blyden, assumed that there were 'irrepressible race distinctions', and warned missionaries that 'these would rise in intensity with the progress of the mission', but they were not to react 'by charging the natives with presumption and ingratitude' or by 'standing upon their British prestige'; they were to expect that 'as the native church assumes a national character it will supersede the denominational distinctions which are now introduced by Foreign Missionaries'. But the wise policy and perspicacious advice of Venn did not find favour with European missionaries, and in Sierra Leone, as elsewhere, missionary work fell far short of what he had recommended.

But Venn himself had provided Africans with the grounds for criticizing European missionary shortcomings and had set them the unequivocal goal of a 'national' independent church. In Sierra Leone on All Saints' Day, 1861, a Native Church Pastorate was formed with nine pastors in charge of as many parishes, but contrary to Venn's recommended policy remained under direct European supervision. It was left to enlightened Africans to attempt to bring to pass Venn's goal of an independent African Church which they had adopted as their own. And it is significant that in a sermon preached on 31 May 1871, during the celebration of the tenth anniversary of the Native Church Pastorate, J. H. Davies, one of the African pastors, emphasized the need for an independent African Church: 'We are pleading for an institution . . . which alone can bring true liberty to the soul and body of man. . . . We request you to aim at establishing at Sierra Leone a pure Native Church . . . not only for our own and children's use, but for the use of Africa at large.'[7]

In like manner, the recommendations of the 1865 Parliamentary Committee had tended to encourage greater African assertion in their own affairs, and although the British Government did not find it convenient to implement the recommenda-

[7] C.M.S., CA1/09, *Tenth Annual Report of the Sierra Leone Native Pastorate.*

tions, they affected the thinking of colonial Governors in British West Africa for at least a decade. Thus, during his second governorship of Sierra Leone (1868–72), Sir Arthur E. Kennedy implemented a policy of appointing qualified Africans in preference to Europeans to vacant Government positions.[8] Among these new appointments was that of the Rev. George Nicol to the colonial chaplaincy of the Gambia—the first African to be appointed to such a position. In a letter of gratitude to Kennedy, the African pastors of Sierra Leone saw the appointment 'as an era in the history of West Africa', and hoped that it heralded 'a happier day . . . when the prejudices of race will end'.[9] In addition, Kennedy had increased African representation on the Legislative Council from one to two, and shortly before his governorship ended, prompted, with success, educated Africans to form a Sierra Leone Native Association to promote their own interests. For their part, educated West Africans had immediately endorsed the recommendations of the 1865 Parliamentary Committee. One of the most articulate endorsements came from James Africanus Horton, a Sierra Leonean medical doctor trained at the University of Edinburgh, who became an admirer and friend of Blyden on a visit to Monrovia in 1866.[10] Horton described the recommendations as 'a grand conception', and looked forward to the time when 'West African nationalities will occupy a prominent place in the world's history, and when they will command a voice in the councils of nations.'[11] And Blyden himself was to cite the recommendations of the 1865 committee and their reputed tradition of humanitarianism in West Africa, in his attempts to persuade the British to extend their jurisdiction far and wide in this area, which process together with Liberia's efforts, he envisaged as culminating ultimately in the formation of a large West African state which he hoped would command world-wide attention.

On fleeing Liberia, Blyden had gone to Sierra Leone and after a few weeks there had left for England. In Salisbury Court, London, the headquarters of the C.M.S., Blyden met Venn, that great product and representative of the liberal British evangelistic

[8] *African Times*, X, 21 May 1871.
[9] Native Pastors to Sir A. E. Kennedy, Nov. 1869, quoted in J. A. B. Horton, *Letters on the Political Condition of the Gold Coast*, London 1870, 164–5.
[10] J. A. B. Horton, *West African Countries and Peoples . . .* , London 1868, 15–18, 269, 271.   [11] *Ibid.*, 68–9.

and humanitarian movement, and a man much revered by Christian West Africans. Blyden was interviewed by the C.M.S. Committee and was able to persuade its members to agree to push the Society's work and influence into the interior. Highly impressed with Blyden's ability as a linguist, members of the committee offered him a position in this capacity in the C.M.S. at Sierra Leone, and regarded him as a key figure in the contemplated interior work.[12] In preparation for this, Blyden was to teach Arabic to select African students at Fourah Bay College, and himself to study and reduce to writing the Fula tongue. Blyden left England in early August with great enthusiasm for his new job and with high hopes of the results. Once within the C.M.S., he had hoped to reform its operation by seeking to persuade European missionaries to show greater respect and appreciation for African customs and institutions, to accelerate the process of delegation of ecclesiastical authority to trained Africans; and ever to extend their activities into the interior.

But by merely taking up his appointment Blyden created a crisis within the C.M.S. at Sierra Leone. Henry Cheetham, the dynamic new bishop of Sierra Leone, a man with a low opinion of African ability and with no patience for the 'pretensions' of the African pastors towards ecclesiastical independence, was strongly opposed to his appointment, partly because the Negro scholar was already known to have been adversely critical of Christian missions, while lauding the influence of Islam, partly because rumour had reached Sierra Leone from Liberia that Blyden had committed adultery with Roye's wife and had been forced to flee the Negro Republic.[13] In contrast to the cool reception given him by Cheetham and other European missionaries Blyden, no stranger among them, was enthusiastically received by the African pastors and educated laymen who ascribed charges of immorality against him to the machinations of his political enemies.[14] The European missionaries refused to co-operate with

[12] C.M.S., CA1/L8, Secs. of the C.M.S. to Blyden, 1 Aug. 1871; Venn to Messrs. Hamilton and Lamb, 4 Aug. 1871. It is proof of the respect of the parent committee of the C.M.S. for Blyden's linguistic ability that members hired him although he was not an Anglican.

[13] C.M.S., CA1/025e, Cheetham to Venn, 10 Aug. 1871.

[14] C.M.S. CA1/024, Petition of the Native Pastors to Venn, Dec. 1871; Blyden had made an eleven day visit (10–20 Jan.) earlier in the year and had then been urged by the local educated élite to take up an appointment at Fourah Bay College.

Blyden who complained thus to Venn: 'I find that there is not much sympathy here for the study of native languages or for the interior enterprise. As a general thing, the European missionary, however ardent his zeal on behalf of "poor benighted Africa" while in Europe, as soon as he comes in contact with the Negro, his ardour undergoes a sensible refrigeration.'[15] Moreover his appointment was terminated before he could start working effectively. On 16 November 1871, the parent committee of the C.M.S., after receiving news of Blyden's alleged adultery, decided to suspend him until 'his name could be cleared', Venn reluctantly concurring in the decision.[16] Blyden's suspension won him the sympathy of educated Africans and increased his influence among them. He had also become well-known and popular among the Muslims of Freetown.[17]

If Blyden could not influence the policy of the C.M.S. as it affected the African from within, he was determined to do so from without. Indeed, by the time of his suspension, and perhaps anticipating it, he had already decided to found a newspaper to propagate his views. In this he had the financial support of five African merchants: Syble Boyle, William Grant, T. J. Sawyerr, Thomas Bright, and T. J. Macaulay—all wealthy and race-proud sons of Recaptive parents. Their support made this 'completely Negro venture' possible, and Blyden wrote with pride to Venn that 'Not one European has given anything towards establishing the paper.'[18] The newspaper with Blyden as editor was due to start publication in April 1872.

In the interim, Blyden continued to show interest in linking Sierra Leone with its hinterland and himself conducted an expedition thither. Even before his suspension from the C.M.S. mission Blyden had urged Governor Kennedy to permit the Liberian, Benjamin Anderson, to explore the territory between the colony 'and the head waters of the Niger'.[19] Blyden's letter was forwarded by Kennedy to the Colonial Office and created 'much interest' there. One of the minutes labelled it 'very interesting and

[15] C.M.S., CA1/047, Blyden to Venn, 16 Oct. 1871.

[16] C.M.S., CA1/L8, Venn to 16 Nov. 1871.

[17] C.M.S., CA1/047, Blyden to Venn, 6 Sept., 16 Sept., 11 Oct., and 28 Oct. 1871.

[18] Ibid., Blyden to Venn, 17 April 1872.

[19] C.O. 267/312, Blyden to Kennedy, 11 Oct. 1871; also Colonial Office Minutes of 3 January 1872.

a good specimen of what the Negro can attain to', and Lord
Kimberley, the Colonial Secretary, thought it important enough
to have a copy sent to Lord Granville, the Foreign Secretary. But
although Blyden had succeeded in arousing curiosity about himself at the Colonial Office, no action was taken on his letter. Two
months after his first letter, Blyden offered to explore the hinterland of Sierra Leone 'in the interest of geography, ethnology,
history and commerce'.[20] This time his plea succeeded and
Blyden, 'a pure African and a man of high intelligence', was
officially appointed by Governor Kennedy to go on 'a mission of
Peace and Friendship to the Kings and Chiefs of the Falaba and
Sangara Country'.[21]

Blyden set out on his expedition from Freetown on 6 January
1872, determined to show the British why they ought to extend
their influence into the interior. After three days travel he came to
Kambia, 'a trading town of considerable importance situated on
the south bank of the Great Scarcies River', and here discovered
from the Muslim Chief, Almami Al-Hay, and his principal men
that the interior was in a very unsettled state as a result of a
protracted war between runaway slaves led by Bilâli, a native of
Kissy country, and a slave-holding combination led by Almami
Mumineh, Chief of Kukumah in the Susu country. Blyden
reported to Kennedy that the King of Kambia was anxious for
the British Government to restore the peace and security of the
country, and thus pave the way for the revival of trade; the King
requested, too, that schools be set up in his town for the instruction of children in the English language.[22]

After two days of further travel, Blyden reached Kukumah,
the headquarters of Mumineh, whom he sought to persuade to
put an end to the war. He assured the Muslim chief that were he
to desist from his 'aggressive pro-slavery policy', the Government
of Sierra Leone would enter into a treaty of friendship with him.
Mumineh, whose resources had been exhausted by the war,
agreed that the Government of Sierra Leone should act as
mediator in the unsettled dispute. Blyden urged the Acting

[20] C.O. 267/315, Blyden to Kennedy, 21 Dec. 1871.
[21] *Ibid.*, Kennedy to Kimberley, 3 Jan. 1872.
[22] C.M.S. (Copy), CA1/047, Blyden to Kennedy, 10 Jan. 1872. This and other
letters of Blyden to the Government of Sierra Leone while he was on his way to
Falaba are not in the Colonial Office Archives. The copies in the C.M.S. archives
were sent by Blyden to Henry Venn.

Governor, John J. Kendall, to act swiftly on this the 'first ever pacific expression' of Mumineh. He claimed that if the war was settled the whole region would be opened to 'a pacific and lucrative trade'. And to guarantee future peace and prosperity, Blyden suggested that the area be colonized by 'Africans from Sierra Leone or the Western hemisphere . . . men willing to engage in agriculture and of moderate training. . . .'[23]

In his next despatch, Blyden again sought to impress the Governor with the potential richness of the country. He reported that most of it was fertile prairie land 'where thousands of cattle might easily feed and fatten' and tropical vegetables could be produced 'in unlimited quantity'; also, that iron ore 'of the greatest purity' was widely distributed and that his party had seen 'several furnaces where large quantities of that useful metal' was produced. As a prerequisite to the development of this area, Blyden recommended 'the construction of good common roads in the first instance and of railroads at no distant period'. He assured that the terrain would present no major engineering difficulties. He insisted, optimistically, that the financial outlay for the development of the area need not be great, but that it would 'enrich the shareholders . . . and develop to an extent incomprehensible, the commercial importance of Sierra Leone'.[24]

From Kukumah, Blyden's expedition passed in a northerly direction through the trading towns of Ganjah and Sumatra, and thence in an easterly direction into territory terrorized by 'an impudent and warlike' Muslim people—the Houbous.[25] The disordered state of this territory Blyden cited as another reason for the pacification and development of the area by the British.

Blyden reached Falaba on 1 March, after an eventful journey through an hitherto untraversed route. On behalf of the Sierra Leone Government he entered into a treaty of friendship with the King. He reported, too, that the King was willing to 'put himself and his country under the protection of the English'.[26]

In his official report Blyden again made a strong plea for the establishment of a vast protectorate over the hinterland of Sierra Leone by appealing to the 'humanitarian and commercial

[23] *Ibid.*, Blyden to Kendall, 26 Jan. 1872.
[24] *Ibid.*, Blyden to Kendall, 5 Feb. 1872.
[25] *Ibid.*
[26] *Ibid.*, Blyden to Kendall, 19 Feb. 1872.

instincts' of the British. First, he stressed the need of the interior for civilized contact:

The route adopted by the Expedition from Kambia to Falaba must be considered the darkest portion of the interior accessible from Sierra Leone. No foreigner had ever traversed it. . . . The people are, as a rule, besotted pagans, entirely at large from the influence of Mohammedanism. Indolence has long been their habit. They live together by the labour of their slaves and extorting heavy taxes from the poor interior traders who happen to pass through their towns. The ordinary instincts of human nature which suggest plans for growth and improvement have not been developed in them. They have existed for ages under conditions altogether incompatible with human progress.[27]

He dared the British Government to accept the challenge of developing the area:

a great work devolves upon the Government of Sierra Leone—a work with which the commercial prosperity of the colony and the civiliza-tion of millions are connected. England stands foremost among nations as the energetic promoter of whatever concerns the welfare of the African continent. Her colonial possessions on this coast and her commercial and moral ascendancy especially qualify her through her Agents . . . to contribute largely towards rescuing tribes accessible to her influence from their present abject condition and assist them to take part in the work of the world's progress.[28]

The Colonial Office was clearly impressed with Blyden's Report and its recommendations but a stringent financial policy would not permit it to go beyond granting stipends to the more impor-tant chiefs of the interior.

Blyden also appealed to missionary societies to extend their operations into the interior. He wrote to Venn: 'I think that a Christian missionary would be welcomed at Falaba; and it would be an important centre for the aggressive operations of the Church of Christ. I beg most earnestly to call the attention of the C.M.S. to Kambia and Falaba as important outposts and strategic points in the great warfare which is to restore the kingdom of this world to their legitimate heir.'[29] But this carefully phrased appeal, too, met with no response.

Paradoxically, although Blyden invited the missionaries to

[27] C.O. 267/316, Blyden to John Pope-Hennessy, 4 March 1872: Report of the Expedition to Falaba.
[28] *Ibid.*   [29] C.M.S., CA1/047, Blyden to Venn, 11 Feb. 1872.

extend their operations into the interior, he remained highly critical of their activities on the coast. Before he left for the interior, he had given a clear indication that his clashes with European missionaries was by no means at an end. In a letter of 5 January 1872, to the Hon. William Grant, a well-to-do merchant, and a member of the Legislative Council, Blyden charged that European missionary education had failed to develop 'pride of race' in Africans, an attribute which had given another downtrodden people—the Jew—their 'unquenchable vitality'. To supply this want, he advocated the establishment of a West African University in Sierra Leone to be 'conducted by earnest and well-cultivated Negroes'. He optimistically assured Grant that: 'You will find that, with such an institution here, in a short time, there will be a general diffusion of that higher intelligence which originates public measures, which stimulates the people, moderates their impulses, sustains and gives weight to noble enterprises, creates and expounds a healthy public sentiment and accelerates the moral and spiritual progress of the race.'[30]

On his return from the interior Blyden found unexpected support for his 'nationalist' ideas from the new Governor, John Pope-Hennessy, who had succeeded Kennedy in February 1872. Pope-Hennessy was a highly controversial Irish-Catholic who, as an Irish member of the British House of Commons, and as Governor of Labuan, had established a reputation for espousing the cause of the under-privileged.[31] He continued this aspect of his career in Sierra Leone: although his was an interim governorship which lasted only one year, he proved himself to be the most enthusiastic exponent of the recommendations of the 1865 Parliamentary Committee by his strong and open support for African aspirations.

Back in Freetown, Blyden began his newspaper. It was meant to 'herald a new departure'; it was the first newspaper in Sierra Leone designed to 'serve the race purpose'.[32] Its very title—the *Negro*—hitherto used in Sierra Leone only as a term of abuse, was intended to promote racial unity and solidarity. The strong objection which was in fact registered against the title was anticipated and rebutted in the first issue:

[30] *The West African University: Correspondence between E. W. Blyden and His Excellency, J. Pope-Hennessy*, Freetown 1872, 2–3.

[31] See James Pope-Hennessy, *Verandah: Some Episodes in the Crown Colonies, 1867–1889*, London 1964, Book III.

[32] *Sierra Leone Weekly News*, VI, 6 Sept. 1890, article on 'The West African Press'.

It has been called the *Negro* (if explanation be necessary) because it is intended to represent and defend the interest of that peculiar type of humanity known as the Negro, with all its affiliated and collateral branches whether on this continent or elsewhere.

'West African' was considered definite enough, but too exclusive for the comprehensive intentions entertained by the promoters of the scheme—viz.: to recognize and greet the brotherhood of the race wherever found. . . .

The term is perfectly legitimate and under our circumstances indispensable.[33]

One year later, Blyden made the proud claim that 'The title of this paper, at first misunderstood, we now know to be generally accepted and cordially approved by all thinking members of the race in West Africa, in the West Indies, and in the United States, and we have constant proof of their heartfelt sympathy with the views to which we are committed.'[34]

Assured of the sympathy of Pope-Hennessy, Blyden became more uncharitable than ever in his condemnation of European missionary influence on Africans. On 6 December he wrote thus to the Governor:

The system or want of system to which the natives of this country have been subjected in consequence of the conflicting dogmatic creed introduced from abroad, has unduly biassed their development and hampered progress. All efforts here . . . seem to have been directed mainly to a solution of the question of who shall be uppermost; hence denominational rivalry and the wasting of time and energy in localities already occupied, instead of carrying the Gospel to 'regions beyond' and proclaiming it to every creature. Free learning has with very few exceptions, been substituted by the narrow and dwarfing influence of ecclesiastical dogmatism. We have been torn into discordant and unprofitable sectaries by our pretending to understand the different elaborate creeds brought to us from Europe, and confusing ourselves with ecclesiastical quarrels handed down from a remote antiquity, which even in Europe only those who are learned in a particular department can grasp and comprehend.[35]

This largely-justified criticism was not an argument for the withdrawal of foreign missionaries. It was an appeal for a change in

[33] Quoted in *Proceedings of a Banquet in honour of E. W. Blyden, LL.D.*, London 1907, 52–3.
[34] C.O. 267/324, No. 978, enclosure: *The Negro*, II, 16 April 1873. This is the only copy of the *Negro* known to have survived.
[35] *The West African University*, 7.

their attitudes and methods, for Blyden believed that Christianity, in its simple essence, taught by men who understood or attempted to understand African customs and institutions, was the highest influence to which the Negro could be exposed.

He also continued his campaign for an independent secular West African University. In his letter of 6 December to the Governor he had written:

If in the Government of the Settlements, native agency is to be welcomed and encouraged and not despised and excluded, if the people are ever to become fit to be entrusted with the functions of self-government, if they are ever to become ripe for free and progressive institutions, it must be by a system of education adopted to the exigencies of the country and race; such as shall prepare the intelligent youths for the responsibilities which must devolve upon them, and without interfering with their native instincts and throwing them altogether out of harmony and sympathy with their own countrymen, shall qualify them to be efficient guides and counsellors and rulers of the people. . . .

From the dubious premise that each race had peculiar, inherent attributes, Blyden deduced that each should receive special education designed to 'bring out . . . [race] individuality and originality'. This was why, although he asked for Government aid in building a University, he wanted it run by Negro scholars 'from different parts of the world'.[36]

In a second letter to the Governor on 9 December, Blyden emphasized that 'a government which is more inert in developing the intellectual and moral character of these tribes than in availing itself of the material resources of the country is of doubtful utility to the race'. He gave as an added reason for the founding of a University the need for an indigenous literature which he hoped would 'silently but effectually transform the moral and intellectual condition of the people'.[37]

Though sympathetic, Pope-Hennessy replied that because there had been so many 'monuments of benevolent failures' in Sierra Leone, the initiative for founding such a University must come from Africans themselves.[38] Blyden, aware that there would not be enough public support for such a scheme, conveniently attributed this to 'the warping influence' of missionary education. He

[36] *Ibid.*, 6.   [37] *Ibid.*, 7.   [38] *Ibid.*, 12.

claimed that Europeans 'owed Africans a great debt for un-
requited physical labour', and so Africans did not 'simply ask it
as a favour but claimed it as a right' that European governments
should aid in 'unfettering and enlightening the Negro mind, and
placing him in a position to act well his part among the productive
agencies of time'.[39] After further discussion of the subject with
educated Africans, Pope-Hennessy transmitted the correspondence
between himself and Blyden to the Colonial Office, adding his
own plea for 'the establishment of a West African University
founded on a humble basis'.[40] Blyden was hopeful that the
Governor's recommendation would be implemented and already
he anticipated the results: 'The tropical blood that beats passionately in the veins of every Negro will manifest itself in a new
social force, in new institutions, and a new literature. The present
strait-jacket of unmodified European tradition holds back the
mind of many a master.'[41]

The Governor had shared, too, Blyden's enthusiasm for linking
Sierra Leone with the interior. In January 1873 Pope-Hennessy
appointed him Government Agent to the Interior and Blyden set
out on another official expedition, this time to Timbo, the capital
of the Muslim kingdom of Futa Jallon. The Governor and his
retinue accompanied the expedition as far as Kambia whither the
leading Susu, Limba and Temme chiefs had been summoned in
an attempt to settle the Bilâli War.[42] At a public meeting attended
by some 2,000 Africans, the Governor spoke 'on the great subject
of the promotion of African interest'.[43] The Hon. William Grant,
a member of the Governor's party, spoke 'on the importance of
peace and harmony in the country for the development and
organization of the great African nationality which must be
established in this country'.[44] And when Blyden 'saw the
enthusiasm of the crowd, he was encouraged to think that a great
civilized state in the tropics will yet come to pass'. No doubt he
saw proof of this, too, in Billeh, 'a University town—the Oxford of
the region', in a 'sequestered position' on the bank of the Scarcies
river.[45] Members of the expedition and of the Governor's party

[39] Ibid., 13.
[40] C.O. 267/317, Pope-Hennessy to Kimberley, 31 Dec. 1872.
[41] The West African University, 6.
[42] CA1/047, Blyden to Venn, 9 Jan. 1873.
[43] Blyden to Coppinger, 11 Jan. 1873, A.C.S. Papers, Vol. 16.
[44] Ibid.   [45] Ibid.

visited the 'Muslim University' where 500 young men studied, to pay their respects to Fode Tarawally, its President, and 'the great literary celebrity of this region'. The President showed his visitors 'a wonderful collection of Arabic manuscripts on various subjects—some copies of books brought from Arabia, and some original African compositions'.[46] This, for Blyden, was proof of the salutary influence of Islam on West African Negroes.

Everywhere on his way to Timbo, Blyden found evidence which he thought proclaimed the superiority of the Muslim Negro over the Christian Negro on the coast. At Moala, sixteen miles north-east of Melakori, Blyden witnessed another manifestation of Muslim Negro ability. When he arrived here on 17 January, he found that thirteen chiefs from an area 'extending 150 miles from the coast to the borders of Futah Jallon' had already been in deliberation six weeks in an attempt to bring the wars of the area to an end. Blyden felt pride in the conference and its proceedings. He commented:

I should have liked to have taken for the use of the Government a photographic representation of the chiefs in Council. They were all men of intellectual physiognomy and all Mohammedans. Their discussions were conducted with as much gravity as those of any deliberative assembly in foreign countries. If they do not display lofty statesmanship, they give honest expositions of their views; they have not yet risen to the art of diplomatic mystery and enigmatic declarations.[47]

From Moala the expedition went on to the slave town of Fansiggah. Blyden had praise for the practice here of facilitating the conversion of pagan slaves to Islam. He reported that the king had built a mosque among the pagan slaves and made it compulsory that the children be taught the Koran, and optional for adults to attend prayers. This seems to have been a widespread practice among Muslim chiefs.

Blyden's expedition reached its destination on 4 February. Timbo, like Billeh, demonstrated aspects of African life which commanded respect. It was strategically located at 'the western base of a high hill facing a beautiful plain', and although comparatively small, it owed its tremendous importance to the fact that it was both the administrative centre as well as the paramount seat of the Muslim faith and learning in Futa Jallon.

[46] C.O. 267/320, No. 6209: Report on the Timbo Expedition.   [47] *Ibid.*

Blyden advised that the co-operation of Timbo would be 'indispensable' in any attempt of the Government to establish intercourse with West Central Africa.[48]

On 5 February, Blyden completed negotiations for 'a Treaty of Perpetual Peace and Friendship between Alimami Ibrahima Suri, King of Futah Jallon, and his successors on one part, and the Governor of Sierra Leone and his successors on the other'. The treaty stipulated that the King was to be paid a stipend of £100 annually. In his report Blyden made familiar recommendations: steps should be taken to increase trade links between Sierra Leone and the Muslim interior, with consular agents appointed to superintend the commercial interests of the Government; missionaries, too, should not overlook 'so interesting a field of effort'. The pattern was familiar to the end: the Colonial Office found Blyden's report 'well-written and interesting' but could not act on it.[49]

On the coast itself, the African pastors stimulated by Blyden became bolder in their agitation for an independent African church. This agitation was led by James Johnson, the most race-conscious and the most outstanding of the young African pastors. As pastor of Christ Church, Pademba Road, Johnson had given ample evidence that he believed that Christianity as taught by Europeans required modifications to suit the needs of Africans.[50] In Blyden's absence in the interior, Johnson edited the *Negro*, and like his lay associate, deprecated 'the mistaken benevolence of Protestant Missionary Societies', emphasized that 'the Church of England is not our Church', and kept in view the goal of an independent African Church.[51]

When Bishop Cheetham returned to Sierra Leone late in January 1873, after six months' furlough in England, he found a new militancy among Africans. He complained that 'the influence of Mr. Hennessy's administration and the presence of Mr. Blyden . . . have produced most important and unfortunate results on the minds of the native pastors and some of the other upper natives'.[52] He claimed that 'national feeling . . . is not finding expression in the *Negro* but the *Negro* is spreading it on thick

[48] *Ibid.*,   [49] *Ibid.* Colonial Office Minutes.
[50] Fyfe, *History of Sierra Leone*, 352.
[51] CA1/025e, quoted in Cheetham to Venn, 1 Feb. 1873.   [52] *Ibid.*

before the people are ready'.[53] He charged that 'the great source
of evil is Mr. Blyden; he has so dwelt upon this race feeling that
. . . a most strong and virulent anti-white feeling has arisen'. The
bishop was horrified, too, 'to find the place ablaze with a scheme
for a godless West African University under Government and
Negro control'. He saw Blyden's advocacy of a secular University
merely as an attempt to 'feather his own nest'.[54]

Cheetham was further upset by the fact that the African
pastors, and especially James Johnson, had openly associated
themselves with Blyden's views, and sought ways of making them
capitulate. He threatened to withhold from the Native Pastorate
funds which he had collected on its behalf in England,[55] an effective threat in view of the fact that the Pastorate was perennially
in financial difficulty. For, while Blyden and the pastors were loud
in calling for an independent African Church, Africans themselves contributed a negligible sum towards the upkeep of
the Native Pastorate, which they regarded as the nucleus of the
desired African Church. The main source of income for the
Pastorate was an annual grant of £500 received from the Sierra
Leone Government since 1866. It was the only religious body of
the colony so favoured. But the attack of Blyden and the African
pastors on sectarianism, had brought a serious counter-attack by
Benjamin Tregaskis, the ebullient Superintendent of the thriving
Wesleyan Mission in Freetown, who argued that the Pastorate
grant was a use of public money to favour one religious body 'to
the serious disadvantages of the others', making 'peace ecclesiastical' impossible.[56] Tregaskis was an especially dangerous opponent because he was generally popular among Africans for having
persuaded Pope-Hennessy to abolish the 'oppressive' Road and
House and Land Taxes which his predecessor had imposed; and
among his carefully cultivated African proteges was Samuel
Lewis, a young and promising lawyer. The grant survived
Tregaskis' determined attack but was abolished in 1876 for reasons
of economy.

Another weapon which Cheetham used in his battle against the
African pastors, was his refusal to recommend any of them for

[53] *Ibid.* Cheetham to Venn, 9 April 1873.
[54] *Ibid.* Cheetham to Venn, 13 March 1873.
[55] Cheetham to Venn, 1 Feb. 1873.
[56] C.O. 267/324, No. 978, enclosure: Tregaskis to Pope-Hennessy, 20 Nov. 1872.

promotion. Thus, when Pope-Hennessy recommended Henry Johnson, a talented African and an especially able linguist, for a vacant position of Colonial Chaplaincy, Cheetham opposed his appointment, averring that although he was 'a promising native, Mr. Blyden and race feeling have damaged him',[57] and instead recommended a European missionary for the position. Under strong pressure from the Bishop and the Missionary Leaves Association,[58] an English organization formed to aid Native Pastorates, the African pastors, with the exception of James Johnson, disclaimed the views of the *Negro* as their own, and even admitted that they did not endorse many of its sentiments but still insisted that they 'contemplated the growth of their church into a national institution'.[59]

As a result of the controversy between the African pastors and European missionaries, the parent committee of the C.M.S. decided to invite James Johnson to England to confer with him on 'the state of things in Sierra Leone'.[60] This invitation fired the imagination of Sierra Leoneans as to the possible outcome: rumours were rife in the Bishop's words 'that Johnson was going to plead for a black Governor to be sent; a black bishop in a little while, and with the Society on behalf of the African University'.[61] The *Negro* assured that Johnson would discuss 'questions of vital importance to the perpetuity of their political and ecclesiastical institutions'.[62] And both the educated laymen and clergymen sent letters of support and congratulation to Johnson in which they expressed the hope that his visit would be 'productive of much good to Africa at large, and to the Sierra Leone Church'.[63]

No sooner had Johnson left for England than the struggle between the two forces centred on the issue of the appointment of a Director of Public Instruction in Sierra Leone. The position

[57] C.M.S., CA1/025e, Cheetham to Henry Wright, 5 Feb. 1873.
[58] C.M.S., CA1/09, Address of the Missionary Leaves Association to the Native Church Pastorate, 4 April 1873.
[59] *Ibid*. Native Pastors to the Secretary of the Missionary Leaves Association, 29 May 1873.
[60] C.M.S., *Minutes of the Committee of Correspondence*, XXXIX.
[61] C.M.S., CA1/025e, Cheetham to Secretary of the C.M.S., 21 April 1873.
[62] C.O. 267/324, *The Negro*, 16 April 1873.
[63] C.M.S., CA1/025e. S. Boyle, J. L. Fitzjohn, T. J. Sawyerr and J. P. Bull to Johnson, April 1873; Native Pastors to Johnson, 19 April 1873. This letter was signed by the Revs. Moses Taylor, George J. Macaulay, John H. Davies, Moses Pearce, Thomas C. Nylander, J. Robbin, G. Williams, and J. Wilson.

was first created in September 1870, and the duties consisted of inspecting government schools and recommending the amount of grant to be awarded to each. In view of the recent controversy on education, it was certain that both sides would take an unusually keen interest in the appointment. Blyden, as one 'deeply interested in the work of educational reform in West Africa', and mindful of the recommendation of the Select Parliamentary Committee of 1865, applied for the position. The application of the Negro scholar was strongly endorsed by the acting Governor, Major Alexander Bravo, who thought that Blyden 'as a highly educated Negro' with 'an unobtrusive manner' and 'temperate habits' was well qualified for the position.[64]

Bishop Cheetham, predictably, thought otherwise. When he heard that the Negro scholar had applied for the position, he prayed that 'the Lord guide us in this matter and avert Mr. Blyden getting it'.[65] Not trusting entirely in the efficacy of his prayer, he sought to use his influence to prevent Blyden from being appointed. The Colonial Office seemed to have taken his opinion into serious consideration, for although Blyden was easily and undoubtedly the best qualified candidate for the position, his application was turned down because officials feared that his appointment would 'probably create a disturbance in Sierra Leone'.[66] Ostensibly on the grounds of ill-health, but probably because he had not received the appointment of Director of Public Education, Blyden resigned as Agent to the Interior on 22 October 1873, and shortly thereafter returned to Liberia.

If in Sierra Leone Blyden met with disappointment, James Johnson was no more successful in England. The parent committee of the C.M.S. told him that they thought it would be premature to grant ecclesiastical independence to Africans, and to ensure that the controversy in Sierra Leone come to an end, transferred Johnson to the Breadfruit Mission, Lagos, in defiance of the protests of the African pastors of Sierra Leone.[67] Nor were Johnson's negotiations with the Colonial Office very much more successful. He had demanded that that Office co-operate with the C.M.S. in converting Fourah Bay College into a West African

[64] C.O. 267/321, Blyden to Bravo, 13 May 1873.
[65] C.M.S., CA1/025e, Cheetham to Secretary of C.M.S., 24 May 1873.
[66] C.O. 267/321, Colonial Office Minutes, 18 July 1873.
[67] C.M.S., CA1/024. Petition by Native Pastors to Secretary of C.M.S., 7 April 1874.

University, in founding a teacher's training college, elementary
schools, and a secondary school for girls; that it establish a technical school; that it set up a system of municipal governments
which would 'give the people real interests in their towns, lead
them to take care of them, and make them self-reliant'; that
communications within the colony be improved and steps taken
to survey its natural resources 'and open new sources of wealth to
the people'; finally, that qualified West Indians be brought in to
take the place of Europeans 'whose frequent return home on
account of failing health hinder the progress of the colony'.[68]
Of all these demands action was taken only on that of providing
some form of higher education: on 1 February 1876, Fourah Bay
College became affiliated to Durham University.

Blyden's failure to get the appointment of Director of Public
Education and Johnson's to win support for his programme, had
shown unmistakeably that it was not the primary concern of the
British Government to prepare the Africans for self-government
as recommended by the Select Parliamentary Committee of 1865,
and with the departure of the two Negro patriots from Freetown,
thrustful African assertion in Sierra Leone came abruptly to an
end.

But Blyden continued to cling to the hope that the British
might yet be badgered into conscientiously assuming greater
imperial responsibility in West Africa. On the very day of his
resignation, he wrote a long letter to Lord Kimberley, offering
advice, not altogether unfamiliar, for the formulation of a new
policy for British West Africa.[69] He informed the Colonial Secretary that 'England has been marked out for the future work of
civilization in Africa', and that this policy might best be accomplished by pursuing 'a uniform and persistent policy'. He urged
the appointment of governors who would show a sympathetic
appreciation of the African character and were keen on seeing the
African improve. He deprecated 'the frequent interruption in the
office of Governors-in-chief' which often resulted in a discon-
tinuity of policy. He advised the implementation of measures
which would remove from the chiefs of the interior 'the idea of
vacillation or indifference on the part of the government', and to
him the most effective way for the British Government to do this

[68] C.O. 879/8, Johnson to Kimberley, 21 Jan. 1874.
[69] C.O. 267/324, Blyden to Kimberley, 22 Oct. 1873.

was 'to take charge of the Western Soudan'. Once again he recommended that the British Government extend its 'educational influence' throughout its colonies:

Some means ought to be provided by which, under Government's patronage and supervision, a thorough education may be brought within the reach of the masses in the settlements, as well as of the children of influential natives of the interior. . . .

There is hardly an element of life of the people which does not depend upon this question of education, whether trade, agriculture, interior affairs, ecclesiastical institutions or sanitary improvements. And any Government which will give to these settlements an efficient and comprehensive system of education will add to the imperishable claims by which England has deserved the gratitude of the African race. . . .

Not unexpectedly, the Colonial Office again diplomatically rebuffed Blyden. The Parliamentary Under-Secretary, Edward Knatchbull-Hugessen, considered his recommendations 'somewhat impractical and visionary'. And Lord Kimberley added somewhat gratuitously that 'taking charge of the Western Soudan' was 'a project of considerable magnitude and audacity', and one to which 'Just now the British Government does not seem much disposed'.[70]

Blyden had used the opportunity of his stay in Sierra Leone and what seemed like favourable circumstances to attempt to advance the interest of his race. But he met with little tangible results. This was because his ambitious programme—an independent African Church, a secular University, and the extension of Sierra Leone's rule over its hinterland—depended wholly for its implementation on the support and co-operation of the British Government and the C.M.S. But despite the sympathetic gestures of such Governors as Kennedy and Pope-Hennessy, the British Government, whose policy in West Africa was guided by the strictest parsimony, never sought 'to prepare the natives for self-government', much less increase its imperial responsibilities in West Africa. No serious attempt had even been made to implement Venn's policy and there was little or no likelihood of such an attempt being made after his death. Further, the support which Blyden received was confined to a small group of educated Africans, primarily successful members of the Recaptive group; his 'movement' had no

[70] *Ibid.* Colonial Office Minutes.

'mass support', and there was certainly never a chance of raising adequate funds for the support either of an independent African Church or University. However, the ethnocentrism which Blyden inspired is significant as marking the first major revolt in West Africa against western cultural dominance, and the beginning of cultural nationalism—the most characteristic form of African assertion in the nineteenth century.

6. 'Pure Negroes' only for Africa

In formulating his theory of race[1] Blyden had been influenced by his experiences in the United States: he had correctly discerned and resented the fact that leadership of Negroes there lay, for the most part, with mulattoes, and that within the designated 'American Negro' world, there was a social hierarchy based partly on colour—with the blacks occupying the lowest rung.[2] His own concept of race had permitted him to exclude mulattoes from the Negro race and hence to deny them 'the right and privilege to repatriate to the fatherland'. But he never gave up hoping that 'the race instincts of genuine Negroes' would impel them to return to Africa. This chapter will discuss his relations with American Negroes and his attempt to promote the emigration of 'pure' Negroes only to Africa.

It was during his fourth visit to the United States, in May 1874, in a speech delivered at Hampton Institute, Virginia, that Blyden first publicly stated that 'there was a significant difference between the Negro and the mulatto'.[3] It is interesting to note, too, that in 1874 he no longer fulminated, as he did in 1862, against white discrimination; he now accepted it as 'natural'. Thus, when he was refused accommodation at a hotel in Hampton, although he was the guest of General O. O. Hampton, the white Principal of Hampton Institute for Negroes, he accepted this without protest.[4] He spent only one month in the United States during which, besides his visit to Hampton, he lectured to students at Howard, Lincoln and Harvard Universities.

Shortly after his return to Liberia, Blyden set out to persuade the American Colonization Society that it should settle only 'genuine Negroes'. In a long letter dated 19 October 1874, he

[1] For a discussion of this, see Chapter Four.
[2] See E. Franklin Frazier, *The Negro in the United States*, New York 1957, chap. 12; Edward Byron Reuter, *Race Mixture*, New York 1931, 154–7; and Gunnar Myrdal, *An American Dilemma*, New York 1944, 696–9.
[3] Blyden to Coppinger, 21 Oct. 1875, *A.C.S. Papers*, Vol. 17.
[4] Blyden to Lowrie, 17 Dec. 1875, *P.B.F.M. Papers*, Vol. 10.

first made a direct appeal to the Secretary of the American
Colonization Society to exclude mulattoes. He told of his experience of the mulatto in the United States:

The European side of his nature appears in his social affectation.
I found generally . . . that Negroes were indifferent to mixed school
and some opposed to it, but the mulatto thought it was a natural and
inalienable right for which he was bound to contend: and so he
confuses the instincts of his black brother who while anxious to stand
upon his race individuality and independence, is harrassed by the
mulatto who is always restless and dissatisfied.

He charged that mulattoes thought themselves superior to the
blacks and formed themselves in cliques. He instanced Howard
University, where, he claimed Negro and mulatto Professors rarely
mixed socially off campus. He further charged that 'in all the
Negro's trouble in the South, he is led on by his bumptious half or
one-fourth brother'. He claimed that the mulatto was also a
trouble-maker in Liberia and pleaded passionately for his exclusion from the Republic:

You are planting here a nest of vipers who hate the country and the
race. Do save us from this inundation. They keep us feeble all the
time and manage to get into leading positions where they only draw
money and do nothing. They oppose all interior openings and no not
disguise the most impetuous contempt for the natives except in their
public speeches for foreign consumption.[5]

In almost every subsequent letter to Coppinger over a period of
well-near three decades Blyden let off his venom against mulattoes
and pleaded that they be kept in America. While it was undoubtedly true that within 'Negro America' and Liberia, there
existed a social hierarchy based to a large extent on colour, it was
equally certain that Blyden's assumption that 'the unimpaired
race instincts' of the blacks qualified them as 'good' emigrants,
while the 'confused instincts' of mulattoes disqualified them for
race work in Africa, was invalid. Culturally both black and brown
Americans were from the same mould, and there seem to have
been no really significant difference in their attitude to emigration
to Africa.

Blyden's insistent warnings that mulattoes should be kept out
of Africa was actuated by the ever-present possibility of a large-

[5] Blyden to Coppinger, 19 Oct. 1874, *A.C.S. Papers*, Vol. 17.

scale emigration of non-whites from America to Africa. The promise of the full rights of citizenship which the early years of the Reconstruction had held out to the Negro was not fulfilled. The white South was determined to make a pariah of the Negro, once it discovered that it did not have much to fear from the North. At first Southerners were content to strike stealthily. Just one month after the passage of the first of the Reconstruction Acts (2 March 1867) the Ku Klux Klan, a secret organization which was to become the great dread of the Negro, was formed. Other secret societies soon proliferated. After a while, this operation to reduce Negroes again to impotence became open, and helped by Northern connivance, grew into one of the most ruthless operations in United States' history. By 1871, the white South, for all practical purposes, had regained its lost powers and privileges; correspondingly, Negroes were being terrorized out of their rights.[6] Nor could Negroes any longer expect help from the North: it had grown weary of crusading on their behalf, and was becoming more and more concerned with establishing a *modus vivendi* with the white South. This purely pragmatic approach reached its climax in February 1877, when Rutherford B. Hayes came to an agreement with white representatives of the South which was to secure his election as President in return for the withdrawal of Federal troops from the South. The 'Negro Betrayal' had taken place; and Southern Negroes were doomed to lose their recently acquired rights and privileges.

As could have been predicted, the number of Negroes wanting to emigrate again rose sharply as the white South perpetrated its systematic terrorization. By 1875, the numbers wanting to emigrate had reached a considerable proportion, but the Society embarrassed by a shortage of funds could send out only a small number of emigrants, some of them paying part of their expenses. By 1877, prospective emigrants had exceeded the numbers wanting to emigrate before the Civil War. Coppinger reported that almost every state had 'one or more organizations for removal to Liberia while the "Exodus Association" of Charleston, S.C., claim to have 60,000 ready for passage, and the Colonization Council of Shreveport, Louisiana, reports 69,000 men and women who wished to be colonized'.[7] The two organizations mentioned

[6] Franklin, *op. cit.*, 338.
[7] Coppinger to Blyden, 12 Sept. 1875, *Coppinger Letter-Book*, Vol. 16.

by Coppinger, as well as others, were acting independently of the American Colonization Society.

The most important of these new organizations was the Liberian Exodus Company of Charleston, South Carolina, which was formed not only for sending emigrants to Africa, but also for trading between Negro America and West Africa.[8] Acting as its Secretary was Martin R. Delany, who, after abandoning his plans to emigrate to the Niger in 1862, had served in the Union army as a Major, and later as an agent of the Freedman's Bureau and School Principal in Charleston, South Carolina. With the tables turned once more on American Negroes, he was again planning to leave for Africa. In 1878, the Company bought the bark *Azor* which was consecrated at an impressive ceremony at which Delany and Henry M. Turner, a new champion of American Negro emigration to Africa,[9] were present. The *Azor* left on its first trip for Liberia on 21 April, with 206 emigrants. Unfortunately, the promoters did not take elementary precautions to safeguard the health of the emigrants and twenty-three died at sea. No other trip was undertaken: the company itself collapsed in 1879 partly as a result of its own mismanagement, partly through the harrassment and duplicity of Charleston whites, who were opposed to Negroes returning to Africa because it meant a loss to them of cheap labour.

Blyden received this news of renewed interest in emigration to Africa without enthusiasm. He knew that any such major emigration to that continent would bring with it a large number of mulattoes, an occurrence which, he maintained, would be calamitous to Africa. When the news reached him that the Liberia Exodus Company had failed he remarked with relief that this was 'a blessing to Liberia; the Republic wanted no rubbish'.[10] He wanted the conduct of Negro emigration to Liberia left solely to the American Colonization Society whose policy he hoped to influence through his close friendship with Coppinger.

[8] George Brown Tindall, *South Carolina Negroes, 1877–1900*, Columbia 1952, chap. 8; C. L. Simpson, *Memoirs*, London 1961, 50–4, Delany to Coppinger, 18 Aug. 1880, *A.C.S. Papers*, Vol. 240.
[9] See Edwin S. Redkey, 'Bishop Turner's African Dream,' *Journal of American History*, LIV, 2, 1967, 271–290.
[10] Blyden to Coppinger, 20 Nov. 1879, *ibid.*, Vol. 17.

Although the Society had not been sending large numbers of emigrants, Blyden was pleased that Coppinger had been making an effort to send 'the right sort'. In a letter of 28 October 1876, Coppinger informed him that 'the emigrants sent on the last expedition were very generally Negroes'.[11] A pleased Blyden read into this an official endorsement by the Society of his views on emigration. 'Upon this fact' he replied, 'almost the first on record in the history of emigration to this country, I must congratulate the Republic of Liberia and the continent of Africa. It is to small, unnoticed beginnings of this nature that great events owe their origins.'[12] And the following year when Coppinger pointed out to him that a company of seventy sent out by the Society were 'almost without exception blacks',[13] Blyden was again quick to express his approval: 'I am glad that you have now concluded to send out only such persons whose interest and feelings will be thoroughly identified with Africa and the race, and who will have no means of hankering after fathers who spurned them. . . .'[14] So long as the American Colonization Society attempted earnestly to comply with his demands that only 'pure Negroes' be sent to Liberia, Blyden regarded it as the most important single agency working for the regeneration of Africa.

But he remained in constant dread that American 'Coloureds' might take action independent of the American Colonization Society which would result in a large number of them emigrating to Africa. Thus, in 1878, prospective emigrants from Kansas, many of whom had originally fled from the South, sent out two commissioners, Dr. A. L. Stanford and Charles H. Hicks, to Liberia to investigate its suitability as a future home.[15] But before the commissioners could return, about 100 of them led by Richard Newton found their way to New York in their endeavour to get to Liberia.

Blyden first heard of the Kansas refugees from a *Times* report while he was in London, England, on his way to the United States as President-elect of Liberia College.[16] He arrived in New York

---

[11] Coppinger to Blyden, 28 Oct. 1876, *Coppinger Letter-Book*, Vol. 17.

[12] Blyden to Coppinger, 14 March 1877, *A.C.S. Papers*, Vol. 18.

[13] Coppinger to Blyden, 22 July 1888, *Coppinger Letter-Book*, Vol. 19.

[14] Blyden to Coppinger, 31 Aug. 1878, *A.C.S. Papers*, Vol. 18.

[15] *African Repository*, LVI, July 1880.

[16] Blyden to Coppinger, 11 May 1880, *A.C.S. Papers*, Vol. 239; cf. *The Times*, 15 April 1879.

on 10 May 1880, and was relieved to find that they were 'suitable' emigrants. He was pleased, too, to see that Henry Highland Garnet, 'a Prince among his people', was again actively favouring emigration and had been the mentor of the refugees while they were in New York. Blyden, of course, warned the migrants of 'mulatto machinations' and 'did not fail to point out to them the difference between such men as Garnet, inspired and guided by self-sustaining consciousness of ultimate success in the Fatherland, and mulatto doubters and traducers. . . .'[17] Blyden was able to persuade Edwin R. A. Seligman, a New York banker and literary figure, whose guest he had been, to donate a hundred dollars towards buying agricultural equipment for the Kansas refugees.[18] On Sunday 16 May, he preached to a large audience in Garnet's church, and 'set New York Negroes thinking' when he impressed upon the Kansas migrants the high responsibility which awaited them in Liberia and the need to remember that mulattoes had no genuine interest in Africa.[19]

This, Blyden's fifth visit to the United States, lasted two and a half months and provided further proof of his detestation of mulattoes. At Madison, Wisconsin, where was held the, as yet, 'largest and most distinguished' Presbyterian Assembly, Blyden delivered a brilliant address on 'Africa's Service to the World', before a 'select and intellectual audience', including Hon. W. E. Smith, Governor of Wisconsin, and Professors from the State University.[20] This address was enthusiastically received; his old friend, Rev. John Knox, whom he had met again after thirty years, thought it the best delivered at the Assembly. But Blyden's enjoyment of the conference was marred by the presence there of three mulatto delegates, who had 'contrived to find engagements elsewhere' when he was to speak; in contrast, the three black delegates, also from the South, were proud that he had been 'heard on Africa', and had made a good impression.[21]

During a two days' stay in Chicago, Blyden met 'nearly all the leading coloured men' who were in the city for the Republican Convention, and grudgingly accepted an invitation to dine with

[17] Blyden to Coppinger, 11 May 1880, *op. cit.*

[18] 'The Diary of a Liberian in America', *Monrovia Observer*, III, 14 Oct. 1880.

[19] Blyden to Coppinger, 14 June 1880, *A.C.S. Papers*, Vol. 239.

[20] 'The Diary of a Liberian in America', *Monrovia Observer*, III, 14 Oct. 1880; 'The Journal of John P. Knox', cited in Holden, *The Story of Blyden*.

[21] Blyden to Coppinger, 10 June 1880, *A.C.S. Papers*, Vol. 239.

them. Among them were Frederick Douglass, Blanche Kilso
Bruce, a United States Senator from Missouri during the Reconstruction; James Milton Turner, the first United States Minister
to Liberia; and Dr. Robert Purvis, leader of Pennsylvania
Negroes. It was Blyden's first meeting with all of them except
Turner. He reported being well-received by this 'mongrel tribe',
but with the exception of Douglass whom he found 'splendid in
conversation when he chose to let himself out', he was unimpressed: he declared them 'as light and empty as men profess-
ing to lead a race could well be'. Blyden felt compensated in
meeting Robert B. Elliot, the young and brilliant Negro scholar
and politician from South Carolina, and sought to persuade him
to 'give his time and person to Africa'. In Philadelphia Blyden
made the acquaintance of Benjamin Tucker Tanner, an influential mulatto bishop of the African Methodist Church, and
editor of the widely circulated weekly newspaper *Christian
Advocate*, through which he expressed uncompromising opposition to Negro colonization in Africa. Blyden regarded him as a
fine example of a man of mixed blood who used his influence to
hinder the progress of Negroes.[22]

In Washington, where there was probably the largest concentration of the coloured elite in the United States, Blyden again
met several mulatto leaders. He actually came to think well of a
few of them, but was careful to attribute whatever excellence they
possessed to their Negro blood. Of Douglass he noted:

He shows polish of society and the culture of extensive reading. He is
strongly Negro, although of mixed blood. His genius and power come
evidently from the African side of his nature. He reminds me in his
manner and bearing more of some aristocratic African chief such as I
have seen in the distant interior, rather than of any cultivated
European I have ever seen.[23]

Blyden was also impressed with Henry M. Turner, who had
recently been made an A.M.E. bishop. Like other American
Negro leaders, Turner had confidently hoped that the post civil-
war period would bring substantial improvement in the status of
the Negro. During the war he had been commissioned as the first
Negro chaplain. After the war he entered politics in Georgia and
was elected to the House of Representatives in 1868. But like

22 'The Diary of a Liberian in America', *Monrovia Observer*, III, 26 Oct. 1880.
23 *Ibid.*, 11 Nov. 1880.

other coloured politicians in the South, he was pushed out of
active politics. By 1874, he had become an advocate of Negro
emigration to Africa, and a supporter of the American Colonization Society. In 1876 he was elected as one of the first two Negro
Vice-Presidents of the Society.[24] Of him Blyden noted that despite
'his light complexion . . . his hair is . . . unmistakably African—
his instincts strongly of the race: and he has all the peculiarities of
an uncontaminated Eboe'.[25] For Blyden, Douglass and Turner as
men of 'strong Negro instincts', were exceptions which did not
invalidate his theory of race.

Other mulattoes with whom Blyden found it tolerable to have
social intercourse were the following non-emigrationists: Rev.
Francis Grimké, the influential pastor of the fifteenth street
Presbyterian Church, attended by 'the colored aristocracy of
Washington'; Richard T. Greener, the first coloured graduate of
Harvard, and Dean of the Law School at Howard University;
James Wormley, the intelligent and energetic owner of Wormley
Hotel, 'the home of leading members of Congress' and where
Blyden himself stayed; and John W. Cromwell, historian of the
Negro, and editor of the *People's Advocate*. He also saw much of
the two Negro leaders, R. B. Elliot, whom he reported as being
'decidedly in favour of emigration to Liberia', and Alexander
Crummell, who had apparently 'not given up the idea of return-
ing to Liberia'.[26]

Although he was determined to prevent mulatto emigration to
Africa, he could not express his viewpoint openly: the American
Colonization Society which he regarded as the only safe avenue
for Negro emigration to Africa, would not permit him to express
views it regarded as highly impolitic. But it is certain that his
public utterances relating to Africa were directed only at Negroes
'pure and simple'. In his lectures he sought to excite their pride
in the past of the race in Africa as well as in the New World. He
pointed to the efforts being made by other peoples—the Germans,
the Italians and the Slavs—for solidarity and national unity.
Africa he contended, was the true home for Negroes. He warned
them not to be side-tracked from the goal of emigration to Africa
by the temporary advantages which 'the exigencies of party

[24] *African Repository*, LII, July 1876, 84–6.
[25] 'The Diary of a Liberian in America', *Monrovia Observer*, III, 9 Dec. 1880.
[26] *Ibid.*

politics' might dictate. Nor were they to be deceived by acts of generosity on the part of white liberals because even the most well-meaning of them did not accept the Negro as an equal. Blyden convincingly explained the ambivalence of whites towards Negroes:

Among the phenomena in the relation of the white man to the Negro in the house of bondage, none has been more curious than this: that the white man, under a keen sense of wrong done to the Negro, will work for him, will suffer for him, will fight for him, will even die for him, but he cannot get rid of a secret contempt for him.[27]

Blyden had hoped that the United States Government, working in co-operation with the American Colonization Society, would undertake to colonize American Negroes in Africa. While in Washington, he and his close friend, John H. Smyth, the United States Minister to Liberia, had several interviews with top American politicians and officials, including President Rutherford B. Hayes, and his private secretary, Colonel W. K. Rogers; William H. Ewarts, Secretary of State, and Carl Schurz, Secretary of the Interior, during which he advocated that the United States Government sponsor and finance Negro emigration to Africa.[28] Later, he publicly and unrealistically pleaded for that Government to 'stretch a chain of colonies of her own (black) citizens through the whole length of the Soudan, from the Niger to the Nile—from the Atlantic to the Indian Ocean'. He painted a poetic and romantic picture of the results of an anticipated exodus:

In visions of the future, I behold those beautiful hills, the banks of those charming streams, the verdant plains and flowery fields, the salubrious highlands in primeval innocence and glory, and those fertile districts watered everywhere.... I see them all taken possession of by the returning exiles from the West, trained for the work of rebuilding waste places under severe discipline and hard bondage. I see, too, their brethren hastening to welcome them from the slopes of the Niger, and from its lovely valleys—from a sequestered nook, and from palmy plain—Mohammedans and pagans, chiefs and people, all coming to catch the inspiration the exiles have brought—to share in the borrowed jewels they have imported, and to march hand in hand with their returned brethren towards the sunrise for the regeneration of a continent. And under their united labour, I see the

[27] Blyden, 'Echoes from Africa', *Christianity, Islam and the Negro Race*, 153.
[28] 'The Diary of a Liberian in America', *Monrovia Observer*, III, 11 Nov. 1880; also Blyden to Coppinger, 19 June 1880, *A.C.S. Papers*, Vol. 239.

land rapidly reclaimed—raised from the slumber of the whole world. . . .

But until this predicted exodus with its glorious results took place, Blyden invited Negro churches to 'increase their efficiency and . . . develop their central strength by taking a wider, deeper and more practical interest in the land of their fathers, in their kith and kin'.[29]

Although possessing 'a conservative manner of address' Blyden was an effective and evocative speaker, able to stir the emotion of his audiences. Thus, after hearing one of his sermons on Africa, a Negro clergyman, the Rev. H. C. Cook, who had hitherto strongly opposed American Negro emigration to Africa, felt 'like going through the land and preaching in its favour'.[30] Undoubtedly, Blyden had helped to keep alive the spirit of emigration among Negroes to whom he had lectured and preached, and perhaps had even helped to create that feeling; and yet he had not at all influenced actual emigration nor was he any closer to a solution of the problem he had set himself of how to separate 'pure Negroes' from the coloured population and colonize them in appreciable numbers in West Africa.

In July 1882, Blyden returned to the United States partly for the purpose of acting as the travelling agent of the American Colonization Society in the 'great work of colonization'.[31] He spent nine months in the United States—his longest uninterrupted stay—during which, for the first time, he travelled and lectured in the deep South. In the two years which had elapsed since his last visit the situation of non-whites had not changed. In his inaugural address of 1881, President Garfield had promised that there would be 'no middle ground for the negro between slavery and equal citizenship';[32] but he had died early in office and his promise had never been put to the test. His successor, President Arthur, had adopted a policy of accommodation to the white South, and with this connivance, it had continued its systematic subjugation of Negroes, and they had continued to react by migrating or talking of emigration.

The pattern of Blyden's activities was the same as his previous

[29] Blyden, 'Africa's Service to the World', *Christianity, Islam and the Negro Race*, 148.
[30] Rev. H. C. Cook to Coppinger, 21 June 1880, *A.C.S. Papers*, Vol. 239.
[31] Coppinger to Blyden, 5 April 1882, *Coppinger Letter-Book*, Vol. 23.
[32] Quoted in Rayford Logan, *The Negro in American Life and Thought: the Nadir, 1877–1900*, New York 1954, 38.

visit; lectures to both black and white in the North and South to
dispel their 'astonishing ignorance of Liberia', and win their
co-operation in sending Negroes back to Africa;[33] as before, he
could hardly hide his dislike for mulattoes. During his first five
weeks, spent in New York, he suffered from bronchial infection
and had to curtail his public engagements. His stay was further
aggravated by the fact that he lived among mulattoes. He complained to Coppinger of having to put up with 'empty . . .
bumptious . . . impudent and prejudiced mulattoes' at Porter's
Hotel, as the only black man there.[34] So irritated was he that he
wished to return to Liberia but remained only in order to 'make
some effort on behalf of my people in bondage here and of our
fatherland'.[35] In Philadelphia, he made an appeal for 500,000
Negroes for Africa in Tanner's *Christian Recorder*. In Boston he
spoke of the American Negro as the instrument of Africa's
regeneration. In Cleveland, Ohio, he addressed the annual meeting of the American Missionary Society, presenting Liberia 'fully
and squarely' and tried to 'kill the old abolitionist opposition to
colonization'.[36] Blyden's tour of the South, starting in early
November, lasted about six weeks during which he visited Negro
institutions of higher learning in an attempt to persuade Negro
students who intended to work in Africa to get their training at
Liberia College.

Blyden's most important public statement on his American visit
was made in an address, 'The Origin and Purpose of African
Colonization', delivered in Washington, D.C., on 4 January 1883
at the sixty-sixth anniversary of the American Colonization
Society. Whereas before it had been customary to have 'two or
three distinguished speakers . . . occupy the evening', Blyden was
allotted the entire time.[37] His main concern was ostensibly to
arouse public support for Negro emigration to Liberia. He began
by pointing out that the establishment of a Negro nation which
had been moderately successful, and which could yet grow into a
great nation, was sufficient vindication of the work of the American Colonization Society. He argued that the strategy of all Negro
leaders should be to bring about a mass Negro emigration to

[33] Blyden to Coppinger, 19 Aug. 1882, *A.C.S. Papers*, Vol. 248.
[34] Blyden to Coppinger, 20 Sept., *ibid.*
[35] *Ibid.*
[36] Coppinger to Blyden, 31 July 1882, *Coppinger Letter-Book*, Vol. 24.
[37] Coppinger to Blyden, 18 Oct. 1882, *ibid.*

Africa; it was the only 'statesmanlike' thing to do. He claimed that Bishop Turner was one of the few Negro leaders who had seen the correct solution to the problem of the American Negro. He predicted that as the Negro masses became educated they would grow impatient with their circumscribed lives, and must then feel 'an irrepressible desire to return to the Fatherland'.

The Negro youth—as a result of the training which he is now generously receiving in schools—will seek to construct states. He will aspire after feats of statesmanship and Africa will be the field to which he will look for the realization of his desires.[38]

In an oblique attack on mulattoes, he deprecated 'the general practice among superficial politicians and colored journalists to ignore the craving for the fatherland among American Negroes'; he averred that it was neither 'indispensable' nor 'desirable' that all six million coloured Americans should go: he estimated that one-tenth (which was roughly the percentage of the 'pure Negro' population) would suffice to accomplish the task to be done in Africa. In a passage of pathos and romance, he assured that:

There are Negroes enough in this country to join in the return— descendants of Africa enough, who are faithful to the instincts of the race and who realize their duty to the fatherland. I rejoice to know that here where the teachings of generations have been to disparage the race, there are men and women who will go, who have a restless sense of homelessness which will never be appeased until they stand in the great land where their forefathers lived; until they catch the glimpses of the old sun, and moon and stars, which still shine in their pristine brilliancy upon that vast domain; until from the deck of the ship which bears them back home they see visions of the hills rising from the white margin of the continent, and listen to the breaking music of the waves—the exhilarating laughter of the sea as it dashes against the beach.[39]

He was hopeful that American Negro emigration would transform Africa in his own life-time:

It may be our happiness to see those rise up who will formulate progress for Africa—embody the ideas which will reduce our social and political life to order and we may, before we die, thank God . . . that the Negro has grasped with a clear knowledge his meaning in the world's vast life—in politics, in science and religion.[40]

[38] Edward W. Blyden, *The Origin and Purpose of African Colonization*, Washington 1883, 15.   [39] *Ibid.*, 17.   [40] *Ibid.*, 18.

Blyden expressed his disappointment that, despite frequent petitions from Negroes themselves and from the American Colonization Society, the United States Government had refused to undertake the colonization of Negroes in Africa. He felt that the time had come when 'an earnest and united effort should be made by all sections of this great country' to persuade the United States Government to do so. Alternatively, the American public could give its support directly to the American Colonization Society; to his mind there was 'no philanthropic institution before the American public that has more just and reasonable claims upon private and official benevolence than the American Colonization Society.[41] But despite the accustomed brilliance of his speech, Blyden had made no new or realistic idea for promoting 'pure Negro' emigration to Africa. It ought to have been clear to him that neither the United States Government nor public was likely to provide financial support for schemes of Negro emigration to Africa.

Five months after Blyden left the United States, a thunderbolt at least as shattering as the Fugitive Slave Bill or the Dred Scott Decision was hurled at Negroes when the Supreme Court declared as unconstitutional the Civil Rights Act of 1875. That Act had specifically been passed to prevent discrimination against Negroes in public places; thus the new decision had, in effect, given legal sanction to segregation. Once again Negroes howled their protests throughout the land at national and local conventions. Blyden had no sympathy with this outcry. Indeed, he approved of every discriminatory measure against the American Negro in the hope that this would drive him to Africa. He expressed this view to Coppinger in 1886:

I think that God who has His hands both upon Africa and America will deepen the prejudice against the Negro in the United States. He will continue to harden Pharoah's heart, until the oppressed shall be driven from the house of bondage, as Israel was from Egypt, to do his work in the land of his fathers.[42]

Almost jubilantly, he watched the South, encouraged by the repeal of the Civil Rights Act, pass new discriminatory measures against the Negro. When in 1887 a bill was passed in the Georgia

[41] *Ibid.*, 22.
[42] 22 June 1886, *A.C.S. Papers*, Vol. 23.

Legislature making 'the co-education of white and colored races' a penal offence, Blyden exulted. He wrote to Coppinger:

Had I been in that legislature, I should have voted *ex-animo* for the bill. All lovers of humanity must rejoice in its passage. . . . I hope that the law will be rigidly enforced in Georgia and throughout the South, then Africa will get back her children, as is evidently God's design.[43]

In a later letter, he added that the Georgia Bill was 'one of the most important supplementary measures adopted since the abolition of slavery',[44] that is, as far as his ultimate goal of getting American Negroes to emigrate to Africa. Blyden also approved, with reservation, the Alabama Criminal Code which forbade intermarriage or fornication between white and non-white; he wanted it extended to forbid marriage or fornication between 'genuine Negroes' and 'half-castes'. 'I feel as many of the white leaders of public opinion in the South on their side of the question —that in Africa and the African work, the marriage of a genuine Negro with a mulatto or quadroon is *ipso facto* null and void,'[45] he wrote bitterly to Coppinger.

The new discriminatory measures which Southern state legislatures began passing against the Negro in the 1880's, and which were perfected in the next decade, had caused the talk about emigration to rise to a crescendo, with Bishop Turner hitting the highest notes of stridency. But as before, neither Turner, nor any other Negro leader could capitalize on this feeling, and over-coming all obstacles, turn it into a creative historic force by organizing a major back-to-Africa movement. As always, this discussion about emigration created a cleavage among American non-whites. There were those leaders who were totally opposed to any emigration abroad, others, while opposing the idea of a mass exodus to Africa as either undesirable or impracticable, favoured the emigration of select groups who had no illusions about the challenge which Africa presented; Bishop Turner remained alone in still wishing all non-white Americans with Negro blood to return to Africa. These divisions reflected themselves in the press: as a general rule mulatto opinion was opposed to emigration to Africa; Negro editors tended to be sympathetic to selective Negro emigration, while not necessarily endorsing a mass exodus.

[43] Blyden to Coppinger, 29 Aug. 1887, *A.C.S. Papers*, Vol. 24.
[44] Blyden to Coppinger, 12 Sept. 1887, *ibid*.
[45] Blyden to Coppinger, 3 Dec. 1888, *ibid*., Vol. 25.

After the Berlin Conference, which signalized the beginning of the partition of Africa, the anti-emigrationist editors claimed tirelessly that American Negroes emigrating to Africa would be making a great sacrifice to exchange one form of despotism for another. Blyden did not agree that the European partition of Africa in any way altered the case for American Negro return to that continent: Liberia could settle thousands of them; in addition, he maintained that European powers—temporary agents in Africa—would regard westernized Negroes as assets in their colonies—a viewpoint that seemed to have been based solely on the interest of the Congo state in American Negroes as emigrants.[46] At any rate, from alleged mulatto opposition to emigration to Africa, Blyden hopefully but wrongly predicted that 'there will be two camps formed in America before long—a mulatto and a Negro camp—the one favouring, the other opposing colonization to Africa'.[47]

In the meantime Blyden urged the American Colonization Society 'to have a definite Negro policy for a definite Negro work in Africa'. In the past he had been content to have the Society merely follow a policy of sending only Negroes to Liberia, now he was urging that such a policy should be openly proclaimed: he wanted the word 'Negro' substituted for the word 'colored' in the second article of the Constitution of the Society, to make it clear that in future it would colonize only 'pure Negroes' in Africa.[48] But the Society continued to be reluctant to endorse publicly Blyden's views on race and colonization: in the minds of the benefactors of the Society there was no distinction between the Negro and the mulatto, and for the Society to have openly proclaimed such a distinction would have been for it to alienate whatever little support it still received.

However, in 1888 Blyden came close to having the Society officially endorse his views. In a letter of 30 March, Coppinger reported to Blyden that 'half-breed' editors had increased their attacks on the Society and requested him to counter.[49] Glad of this opportunity, Blyden wrote a long article entitled 'The Two Voices'—the one Negro, the other mulatto—which was

[46] Edward W. Blyden, *The African Problem and other Discourses*, London 1890, 23.
[47] Blyden to Coppinger, 29 Aug. 1887, *A.C.S. Papers*, Vol. 24.
[48] Blyden to Coppinger, 19 Nov. 1887, *ibid*.
[49] Coppinger to Blyden, 30 March 1888, *Coppinger Letter-Book*, Vol. 30.

published as an editorial in the July issue of the *Repository*. For the first time the mulatto-Negro conflict was reflected in the pages of the *Repository*; the article required justification:

We have noticed from time to time ... attacks on our works, which have appeared uncalled for and gratuitous. ... In view of the increasing importance of the African question and the stand which the genuine Negroes are taking on behalf of their Fatherland, we deem it necessary to point out the aspirations and utterances of the genuine Negro and those of the persons allied both to the Negro and to the Indian or to the Negro and the white man.[50]

The article went on to prove its point by quoting from the editorials of newspapers with both Negro and mulatto editors.

Coppinger admitted to Blyden that the publication of the 'Two Voices' in the *Repository* had committed the Society to a policy of sending only Negroes to Liberia.[51] Blyden applauded what he called 'the new policy' of the Society.[52] In fact, for some years now, the Society had sent out only emigrants who were not obviously hybrid. But even so, it was impossible to avoid sending some emigrants who did not meet Blyden's uncompromising racial standards. This Coppinger pointed out in a frank censure of the Liberian:

I am heartily with you in your cry of Africa for the Africans. ... I carry this principle in action as far as emigration was concerned. ... (But) There is much of the impracticable and the impossible in your demand. The emigrants often go in families and communities. To eliminate those with 'white reinforcements' ... would be to stop all emigration, for there are mighty few families offering for Liberia, who are all, father, mother, and children, pure blacks. ... [53]

Blyden's article had caused 'quite a roar' in the mulatto press. Typical of the reaction was the following excerpt from an editorial in the *South Western*, whose editor was of French and Negro extraction: 'The man that seeks to propagate the doctrines set forth in the *Repository*'s "Two Voices" is a dangerous enemy who threatens the peace and welfare of four-fifths of the Negro families of this land and inspires father and mother to rise against their children, brothers and sisters, and husbands and wives, to

[50] *African Repository*, LXIV, July 1888, 97.
[51] Coppinger to Blyden, 30 March 1888, *op. cit.*
[52] Blyden to C. T. O. King, 8 Aug. 1888, *A.C.S. Papers*, Vol. 25.
[53] Coppinger to Blyden, 13 June 1891, *Coppinger Letter-Book*, Vol. 34.

rise against each other.'[54] But this reasonable comment Blyden set down as 'mongrel insincerity'.

As yet, nothing would convince Blyden that a 'black Moses' would not still rise to lead an exodus from America to Africa. He gave Coppinger a description of what such a leader would be like:

> The Negro leader of the exodus, who will succeed, will be a Negro of the Negroes, like Moses was a Hebrew of the Hebrews—even if brought up in Pharaoh's palace he will be found—No half-Hebrew and half-Egyptian will do the work—he will have brass and assurance enough—for this work, heart, soul, and faith are needed.[55]

Blyden's prediction was almost fulfilled in the remarkable career of Marcus Garvey, the charismatic Jamaican Negro who in the half a dozen years after the first World War, led the first genuine American Negro mass movement, one of whose goals was a return to Africa.[56] Although Garvey, too, claimed to be a 'pure Negro' and had as strong a pride of race as Blyden, unlike the latter, he never suggested that only 'pure Negroes' were qualified to return to Africa. However, Garvey's efforts were thwarted by the powerful vested interests of American Negro middle-class leadership and European imperialists and consequently his movement failed.

But if by the mid-eighteen-eighties Blyden was still hopeful that a Negro exodus would take place, his views on the role that American Negroes were to play in Africa underwent a marked change: earlier he had held the view that in the task of the regeneration of Africa, westernized Negroes would provide both the stimulus and the leadership, but now, while he still believed that New World Negroes had an important role to play in Africa using the skills they had learned, he was firmly of the opinion that the leadership of the race in Africa must come from native Africans themselves. One of his most explicit statements on this point was in a letter to Coppinger dated 1 October 1888:

> The American Negro has his place in the work of Africa's regeneration—an important place; but he is incompetent to lead the work of the race on this continent. He has been too demoralized by his oppression of two hundred years to lead; but he will furnish indispensable material aid in the work of constructing a nation on civilized principles . . . although not according to the form in every respect

---

[54] Quoted in Blyden to Coppinger, 1 Oct. 1888, *A.C.S. Papers*, Vol. 25.

[55] Blyden to Coppinger, 3 Oct. 1887, *ibid.*, Vol. 24.

[56] See Edmund David Cronon, *Black Moses*, Madison 1955.

which he has seen in the land of his exile. But he will be forever striving to reproduce the form which he has left behind, and he will be forever blundering and failing. The trained aborigine must take the lead to give the superstructure—the form which the untrammelled and unimpaired genius of the race will suggest and dictate.[57]

Blyden had come to this conclusion because educated 'pure Negroes' had not responded to Africa in the way that he had hoped and predicted that they would, and the few who did go had not 'amalgamated' with the natives, or evinced patriotic race leadership. All the evidence had contradicted Blyden's theory that strong racial instincts would impel pure Negroes to separate themselves from an alien race and culture, and 'hie them hither' to the congenial fatherland of Africa, yet he clung to it.

But he did offer an explanation for the lack of meaningful Negro response to Africa, one which caused him to reverse his position on the education of Negroes in America. Earlier he had held that the education of American Negroes would make their circumscribed lives intolerable, and would hasten their return to Africa, but in the absence of such a response he concluded that an alien educative and acculturative process had dulled and diminished the race instincts of Negroes. From this, Blyden came to the further and grave conclusion that Negroes in America should be deprived of higher academic education—a viewpoint, paradoxically, which coincided with that of white Southerners. Not that Blyden was against higher education for Negroes, but he believed that this could be beneficial only if received in institutions on African soil run by 'properly educated' Negroes. This fantastic point of view Blyden thus confided to Coppinger in a letter of 22 June 1886:

If I were a white man . . . I should oppose, seeing clearly the possibilities and the actualities of the Negro in America—and his possibilities in Africa; the erecting of costly buildings and the establishment of elaborate machinery for his literary education. I should abolish Lincoln, Howard and Fiske Universities and other similar pretensions, and would establish elementary schools, with every possible appliances for their industrial and technical training. I should use the money for the promotion of wide and deep culture in Africa in the Republic of Liberia where circumstances will give practicality and reality to such education.[58]

[57] Blyden to Coppinger, 1 Oct. 1888, *A.C.S. Papers*, Vol. 25.
[58] Blyden to Coppinger, 22 June 1886, *ibid.*, Vol. 23.

No one, of course, would quarrel with Blyden's advocacy of 'industrial and technical' training for Negroes. Indeed such training was rather the vogue of the time. But he fully recognized that his counsel to abolish American Negro Universities could hardly be uttered publicly and that if American Negroes knew of it 'the whole multitude of them would have been prepared to stone him'.[59]

Blyden, then, had strangely concluded that educated American Negroes, like mulattoes, were unfit for 'race work' in Africa. His favourite emigrant had become the black man who combined great physical strength with 'industrial know-how'. And it was this kind of emigrant, albeit in small numbers, that was disembarking from the society's ships. Some Liberians jibed that they were 'woefully inferior Negroes'. But Blyden defended them as having 'the germ of nationality and the law of progress in their nature'.[60]

Blyden's disenchantment with educated American Negroes led him to affirm that they were not suitable to represent the United States Government in Liberia. He had been helped to this conclusion through a breach in his friendship with J. H. Smyth, the first 'pure Negro' U.S. Minister to Liberia. Smyth was like Blyden a 'race man', and initially, they had worked closely together, but the latter's self-righteousness and his uncompromising demand for loyalty to him and his ideas had brought a rupture between them. After this, Blyden peevishly concluded 'there was no Negro in America yet fitted for a high diplomatic position', and asked the executive committee of the American Colonization Society, who were consulted by the United States Government in affairs relating to Liberia, to use its influence to ensure that only white men be appointed as United States Minister to Liberia. Blyden argued that an American Negro or coloured man could not be 'an impartial and prudent representative', and was very likely to be 'a dividing influence'. On the other hand, a 'well-trained, statesman-like white official' would be 'a steadying influence' and might persuade 'the American Government, without contravening the Monroe doctrine, to exert an important influence in West and Central Africa'.[61]

But Blyden's request was impolitic. Traditionally, the positions

[59] *Ibid.*   [60] Blyden to Coppinger, 2 Sept. 1887, *A.C.S. Papers,* Vol. 24.
[61] Blyden to Coppinger, 18 Sept, 1883, *ibid.,* Vol. 21.

of U.S. Ministers to Haiti and Liberia were given to Negroes or coloured men as political patronage. In September 1885, President Cleveland appointed Moses A. Hopkins to replace Smyth as Minister to Liberia. Coppinger reported to Blyden that the Society 'had taken no part in the hot contest for the office', but commended Hopkins as being 'Negro in blood and instincts'.[62] Blyden consoled himself that if it was obligatory upon the President to appoint a Negro, then he had made the best choice: he had 'steered clear of the corrupt Negro politician on the one hand, and the conceited literary character on the other'.[63] Besides, he had met the 'black and comely' Hopkins on his visits to the U.S. in 1874 and 1880 and had thought well of him. But after Hopkins's early death in office, Blyden persisted in asking Coppinger to have the Society use its influence to have a white man appointed to the vacant position.

In 1889, two years after the publication of his book, *Christianity, Islam and the Negro Race*, Blyden returned to the United States as a much more widely known and controversial literary figure than ever before. His white colonization friends were chagrined at his trenchant criticism and public rejection of sectarian Christianity, and his strong sympathy for Islam, but their attitude was for Blyden further proof that even the most well-meaning of white men could never understand the viewpoint of a Negro patriot. It was widely but wrongly reported in the American press that Blyden had become a Muslim, and he did little to dispel that impression. Indeed, during this stay in the United States, he gave several lectures on the Koran and Islam in West Africa.[64]

Blyden had been invited by the American Colonization Society to work as a temporary agent because applications to it had been more 'numerous and urgent' than ever before.[65] The Society

---

[62] Coppinger to Blyden, 19 Sept. 1885, *Coppinger Letter-Book*, Vol. 27.

[63] Blyden to Coppinger, 2 Oct. 1885, *A.C.S. Papers*, Vol. 23.

[64] Blyden's lauding of Islam brings to mind the present-day Black Muslims sect whose reaction to white American Society was in some ways similar to his: Negro separation from the dominant white society (the Black Muslims setting themselves the impractical goal of an independent Negro nation within the geographic boundaries of the U.S.A.) and the recognition that Christianity has sometimes been used as a tool to oppress or retard Negroes. There are two major studies of the Black Muslims: C. Eric Lincoln, *The Black Muslims in America*, Boston 1961; and E. Essien Udom, *Black Nationalism: A Search for an Identity in America*, New York 1962.

[65] Coppinger to Blyden, 26 Jan. and 3 May 1889, *Coppinger Letter-Book*, Vol. 31.

wished Blyden to act as its travelling agent publicizing the fact
that it was still active and collecting subscriptions on its behalf.
Leaving Monrovia on 16 May he arrived in the United States on
2 August after a short stay in England. He spent the first three
months in the large cities of the North, and then attempted
through lectures and circulars to win the support of influential
white Southerners for the Society.

On 29 November he began a tour of the South in Charleston,
South Carolina. Here his host, Rev. J. S. Lee of the A.M.E.
Church, informed him that 'if he were authorized to do so, he
could at short notice have thousands of Negroes ready to embark
for Africa'. Another Negro minister claimed 'that more than
500,000 Negroes were ready to leave the South for Africa if they
had the opportunity to go'. Blyden himself reported that emigration had the support of the leading Negroes of Charleston,
among them Randall G. George, a 'genuine Negro' and the
richest non-white in the state.[66]

Blyden found in South Carolina and in other parts of the South
much white support for Negro 'repatriation'. This in itself represented a marked change in the attitude of the South to non-white
migration and emigration, and can be explained in terms of federal
politics. The Democratic victory in the presidential election of
1884 had had the effect of reviving Republican interest in the
non-whites of the South. In the election of 1888 they had been
especially wooed and had been promised that their personal rights
and liberties would be secured. As a gesture, President Harrison
proposed in his annual message of 1889 that Congress pass a law
providing for the supervision of federal elections. The passage and
execution of such a law would have greatly revived the political
power of the Negro in the South. It was the fear of this which had
prompted some white politicians to favour emigration of non-
whites from the South. It is significant that, on 12 December 1889,
Senator M. C. Butler of South Carolina, introduced a bill into
Congress 'to provide for the migration of persons of Color from
the Southern states'.[67] In this he was strongly supported by
Senator Morgan from Alabama. But if some Southern politicians
were in favour of non-whites leaving the South, most of them

[66] Blyden to Coppinger, 20 Dec. 1889. *A.C.S. Papers*, Vol. 247; Tindall, *op. cit.*,
128.
[67] Logan, *op. cit.*, 53.

were opposed to this removal through federal finance, and remained confident in their ability to curb and control the coloured population. The state of Mississippi had shown how this could be done. Reacting swiftly to Harrison's threat to provide federal supervision of elections, Mississippi revised its constitution in 1890 'for the express purpose of disenfranchising most Negroes while permitting most whites to vote'.[68] Nor was white Southern fear well-founded: the Lodge Bill which was to provide for federal supervision of elections was killed at the committee stage in the House of Representatives.

But if Southern whites still refused to countenance federal support for Negro emigration, the Republican threat to revive the Negro politically had made them more sympathetic than before to the idea of non-governmental arrangement for this purpose. Thus as soon as Blyden arrived in Charleston, he won the support of influential whites for his scheme for Negro colonization in Africa. Among the first to endorse his views and aid in their dissemination were the editors of both Charleston daily newspapers. Shortly after his arrival, a reporter from the *Charleston World* sought him out and assured him 'that the white people would interpose no objection to enterprising Negroes going where they would better their conditions'; and Blyden found that the views of Major J. C. Hemphill, editor of the *Charleston News and Courier*, coincided with his own: that whites and Negroes could not live together in harmony in the United States and that Federal money should be appropriated to colonize those who wished to go to Africa. Hemphill flatteringly referred to Blyden as the 'Gamaliel of his race' and placed his newspaper completely at the disposal of the Liberian who wrote several editorials in it urging a Negro return to Africa and white support for this.[69]

Blyden had as quickly alienated the mulattoes as he had won the confidence of whites and blacks. On his arrival a delegation of the leading coloured men had called upon him and he had shown a marked partiality for the black members. In addition he had turned down an invitation of the African Methodist Church to attend a conference at Columbia, South Carolina, because he surmised that it was going to be composed mainly of mulattoes and he did not wish 'to cast pearls before swine'. These and other

[68] *Ibid.*, 135.   [69] Blyden to Coppinger, 29 Nov. 1889, *A.C.S. Papers*, Vol. 247.

signs that he could not tolerate mulattoes led to the charge that
he had come 'to divide the people who were living in harmony'.[70]
But the first open and direct attack on him came from Charles
H. J. Taylor, a former U.S. Minister to Liberia, who in an article
in the *Atlanta Constitution* of 1 December, reprinted in the *Charleston World*, charged that Blyden's attempt to promote Negro
emigration to Liberia was 'devilish'. Taylor disparagingly referred
to Liberia as 'that black land of snakes, centipedes, fever, miasma,
ignorance, poverty, superstition and death' and advised that a law
should be passed 'to place in the penitentiary for ten years anyone
who would by word or act invite or encourage individuals to leave
the United States for the Negro Republic'.[71] He further charged,
falsely, that Blyden himself, because of his misdemeanours there,
could not return to Liberia. He followed up this attack with a
further assault on Blyden and the American Colonization Society
in a pamphlet.[72] In addition, he challenged Blyden to a public
debate, but the Negro scholar ignored this averring that 'the
matter was too serious for frivolous controversy'. The *Charleston
World*, however, was interested in Blyden's reaction to Taylor's
newspaper remarks and the Liberian described them as typical of
the venomous dislike of mulattoes for Africa but requested that this
view be not made public.[73] The request was ignored. The appearance of the story in the *Charleston World* served further to widen
the rift between Blyden and the local leaders of mixed blood. But
despite the controversy which he had engendered in Charleston,
or perhaps because of it, his public meetings attracted large
audiences.

Blyden interrupted his stay in Charleston by a visit to Aiken
where he attended the twenty-sixth session of the South Carolina
Conference of the A.M.E. Church, presided over by Benjamin
W. Arnett of Ohio, and composed 'chiefly of Negroes', among
whom were Rev. J. L. Coppin, editor of the *A.M.E. Review*, and
S. J. Campbell, a native of Liberia and Superintendent of the
A.M.E. Church there. Blyden was given a flattering welcome;
and to add to his pleasure, he found that the Conference was responsive to his plea for greater Negro missionary effort in Africa.[74]

[70] Blyden to Coppinger, 10 Dec. 1889, *ibid.* [71] *Charleston World*, 2 Dec. 1889.
[72] Charles H. J. Taylor, *Whites and Blacks or the Question Settled*, Atlanta 1889.
[73] Blyden to Coppinger, 3 Dec. 1889, *A.C.S. Papers*, Vol. 247.
[74] Blyden to Coppinger, 20 Dec. 1889, *op. cit.*; *Sierra Leone Weekly News*, VI,
1 March 1890; *Christian Recorder*, 2 Jan. 1890.

Blyden was pleased with the result of his visit to South Carolina: 'the avenue of my work seems to widen and multiply in this state', he reported to Coppinger. On the eve of his departure from Charleston, he was the guest of a Negro organization, the United Labour Association, which assured him that 300,000 Negroes were ready to emigrate but could not leave because of difficulty in disposing of their property. Before he left that Southern city, too, Major Hemphill gave him letters of introduction to editors of four of the leading newspapers of the South: The *Jacksonville Times Union*, the *New Orleans Pacayune*, the *Times-Democrat* and the *Mobile Register*.[75]

From Charleston Blyden left for Jacksonville, Florida, and while travelling Jim Crow on the train from Savannah took the opportunity to speak to the 'sturdy workmen' with whom he mingled on the 'advantages' of emigrating to Africa. In Jacksonville, he was the guest of Squire English, the wealthiest Negro of that city. Here, as at Charleston, the whites received him enthusiastically. He wrote to Coppinger:

The white people here have been kind to me. Several heard my first lecture and endorsed it. The editor of *Times-Union*, son of a slave-holder . . . made a speech commending my lecture in the most enthusiastic terms. It was moved that the audience express their appreciation of my lecture by a rising vote—everyone rose. I have never had anywhere a more flattering endorsement of my utterances. On the following evening two of the white citizens paid me a complimentary visit and offered to serve me in anyway in their power. Next day I was invited to meet some of the leading white men at the *Times-Union* office, where they urged me to visit every city in the South and lecture. They say they had never before seen so wise, natural and satisfactory a solution of the race problem before them. They asked me if I had money to travel or if I was collecting money. I told them I had enough to travel on. They urged me to return to Jacksonville later in the season as they would like to give me a better reception and make a contribution towards my labour.[76]

The *Times-Union* had referred to Blyden as 'the heaven-appointed medium for helping to solve the (Negro) problem'.[77]

[75] Blyden to Coppinger, 10 Dec. 1889, *op. cit.*
[76] Blyden to Coppinger, 28 Dec. 1889, *A.C.S. Papers*, Vol. 247.
[77] *Florida Times-Union*, 28 Dec. 1889.

Blyden next visited the town of St. Augustine where 'the leading white men welcomed . . . him and thanked him for his utterances as they read them in the *Times-Union*'.[78] His visit to Jacksonville and St. Augustine marked the end of Blyden's tour of the South. It was prematurely ended so that he could fulfil his speaking engagements in the North.

Blyden's visit to the South had confirmed his reputation as a brilliant, enigmatic and controversial figure. But if the promotion of Negro emigration to Africa was his goal then that tour was a failure. He had won the sympathy of influential whites for the idea of Negro 'repatriation to Africa' and yet he did not attempt to get them to give financial support to the American Colonization Society. Neither had he made any attempt to use his obvious influence with Negro leaders either to organize independent schemes for emigration or give whole-hearted support to the Society. The great bulk of Negroes lived in the South and this was really his first attempt to meet the Negro masses, yet he saw fit to curtail his visit for speaking engagements in the North. His paranoid hatred of mulattoes seemed to have inhibited him from seriously seeking to implement any plans for Negro emigration to Africa.

An ambivalent attitude to the promotion of emigration to Africa, borne of his determination to exclude mulattoes from that continent, was also evident in a major address which he made as the main speaker at the seventy-third anniversary of the American Colonization Society held in Washington on 19 January 1890, and attended by 'statesmen and lawmakers of the land'.[79] Here Blyden urged the United States Government and the American public to support American Negro Colonization in Africa, and yet insisted that the time for such an emigration had not come. He began his speech by reporting that 'Two hundred millions of people have sent me on an errand of invitation to their blood relations here. Their cry is "Come over and help us".' He had found among Negroes 'an eager and enthusiastic response' but also discovered that their leaders, the general public and the United States Government were not prepared to promote Negro emigration to Africa. Again he expressed his disappointment that

[78] Blyden to Coppinger, 28 Dec. 1889, *op. cit.*
[79] Blyden, *The African Problem*, 1–23. The material in this and the following paragraph is taken from this source.

those—both Negroes and white—who had fought so earnestly to end slavery could not understand that that was not an end in itself, that they were really releasing agents for the building of a progressive civilization in Africa. Again he expressed his chagrin that 'the American Congress ... would ... begrudge the money required to assist a hundred thousand Negroes to carry on the work that Liberia had begun on a grander and more efficient scale'. As before, he maintained that eventually the Negro exodus must take place: young Negro leaders would arise who would 'catch the spirit of the future, and ... place themselves in accord with it'. He pointed out, correctly, that 'the Negro problem was upon the United States and could no more be ignored than any of her other vital interests'. And he was sure that in time so 'statesmanlike' an idea as Negro 'repatriation' to Africa must eventually gain currency in the public's mind. His insistence that the time was not ripe for a major Negro emigration scheme annulled his stirring pleas for public and governmental support for it, and must have puzzled those Negroes whom he had convinced of the necessity of emigrating to Africa.

Blyden's ambivalent and vacillating attitude towards Negro emigration to Africa can further be seen from a subsequent lecture he delivered 'in various cities of the United States' in which he berated Negro leaders for their lack of organization, and suggested that a demonstration of initiative and earnestness on their part for colonization in Africa would win the support of the American public and Government for the scheme.

There are thousands of Negroes—young men—growing up in this country with no settled purpose, no well defined plan. They have no goal set before them which, with all their energies, they strive to reach. There is in their minds no clear and distinct idea toward which they struggle. They merely drift on the current, and are borne by it whithersoever it flows. They are not masters in life but still slave to their surroundings. ... Here are muscles and brain and will, which, if transferred to the land of their fathers, might do a great work for themselves and for humanity. ... Neither as individuals nor as a community, neither as persons or as leagues have they attracted the attention or diverted the minds of the dominant race to an earnest consideration of their needs and desires as a people. No men of ideas and enthusiasms have yet risen among them whose strong convictions could lift them out of their ordinary selves and prepare them to sacrifice all personal, party or class considerations for the sake of the great cause. They, then, do not shake the world.

There was a good deal of truth in Blyden's analysis which pointed to a sense of frustration, despair and lack of constructive purpose among American Negro youth, yet it can hardly be said that he himself had suggested a practical and realistic programme to get them out of their impasse.

If then, Blyden had failed to use effectively his influence to promote American Negro emigration to Africa, or if his scheme was impracticable because of his determination that only 'genuine Negroes' should be repatriated, he continued to predicate all his thinking and actions upon the conviction that emigration to Africa was the only solution to the Negro problem in America, and that a Negro exodus must ultimately come. This was why he was consistently opposed to the formation of any organization whose aim was the betterment of the Negro in the United States. In February 1890, while still on his visit to the United States such an organization was formed. On a call from T. Thomas Fortune, a quadroon who was editor of the *New York Age*, coloured American leaders met in Chicago and founded the Afro-American League.[80] J. C. Price, the black Principal of Livingstone College, North Carolina, was elected President; Fortune was elected Secretary. Blyden's response to this organization was predictable: he commented, trenchantly, and unfairly that

Its real aim is to secure organizations in which lazy and ambitious mulattoes may obtain easy positions of influence and emolument. And also to gather together a crowd of mulattoes who will assume to represent the colored people on the African question.[81]

But his prediction that the Afro-American League 'could never succeed', proved correct; it never became effective and collapsed within a decade.

Less than two years after Blyden left the United States in 1890, the two most devoted white advocates of American Negro colonization, John B. Latrobe and William Coppinger, died, in September 1891 and February 1892, respectively.[82] Latrobe first as

[80] T. Thomas Fortune, 'The Negro's Place in American Life', *The Negro Problem*, New York 1903, 125.

[81] Blyden to Coppinger, 29 Aug. 1887, *A.C.S. Papers*, Vol. 247.

[82] See John E. Semmes, *John H. B. Latrobe and His Times, 1803–1891*, Baltimore 1917; and *Liberia Bulletin*, No. 1, Nov. 1892, 1–2.

President of Maryland Colonization Society, and from 1853 as President of the American Colonization Society, had served the cause of colonization for more than fifty years. Coppinger's record was even more impressive. First as Secretary of the Pennsylvania Colonization Society, and from 1864 as Secretary and later also as Treasurer of the American Colonization Society he had fully devoted his entire adult life to promoting Negro colonization to Africa. Blyden had long been on terms of friendship with both men, and was particularly close to Coppinger: his friendship with the white colonizationist had extended over forty years, and each expressed his viewpoint to the other freely and fully. Coppinger had been sympathetic to Blyden's views on race, and while reluctant to endorse them publicly, had in practice been largely guided by them. In the last three years before Coppinger's death, the executive committee had made a particularly strenuous effort to revive public support for the Society without substantial success. Yet it was significant and ironic that Coppinger sent out in his last year in office (1891) more emigrants (154) than in any of the previous nineteen years.[83] In the quarter of a century which had elapsed since Blyden first began urging him to send out to Liberia only 'pure Negroes', he had selected and sent off 1256 blacks or 'very nearly Negroes'. The death of Coppinger and Latrobe finally confirmed what had long been evident: that the Society was moribund, and as a private organization would never be an effective instrument for carrying out a Negro exodus from America to Africa.

Succeeding Coppinger as Secretary of the American Colonization Society was J. O. Wilson, a former Superintendent of Schools in Washington, D.C., and a man little known to Blyden. The correspondence which took place between the two men was briefer, less personal and less regular than that between Blyden and Coppinger. Blyden had, of course, acquainted the new Secretary with his views on race and emigration and had found him, too, sympathetic: indeed Wilson had made out a questionnaire to prospective emigrants in which among other questions asked was: 'Are you light or dark colored?' But Wilson, too, pointed out the difficulty of choosing emigrants Blyden considered desirable: what was he to do when prospective emigrants answered that they were 'ginger-colored'? Wilson further suggested that, be-

[83] Staundenraus, *op. cit.*, Appendix I.

cause it was 'not possible to get the busy Anglo-Saxon to stop long enough to study the problem of race' it would be impossible to persuade the American public that mulattoes did not belong to the Negro race.[84] But by the mid 1890's the question had become an academic one: with its funds at an all time low, emigration through the Society had all but ceased: between 1893 and the end of the century the Society sent out only seventy-three emigrants.

Blyden made a final visit of three months to the United States in 1895, arriving in New York on 20 July. The main purpose of his visit was to do research for a projected history of Liberia and had nothing to do with the promotion of Negro emigration to Africa. However, in an article on the 'African Problem' written at the request of the editor of the *North American Review*, Blyden was more emphatic than ever that the time had not yet come for a Negro exodus to Africa.

The present generation of white men and the present generation of black men must pass away. A new generation of each race, strangers to the abnormal fact of slavery and its monstrous offshoots, must arise before any extensive colonization of American blacks in Africa can answer its purpose. The Negro problem must be solved here or it will appear in Africa in a new form. The Negro must learn to respect himself here before he will be able to perform the functions of true manhood there. Should he leave this country now, harrassed and cowed, broken in spirit and depressed, ashamed of his racial peculiarities and deprecating every thing intended for racial preservation, he would be destitute of the tenacity and force, the self-reliance and confidence, that faith in himself and destiny, which ... would guide him in the policy to be adopted toward the man like himself whom he would find on his ancestral continent.

But he still thought it desirable that individual Negro missionary and small colonies should 'go out with some definite object in view for the religious or industrial improvement of the country'. For the bulk of American Negroes who were to remain behind he counselled that they strive to maintain 'peace and harmony' between the two racial groups. He advised them to adopt 'a modest temperateness of behaviour—an unpretentious and un-ambitious deportment...', and to eschew politics as 'barren, un-

[84] Wilson to Blyden, 6 Oct. 1897, *A.C.S. Letter-Book*, Vol. 42.

interesting and often perilous'.[85] This advice must have given small comfort to American Negroes for the alternative paths of action would seem to be to fight manfully for equality in the United States or seek 'manhood' in Africa.

And yet Blyden's opinions and advice were of especial interest because they were being offered at a time when American Negroes were without a recognized leader. Frederick Douglass, the leader of American Negroes for more than thirty years, had died in Washington, D.C., in February 1895. Price, a man with known sympathies for Africa though not an advocate of a Negro exodus to that continent, who had been widely regarded as Douglass's likely successor, had died prematurely. Among the other leaders there was none who was the obvious and undisputed successor to Douglass. Who, then, was to be the new leader? Would he favour Negro emigration to Africa? Would he lead a brave new campaign for Negro equality? Or would he, as part of a temporary strategy, seek to appease the whites by foregoing some of the rights of Negroes as American citizens? The answers were not long in coming: on 18 September 1895, the new leader of American Negroes emerged in the person of Booker T. Washington, the Principal of Tuskegee Institute, Alabama, after his now famous Atlanta Address in which he 'renounced social equality, at least temporarily, conceded a subordinate position for Southern Negroes in politics, urged education for practical ends of gaining a livelihood and emphasized the necessity for Negroes to co-operate with their Southern white friends'.[86] Washington's policy of appeasement had won him the tumultuous applause of the white South, and ironically, had secured him the leadership of Negro America: for, there was no formal procedure for electing a Negro leader, and his choice tended to depend as much on the recognition by white America as on the support of Negroes themselves.

Washington's policy was the same as that advocated by Blyden with one exception: Washington firmly accepted that Negroes were in the United States to stay, while Blyden never gave up hoping that eventually an American Negro exodus to Africa

[85] Edward W. Blyden, 'The African Problem', *North American Review*, CLXI, Sept. 1895, 338.

[86] Logan, *op. cit.*, 314. On pp. 314–40, Logan analyses the entire speech and the national reaction to it. For the most recent analysis of Washington's ideas see August Meier, *Negro Thought in America, 1880–1915*, Ann Arbor 1963.

would take place. Both men already knew of the coincidence of their views. Blyden had met the Negro Principal in Washington, D.C., in 1890, through their mutual friend, Francis Grimké. But probably the full discovery by Blyden of the coincidence of their views did not come until the Liberian read an article by Washington in the *Southern Workman* of October 1894, in which he recommended that Negroes should eschew politics and instead seek to get a good industrial education. On 28 November, he wrote to Washington expressing his agreement with such a policy:

The Negro in the Southern States cannot afford to be a politician. By this I mean that it is not in his best interest to be one. I hope I am too far away from the scene for any interested motive to be attributed to me in making that remark. Every thinking African on this side acquainted with the subject entertains the view I have just expressed. We believe that the interests of both races will be served if the Negro will eschew politics and political aspirations where every step of the way is hampered and covered with thorns and briars. He is called to a higher and nobler work. The religious and industrial spheres lie open before him, in the latter of which you have shown ... in your admirable letter his possibilities are unlimited. It is a pity that he should neglect the great work which he is so well fitted to do for and upon the dominant race and for himself to pursue an *ignis fatuus* which leads him away from rest and peace into all sorts of difficulties and often to death.[87]

Blyden's whole-hearted support of Washington's policy was all the more comforting to the latter in view of the fact that the Liberian admitted, for the first and only time, that for practical purposes the Negro was in the United States to stay. His letter had continued:

I believe that while there are and will continue to be intense longings on the part of many in the South for Africa, and while there will be now and then small emigrations to the Fatherland, the time for anything like a general exodus is far distant—perhaps three hundred years off[88] so that practically the Negro is in the United States to stay, and should adjust his relation with the white people upon a

---

[87] *New York Age*, 24 Jan. 1895.
[88] Blyden's estimate of the length of time that would elapse before American Negroes returned to Africa varied: his most frequent estimate was within a generation or two. This is the only recorded occasion on which he estimated 300 years.

basis that will ensure peace, harmony and prosperity, at the same
time that he brings his peculiar gifts to the improvement of the
situation.

Blyden ended by assuring Washington that he was on 'God's line
for the race'.[89]

Glad of this enthusiastic endorsement by so distinguished a
Negro of a policy that was bound to be controversial, Washington
ensured that Blyden's letter appeared in print. He had replied to
Blyden thus: 'I am exceedingly grateful for the encouraging manner in which you express yourself concerning the condition and
prospects of the Negro in the South. . . . What you say is so good,
and so entirely in keeping with my own views, that I have taken
the liberty of asking Mr. (T. Thomas) Fortune, editor of the *New
York Age*, to let it appear.'[90] It was some nine months after this
exchange of letters that Washington made his policy of accommodation with Southern whites known to the nation, thereby becoming the leader of American Negroes.

If leaders of the American Negro, including Washington, disagreed sharply with Blyden that the solution to the 'race problem'
lay in Negro emigration to Africa, they were always willing to
honour him as an outstanding Negro intellect. In New York in
August 1895, he was given 'a grand reception at the St. Marks
Methodist Church'. Some eight hundred Negroes, among whom
were some of the most distinguished of the country, attended. The
New York Age described his reception as 'a memorable occasion
in the social and intellectual history of Negroes in New York'.[91]
And just before he left the United States, he was invited to deliver
the annual address before the Bethel Historical and Literary
Society of Baltimore. This honour was reserved only for highly
distinguished Negroes; the year before Douglass had delivered
the address. Blyden's name attracted to the lecture 'an unrivalled
aggregation of Negro talent, wealth and culture'.[92] Blyden's final
visit to the United States came to a premature end when he was
requested by the British Colonial Office to assume an appointment in Lagos as Agent of Native Affairs.

In curtailing his American visit, he experienced one regret: that

[89] *Lagos Weekly News*, VI, 16 March 1895.   [90] *Ibid.*
[91] Reprinted in *Lagos Weekly Record*, VII, 5 Oct. 1895.
[92] *Washington Post*, 14 Oct. 1895.

he could not attend the first American Congress on Africa which was scheduled to be held at Gammon Theological Seminary, Atlanta, Georgia, from 13 to 15 December. The Congress was sponsored by Stewart Missionary Foundation which was established to stimulate American Negro interest in Africa. He welcomed this as a step in the right direction and wrote from London, expressing his regret at being unable to attend, but wishing it success:

The 'Congress on Africa' at this time is most opportune when the world is looking to that continent as a field for political, commercial and philanthropic effort. I hope that the results of the Congress upon the Negro population of your country will be such as to lead them to take a greater practical interest in the land of their fathers.[93]

From 1895 until his death in 1912, Blyden's contact with New World Negroes was through private correspondence or in articles which appeared in the *African Methodist Episcopal Review* and in the *Liberia Bulletin*. Throughout this entire period the lot of the Negro in the United States worsened. In state after state in the South he was stripped of his political rights and discriminated against in every way. The result was that this entire period is endemic with race riots; and Negro lynchings, oftentimes with the connivance of the law, were commonplace. If the age of Booker T. Washington saw the Negro make great advance in industrial education, it also saw him reach the nadir of his power in the United States.[94]

But early in the new century there were already signs that the Negro was on his way to a slow, painful recovery. A new, militant and uncompromising leadership had already begun to emerge, led by the young and brilliant W. E. B. Du Bois, who challenged Washington's policy of compromise and appeasement.[95] It was the efforts of this group, as well as the shock administered to the liberal white conscience by the dastardly white-incited race riot of Atlanta in December 1906, which led in 1909 to the formation of the white-dominated but inter-racial National Association for the Advancement of Coloured People—the first effective national organization fighting for the rights of Negroes.

All during this time Negroes continued to respond to discrimi-

[93] J. W. Bowen, *Addresses and Proceedings of the Congress on Africa*, Atlanta 1896, 16.
[94] This is the thesis of Logan, *op. cit.*
[95] See, for instance, W. E. B. Du Bois, *Souls of Black Folk*, Chicago 1903.

nation by drawing up grandiose plans for emigration to Africa; but as in the previous half-century none of these schemes succeeded. The Negro was in the United States to stay. The force of circumstances which had kept them there even when large numbers showed a genuine desire to emigrate, operated even against the efforts of Marcus A. Garvey, who up to his time was the only charismatic national leader in United States Negro history.

In these years Blyden had no new message for the American Negro. Consistently he advised them that it was in their interest to decline to participate in American politics. In 1896, when the movement to disenfranchise the Negro in the South was gathering momentum, he wrote to a friend, John E. Bruce, a distinguished American Negro journalist, that the elimination of the American Negro from politics was 'the best thing that could have happened to him in the South'.[96] And in 1910, less than two years before his death, he expressed a similar view to another American Negro friend:

It seems to me that the Negro in the black belt of the south where you reside, might be the happiest man in the world, if he would only follow the teachings and methods of Christ. . . . He took upon himself the form of a slave and served humanity from below. He eschewed politics.[97]

This was not an expression of lack of sympathy for the plight of the American Negro, but a statement based on the conviction that the place of the true Negro was in Africa, and that his contribution to world civilization was to be in the religious rather than the political sphere.

In theory, Blyden's case for American Negro return to Africa seemed legitimate. For most of his lifetime the lot of the American Negro was a humiliating one, and apart from the early years of the Reconstruction, there were very few signs that he would ever achieve equality in the United States. But Blyden was impractical in believing, in the first place, that all Americans regarded as Negroes could or should return to Africa, and from the early 1870's in insisting that only pure Negroes were qualified to return. Indeed, his theory of race hampered rather than helped his attempts to foster Negro emigration, and as he himself must have discovered, although he never admitted it, that empirical

[96] Blyden to John E. Bruce, 26 Sept. 1896, *John E. Bruce Papers*.
[97] Blyden to Rev. E. W. Cooke, 3 March 1910, *ibid*.

evidence did not support his theory: 'pure Negroes', because of
their 'strong race instincts' were no more impelled to struggle for
the uplift of the fatherland than mulattoes with their 'confused
race instincts'. Yet his intense race pride and his experiences both
in Liberia and the United States could explain, at least partially,
his attitude to mulattoes. It is a measure of his intense hatred for
mulattoes not so much as individuals, but as products of 'the
raped womanhood' of Africa[98] as reminders of a system which
brought humiliation to the Negro race, and as a group who were
in fact used to perpetuate the myth of 'pure Negro' inferiority
that Blyden could say to a friend near the end of his life 'when I
am dead—write nothing on my tombstone but . . . "He hated
mulattoes."'[99] But any American emigration scheme to Africa
which proscribed mulattoes was from the start doomed to failure.
Moreover, it is certain that any really large-scale emigration of
American Negroes to Africa would have brought serious physical
and cultural conflicts with Africans, and could conceivably only
have been successful if backed by the might of a major power,
American or European; but there was never a possibility that this
would materialize. Although to the end of his life he clung to the
belief that a Negro exodus would yet take place, he never really
thought out or suggested any feasible plan for its implementation.
But it is doubtful as Garvey's efforts showed whether any Negro
no matter how great his tenacity and organizing ability, could
have succeeded in organizing a mass American Negro exodus to
Africa.

But if Blyden's efforts at promoting Negro emigration to Africa
were futile, he did succeed in stimulating, and sometimes creating,
among educated American Negroes an interest in Africa, in dis-
pelling myths about that continent, and in engendering pride in
the past achievements of the race; in this effort he was the forerunner of men like William E. B. Du Bois and Carter G. Woodson. Ironically, he helped the cause and struggle of American
Negroes by himself demonstrating that Negroes could, by outstanding achievements, command the respect and attention even
of those who were inclined to be ill-disposed towards them. And
it is significant that although most American Negro leaders did
not agree with many of his viewpoints, they were always willing
to praise and garland him as an outstanding Negro intellectual.

[98] *Sierra Leone Guardian and Foreign Mails*, VII, 16 Feb. 1912.   [99] *Ibid.*

7. Liberian Educator, Politician and Statesman 1874–1912

After his sojourn in Sierra Leone in 1871–3, Blyden returned to Liberia, and although from 1885 he became an itinerant in West Africa, he retained his belief that the success of the Republic was one of the main hopes of advancing the interest of his race, and so he continued to serve it whenever he had the opportunity. In 1874 he resumed his role as educator and as late as 1900 was actively associated with Liberia College, but his most important educational assignment was as President of Liberia College from 1880 to 1884. He served in the Liberian Cabinet as Minister of the Interior and Secretary of Education (1880–2), and in 1885 unsuccessfully contested the Presidential election. He was Liberia's first accredited diplomat abroad—to the Court of St. James in 1877–8, and again in 1892, and to London and Paris in 1905. This chapter will examine his role as educator, politician, and statesman in Liberia from 1874; his career as a diplomat is significant enough to merit treatment in a separate chapter.[1]

Blyden had returned to Liberia with the object of undertaking educational work in the interior and of pushing the influence of the Republic as far as possible into its hinterland. In late June 1873, 'after repeated invitations' he made his first tentative visit to Liberia since his forced departure in 1871, and to his surprise received a cordial reception from 'leading Liberians', most of whom were his former political enemies, and who assured him of their support for his intended project in the interior.[2] After settling his affairs in Sierra Leone, he finally returned in late October with renewed enthusiasm for work he considered vital to the progress of the Republic. However, President Roberts sought to persuade him to join his Cabinet as Secretary of State. Without

[1] See Chapter Eight which also discusses his plan for saving Liberia from threatened dismemberment by the European imperialist powers, and for its economic development.

[2] Blyden to Coppinger, 14 Sept. 1873, *A.C.S. Papers*, Vol. 16; Blyden to J. C. Lowrie, 19 Sept. 1873, *P.B.F.M. Papers*, Vol. 9.

doubt, Blyden was easily the best qualified Liberian for that position: he was the only one who could translate the communication from all foreign governments, as well as Arabic notes from the interior; and none was more adept than he at drafting letters and memoranda. But two and a half years in Sierra Leone had not diminished his dislike and distrust of mulattoes, and of Roberts in particular. Moreover, he had set his mind on working in the interior, and so declined the President's offer.

Blyden believed that his refusal to accept the Cabinet post 'revived mulatto antipathy' to him. He found that the Negro-mulatto conflict which the 'Roye Affair' had exacerbated, was still potentially explosive and reported to a friend that 'Politically, things are wearing a gloomy and threatening aspect. Everybody is dreading some serious outbreak. The oppressions and bloodshed of 1871, unnecessarily enacted, are not yet forgotten; and the party who considered themselves as injured are seeking every opportunity to revenge themselves.' He described the Liberian Government as 'inefficient and imbecile' and regretted that Liberia College, of which the old and ailing Roberts was still President, was 'falling into decay'.[3] Blyden's picture of a spirit of lawlessness in Monrovia, and of ineptitude both in the conduct of the Government and of the College was confirmed by the reports of other Liberians.[4]

This 'degenerate state of affairs' in the Negro Republic drove Blyden to his characteristic admonitions. In a speech delivered in Monrovia on 1 December 1873, he remonstrated with Liberians to 'show yourselves equal to the responsibilities which devolve upon you. Fail not to use every effort to gain a position of prosperity for yourselves, and to open to civilization and Christianity the great continent of which you occupy the border; your unsuccess will only deepen the impression that the Negro is indeed an inferior race, and that the Caucasian will feel justified in scorning him as an equal and a brother.' He urged Liberians to 'amalgamate' with 'the athletic and vigorous' tribes of the interior: the Mandinka, the Fula and Hausa.[5]

[3] Blyden to Lowrie, 10 Feb. 1874, *P.B.F.M. Papers*, Vol. 10; Blyden to Coppinger 7 Sept. 1874, *A.C.S. Papers*, Vol. 17.

[4] The Liberian Board of Trustees to J. J. Roberts, 29 Sept. 1874, *A.C.S. Papers*, Vol. 17; J. Dinery to Lowrie, 21 Oct. 1874, *P.B.F.M. Papers*, Vol. 10.

[5] Edward W. Blyden, 'Problems before Liberia', *African Repository*, L, Aug. 1874, 230.

Liberia's continuing failure caused Blyden to conclude that the Negro Republic 'still needed the example and guidance of white men' as missionaries and educators—a conclusion entirely at variance with that which he had so recently held in Sierra Leone when he had insisted that Negroes should control their own schools and churches. In a long memorandum, entitled 'Liberia a Failure',[6] sent to the Secretary of the Presbyterian Board of Foreign Missions, he recommended that in future American missionary and philanthropic agencies operating in Liberia send out white men to supervise the administration of the work and the expenditure of funds, because Liberians entrusted with this in the past had 'subserved their individual ends without the remotest reference to the public good'. He contended that non-resident white men would be assets to Liberia because 'not having any desire to become prominent and influential citizens of Liberia', they were likely 'to consult the interest of all'. Blyden's impolitic recommendation—one that Liberians were bound to oppose— must have resulted from his keen disappointment that both in Sierra Leone and Liberia there had been very little display of a spirit of patriotism, self-sacrifice and independence, qualities which Negroes needed if their race was to advance.

Much more reasonable and practical were his other recommendations for effective missionary work in Liberia. He urged that each missionary send a report at least once a month, 'describing the condition of his field, its prospects and wants; also conveying intelligence that may be gathered of the native tribes in his vicinty or interior to his station', which would form the basis of future planning; that missionaries abstain from becoming 'mixed up with political or party questions', as also from trading for profit: all their time should be devoted to 'their legitimate work as the religious guides and instructors of the people'; that teachers in mission schools should supply full monthly reports on their classes; that meetings of the Presbytery in Liberia should be held regularly in a central and convenient location to coordinate missionary activities; and that the treasurer of the Presbytery should send out quarterly statements of his accounts. As one of the first steps in instituting his proposed programme of reform, Blyden pressed for the setting up of a Presbyterian Theolo-

[6] Memo. by Blyden: 'Liberia a Failure', 20 Dec. 1873, to Lowrie, *P.B.F.M. Papers*, Vol. 9. The material from this and the next paragraph is from this source.

gical College in Liberia where clergymen could be 'properly' trained.

Blyden also wished the Presbyterian Board to found a lay institution of higher learning in Liberia's interior. He claimed that he could get no help for such a project from the Liberian Government because of the opposition of the small group of powerful traders who feared that the opening of the interior would stimulate greater competition and result in less profit for them, and also because the mulattoes believed that 'the training and incorporation of the natives will lower if not annihilate the prestige which they have so far maintained'. He sought to persuade the Board that it was its duty 'to give to Liberia and interior Africa a comprehensive and effective system of education, and for some years to come should devote itself to training minds which in church and state, on the coast and in the interior, are to control this country'. Blyden offered himself as the head of the prospective 'educational centre not only of Liberia but of West Africa', to which 'leading natives in the British colonies would send their children to be educated by us, and native chiefs of influence in the interior would avail themselves of the opportunity we hope to offer in Arabic and English'. He would make such a school 'contribute as much as possible to its own support' and conduct it 'in the simplest manner—conforming to native usages in clothing and diet to save expense and kill the foolish notion' that the European way of life was best.[7] But despite these assurances, the Presbyterian Board did not undertake to implement Blyden's ambitious project, but instead decided to reopen Alexander High School (which had been closed down after Blyden left it in 1861 to become a Professor at Liberia College), at Harrisburg on the St. Paul's River. Blyden began his educational work in August 1874, and had as his assistant a young Mandinka from Sierra Leone who was fluent in Arabic and in several African languages.

But so perturbed was he by the lawlessness in Liberia, so much did he fear that he might lose his life, so hampered by an uncongenial domestic relationship with his mulatto wife, and indeed, so obsessed with the thought of mulatto opposition to him that he was unable to do any really effective work. He began to appear as a man fickle and without a fixed purpose: his desire for work in the interior alternated with an urge to get away from Liberia

[7] Blyden to Lowrie, 23 Jan. 1877. *P.B.F.M. Papers*, Vol. 11.

and work for two or three years in the United States helping to prepare Negroes there for emigration to Africa. He himself was aware of his own unsteadiness of purpose and in an anguished and pathetic outburst attributed it to a lack of sympathy from his wife and Liberians generally. He wrote confidentially to a friend:

I live among an unsympathetic people—and, I regret to say, an unsympathizing family. My wife seems entirely unimproveable. She is of the mind and temperament of the people around her—sometimes, pressed as I am on all sides, I feel like making my escape to the interior and never allowing myself to be heard from again. Domestically speaking, this has been my life for years. My restlessness and my apparent fickleness is largely due to this. I am persecuted *outside* but more inside. Uncongenial, incompatible, unsympathetic, my wife makes the burden of my life sore and heavy.[8]

Other letters Blyden wrote in this period show him as an utterly frustrated man, poor in health, unable, because of lack of support and his own indecisiveness, to push Liberia's influence effectively into its hinterland, unwilling to participate in a Government controlled by mulattoes, and yet constantly expostulating on mulatto 'misgovernment and rapacity'. Especially did he castigate the Government for its lack of an enlightened policy towards the indigenous peoples, and its refusal to consider their grievances. And when in 1874 the sea-board tribes at Cape Palmas formed themselves into the Grebo Reunited Kingdom and for almost two years repulsed the attempts of the Liberian Government to subdue them, Blyden's sympathy lay with the Africans.[9] He regarded as unfortunate the intervention of an American Man of War which had finally enabled the Liberian Government to overcome the confederacy, and more than hinted that it would have been to the advantage of the Negro Republic if it had been brought under native rule. Blyden consistently maintained that 'a judicious, firm but sympathetic treatment of . . . chiefs would have made them powerful auxiliaries to the Republic'.[10]

At Harrisburg Blyden was adviser and schoolmaster to all who would listen and learn: he taught manual crafts as well as

[8] Blyden to Lowrie, 15 Jan. 1875, *ibid.*, Vol. 10.
[9] Blyden to Lowrie, 20 Sept. 1875, *ibid.*; Blyden to Coppinger, 21 Oct. 1875, *A.C.S. Papers*, Vol. 17; cf. Buell, *op. cit.*, 737.
[10] Blyden to Coppinger, 29 June 1876, *A.C.S. Papers*, Vol. 18.

academic subjects, including Arabic, in day and evening classes, encouraged agriculture, and in all, earned the reputation in Monrovia of 'raising up a black aristocracy on the St. Paul's River'.[11] Occasionally, he visited the capital to deliver public addresses on such characteristic subjects as 'The false conception entertained by our leading men as to their position and work here'.[12] But he preferred to look to the interior. He made occasional visits to nearby Muslim towns and himself received frequent visits from Muslims. In January 1877 he revisited Boporo, and made another attempt to extend Liberia's influence to this Muslim centre by urging the American Colonization Society to plant a colony of American Negroes there, and establish on 'this healthy highland location an educational nucleus ... that will attract aspiring youths from various parts of the coast as well as the interior',[13] but no action was taken. And so Blyden's dream of establishing an outstanding educational centre of higher learning in West Africa as yet remained unfulfilled.

Blyden continued to despair over the fact that Liberia was governed mainly by mulattoes. Roberts died on 25 February 1876, but even with the death of the man he regarded as the great villain in Liberian history, Blyden was no more optimistic of Liberia's future than before, because he believed that the new incumbent, James S. Payne, himself a former President, who had been succeeded by Roye, 'belonged to the same school as Roberts'.[14] But, no doubt, he became better disposed to Payne when the President appointed him as Liberia's ambassador to the Court of St. James, a capacity in which he strove conscientiously to enhance the prestige of the Republic.

On 12 March 1879, Blyden triumphantly returned from his diplomatic duties. At Harrisburg on the St. Paul's River, he was

[11] Blyden to Lowrie, 6 Jan. 1877, *P.B.F.M. Papers*, Vol. 11.
[12] Blyden to Lowrie, 6 Dec. 1876, *ibid.*
[13] *African Repository*, LVIII, July 1877, 91.
[14] Blyden to Lowrie, 1 May 1875, *P.B.F.M. Papers*, Vol. 10. Blyden never forgave Roberts. Later he quoted with relish a verse reputedly composed by Professor Martin Freeman shortly after Roberts' death:

> 'Roberts is dead—so I am told
> His greatest love was the love of gold
> If to heaven he's gone, angels, look sharp
> As you may lose a golden harp.'

See Blyden to Coppinger, 28 April 1888, *A.C.S. Papers*, Vol. 25.

welcomed back as 'a distinguished fellow citizen', and praised for 'the great and noble work' he had been doing. Even more significant was the public reception given him by the Liberian Government in the House of Representatives 'to mark its sense of his merit and recognition of his services' in ably representing Liberia abroad. He was praised as 'one of the rare men of the century' who had undertaken the task of educating the civilized world about Africa and the Negro. Blyden confessed to being 'taken by surprise' and saw the enthusiastic welcome for him as 'a sort of instalment from the future—a glimpse of the hereafter' because he had resigned himself to seeing his work 'generally misunderstood' while he lived. His faith that a new dispensation was in store for the Negro race was reaffirmed, and he was 'thankful' to be both a witness and a participant in what he regarded as an important phase in the history of his race. He expressed these sentiments to a friend thus:

I feel thankful that I was born and grew up just as the shades of Africa's deepest night were melting into the twilight of liberty for the race, when the dead past of her suffering was fast receding, but still before the period of her exaltation had arrived; and I was determined to contribute what I could to assist in forging at least one of the links by which God unites period with period.

The task of working for the Negro race he knew to be a great, noble and arduous one, but he was willing to pay any price in performing it. His patriotic reception he interpreted as a sign that Liberia had started on the path to progress.[15]

Blyden again turned his thoughts to exploring and developing Liberia's hinterland. To Commodore R. W. Shufeldt of the American Naval Squadron, he confided: 'I have dreams of an interior state of Africans from Boporo going back—the world needs such a state and such a state no doubt sooner or later it will have.'[16] In seeking to make his contribution towards the construction of such a state, Blyden had conceived of the ambitious project of building a railway from Monrovia along the St. Paul's River 'over the Kong mountains into the Valley of the Niger and the heart of the Soudan'.[17] He had hoped that a petition by the American Colonization Society to the United States Congress for

[15] *West African Reporter*, V, 16 April 1879; *African Repository*, LV, 108–13.
[16] Blyden to Shufeldt, 18 April 1879, *A.C.S. Papers*. Vol. 19.
[17] Blyden to Coppinger, 23 April 1879, *ibid*.

an appropriation of $25,000 to build such a railway would be successful. In the meantime at Blyden's request and with the cooperation of the Liberian Government, Commodore Shufeldt had ordered two of his officers to conduct a survey of the St. Paul's River. They were assisted by Benjamin Anderson and twenty-seven Africans. But Blyden's 'railway dream', like so many of his others, did not materialize. He ascribed its failure to 'the apathy of the Liberian Government';[18] a more likely explanation was that Liberia could not secure the necessary capital for the construction of such a railway.

PRESIDENT OF LIBERIA COLLEGE

If his railway scheme came to nought, he was compensated in getting appointments he greatly desired. In January 1880 he was offered the Presidency of Liberia College by the local Board of Trustees as well as the position of Minister of the Interior and Secretary of Education in President Gardner's Cabinet. Blyden gladly accepted both, but it was to turn out that the combination of offices as educator and politician was impolitic. This offer of the Presidency of Liberia College was to Blyden like a dream come true. As early as 1874 he had been ambitious to become President of the College: he wrote confiding to Coppinger that he wished to take the place of J. J. Roberts because he believed that mulattoes had used Liberia College 'as a conspiracy against the Negro race'. He had plans for the College if he was appointed President: 'I should at once publish a History and Prospectus of the institutions. I should enter into rapport with some literary institutions in England and America ... I should bring students from Boporo, Musardu, Sierra Leone, Lagos—and make the College a place of learning for Africa and the race,' he wrote.[19]

The College itself had been an abysmal failure. Far from being a centre of academic learning, it had become, as we have seen, one of the battle grounds for the Negro-mulatto conflict in Liberia. Roberts's Presidency of the College had been long and inept, and in his last feeble years, academic activity there sunk to

[18] American Colonization Society, *Sixty-third Annual Report*, Washington 1880, 13; *African Repository*, LV, 83-4.
[19] Blyden to Coppinger, 19 Oct. 1874, *A.C.S. Papers*, Vol. 17.

a low ebb. On Roberts's death in 1876, the Boston Trustees suspended the College on the ground 'that it had failed to be of practical utility for the purpose of education in the Republic'.[20] Blyden had seen the suspension as another 'triumph of the mulatto ring' and felt 'irrepressible indignation . . . at this unfortunate action'.[21] However, in 1877, the Boston Board reopened the College and appointed H. R. W. Johnson as President. Within a year Johnson resigned; and Rev. John B. Pinney, a white man, and Secretary of the New York Colonization Society was appointed instead. Pinney arrived in Monrovia in May, 1878, and decided that the College should be removed into the interior. Blyden, who was at that time in London, was enthusiastic about the appointment of Pinney; he hoped that through him the College affairs would at last be removed from the arena of Negro-mulatto conflict. But Pinney was unable to persuade the Liberian Trustees to agree to have the College set up in the interior, and after six months in Monrovia resigned and returned to the United States. Thus, for more than a year after Pinney's resignation, the College had been without a President. And now Blyden had been offered the Presidency on terms for which he had long fought: state scholarships were to be given to African youths, particularly sons of chiefs; the College was to teach 'agricultural and mechanical arts' as well as literary subjects; and finally, a teacher of Arabic and West African languages was to be employed.[22]

Although Blyden was appointed by the Liberian Trustees to the Presidency of Liberia College, it was by no means certain that his appointment would be approved by the Boston and New York Boards of Trustees. No one doubted his ability but some had misgivings about his suitability because of his paranoic hatred of mulattoes and the fickleness of his temperament. To discuss his own appointment and the reorganization of Liberia College, Blyden was authorized by the Liberia Trustees to visit the United States. During a two month visit he succeeded in removing 'many bad impressions and baseless doubts' from the minds of the trustees, and had his Presidency confirmed.[23] He also got approval

[20] Allen, *op. cit.*, 39.
[21] Blyden to Coppinger, 19 June 1876, *A.C.S. Papers*, Vol. 18.
[22] 'Resolutions Adopted by the Board of Trustees at their Annual Meeting, January 19, 1880, for the benefit of Liberia College', *A.C.S. Papers*, Vol. 19, No. 106.
[23] Allen, *op. cit.*, 47.

for plans to remove the College from Monrovia into the interior.

Blyden returned to Liberia with high optimism: the opportunity he had longed for to establish a superior institution of learning in West Africa was at last given him. He set about his task with vigour. Realizing that the success of Liberia College would depend upon the financial and moral support of as many West Africans as possible, he made every effort to stimulate widespread public interest in the College. He used the custom of the College of having an annual public oral examination to good effect, an unprecedentedly large crowd attending the first public examination conducted under his Presidency. He was the first President to have African chiefs attend the ceremonies of the college.[24] By December, the College had started a course of public lectures, the President himself delivering the first of these on 'Toussaint L'Ouverture, the Emancipator of Haiti'.[25] Already Liberia College had begun to 'excite interest all along the coast' of West Africa.[26]

Blyden's formal inauguration as President took place on 5 February 1881. His address on this occasion was brilliant, purposeful, and in parts at least, controversial.[27] He left no doubt that he expected the College to play a large and important role not only in Liberia, or even West Africa, but on behalf of the entire Negro race. His view of the College was that it was 'only a machine, an instrument to assist in carrying forward our regular work, devised not only for intellectual ends, but for social purposes, for religious duty, for patriotic ends, for racial development'. Mindful of the indifference with which his schemes to promote higher learning had been met by Africans themselves, Blyden saw the first task of Liberia College to be 'generative': 'It must create a sentiment favourable to its existence. It must generate the intellectual and moral state in the community which will give it not only a congenial atmosphere in which to thrive, but food and nutriment for its enlargement and growth.'

Ultimately the role of Liberia College was to counteract the evil influences which European ideas and teachings had had on

---

[24] American Colonization Society, *Sixty-fifth Annual Report*, Washington 1881, 15.

[25] *Monrovia Observer*, III, 25 Nov. 1880.

[26] Blyden to Coppinger, 20 March 1881, *A.C.S. Papers*, Vol. 20.

[27] See Edward W. Blyden, *The Aims and Methods of a Liberal Education for Africans*, Cambridge, Mass., 1882, 30 pp.; republished in *Christianity, Islam and the Negro Race*, 82–109. The quotations and summary which follow are from this source.

the Negro, to correct European misrepresentation of Africa and the Negro, and to play the leading role in interpreting Africa to the rest of the world. Because he believed that the coast was a constant reminder of the detrimental effects on Africans of 'foreign ideas and foreign manners', and that the future of Liberia lay in the interior, he wanted the College removed to the banks of the St. Paul's River. Here, health of body, 'the indispensable condition for health of mind, could be secured'; here, too, 'students may devote a portion of their time to manual labour in the cultivation of the fertile lands which will be accessible, and thus assist in procuring from the soil the means for meeting a large part of the necessary expenses, and where access to the institution will be convenient to the aborigine'.

In Blyden's estimate, the new Liberia College was the only institution of higher learning anywhere that could provide proper education for Negroes. To him, 'The object of all education is to secure growth and efficiency; to make a man all that his natural gifts would allow him to become; to produce self-respect, a proper appreciation of our powers and of those of other people; to beget a fitness for one's sphere of life and action and an ability to discharge the duties it imposes'. But the influence of European teachings on Africans had had the opposite effect: it had produced imitators and men 'lacking in self-respect and efficiency'. This had been so because the method of teaching had been unsuited to the Africans and the information imparted was often false. In Blyden's own words:

... they have taught us books too much and things too little, forms of expression and very little of the importance of thought. The notion common among Negroes ... is that the most important part of knowledge consists in knowing what other men—foreigners—have said about things, and even about Africa, and about themselves. They aspire to be familiar not with what really is, but with what is presented... Hence some of us are found repeating things against ourselves which are thoroughly injurious and false to us, only because we read them in books or have heard them from foreign teachers. The idea never seems to occur to such persons that there are subjects of inquiry, especially in this large and interesting country of theirs, about which the truth is yet to be found out, and peoples and customs and systems about which correct ideas are yet to be formed.

The result of this unquestioning acceptance by Africans of European teaching was that

We have neglected to study matters at home because we were trained in books written by foreigners and for a foreign race ... and from these books we learn that the Negro at home was a degraded being—a heathen and worse than a heathen—a fool; and we were taught everything excellent and praiseworthy about foreigners. Therefore we turned our backs upon our brethren in the interior as those from whom we could learn nothing to elevate, to enlighten, or to refine. A result of this is that we have not yet acted for ourselves. We have had history written for us, and we have endeavoured to act upon it, whereas the true order is that history should be first acted, then written. It is easy to account, then, for the want of genuine life and spontaneity of the people.

Blyden expected that Liberia College would take the lead in reversing this trend:

The African must advance by methods of his own. He must possess a power distinct from that of the European.
    We must show that we are able to go alone, to carve our own way. We must not be satisfied that, in this nation, European influence shapes our polity, makes our laws, rules in our tribunals, and impregnates our social atmosphere. We must not suppose that the Anglo-Saxon methods are final ... We must study our brethren in the interior who knows more than we do the laws of the growth for the race.

But if he inveighed against the adverse influence of the worst aspects of European teaching on the African, Blyden, was prepared to admit that 'the instruments of culture, in its better form at least, was everywhere the same'; he intended using the basic European curriculum after divesting it of its 'distracting influences'. As the College grew he intended to foster more and more purely African subjects. For the time being the basic academic curriculum would consist of 'the earlier epochs of world history'; the classics, mathematics, the Bible without commentaries, Arabic and some of the principal West African languages. It was for good reasons that Blyden would permit the study of history only up to the medieval period. It was not only that he believed that the modern intellectual activities of Europe, even though it had produced 'some of the greatest work of human genius', could not equal those of Greece and Rome at their prime, but more importantly, the modern period was likely to have a harmful effect on African minds because it was during this period that 'the transatlantic slave trade arose and those theories—logical, social, and political—were invented for the degradation and proscription of the Negro'. This was a controversial gap in his curriculum—but a perfectly understandable one coming from a sensitive race patriot. The study of the Greek and Latin languages and literature was permissible because there were in them 'not a sentence, a word, or a syllable disparaging to the Negro'. They could give the Negro mental discipline without 'injecting him with race poison'. Arabic and African languages were, of course, for the purpose of having 'intelligent intercourse with the millions accessible to us in the interior'.

Characteristically, Blyden ended his address by pleading for the support and co-operation of Liberians:

We have a great work before us, a work unique in the history of the world, which others who appreciate its vastness and importance, envy us the privilege of doing. The world is looking at this Republic to see whether 'order and law, religion and morality, the rights of conscience, the rights of property' may be secured and preserved by a government administered by Negroes. Let us show ourselves equal to the task.

The time is past when we can be content with putting forth elaborate arguments to prove our equality with foreign races... The suspicion, disparaging to us, will be dissipated only by the exhibition of the indisputable realities of a lofty manhood as they may be illustrated in successful efforts to build up a nation, to wrest from Nature her secrets, to lead the van of progress in this country and regenerate a continent.

Thus, Blyden expected Liberia College to play an important role in shaping the destiny of the Negro Republic. But there were obstacles in the way of the College developing into an influential institution. The first and major difficulty was that of raising adequate funds for running the College. Blyden, of course, was keenly aware of this difficulty. Shortly after his inauguration as President, he urgently appealed in a circular, to West Africans for donations with which to endow chairs of 'Moral and Physical Sciences,' and of 'Arabic and Native Languages'. He wished to see funds invested on behalf of the College which would bring in a steady income and ensure its continuous development.[28] And in June 1881 Blyden sent a circular to Presidents of several American Universities and Colleges including Harvard, Yale, Princeton, and Amherst requesting aid for Liberia College in any way they saw fit.[29]

Until funds could be raised for constructing new buildings in the interior, Liberia College had to continue to operate in Monrovia. The building here was in a dilapidated condition but repairs and renovations were carried out through communal help. The January term of 1881 opened with twenty-seven students in the Preparatory Department and eight male students, one of whom was from Sierra Leone, in the College itself. A small library contained 4,000 volumes but the reference books were very much out of date. The staff was skeletal: four including the President himself for both sections of the institution. But before long Blyden was seeking to attract Negro scholars from other West African territories: in March, 1881 he offered the Chair of Moral Philosophy to John B. McEwen, a West Indian 'of first class education and culture' who had been a missionary in the Rio Pongo since 1871. The chair of Arabic and West African Studies he offered to Muhammed Wakka, Assistant Arabic writer to the Sierra Leone Government.[30] But he failed to attract them.

If gross inadequacy of funds was one factor militating against the success of Liberia College, another was the character of the President himself. He was essentially a man of ideas, but his attempts to execute them were invariably blundering and unrealistic: in matters in which he considered a principle was involved, he was devoid of tact or diplomacy if he were opposed. He could not overcome his detestation of mulattoes, but the success of Liberia College depended on co-operation with them: of the six members of the Board of Trustees, four were mulattoes. But Blyden, by now conditioned in his reaction to mulattoes, continued to regard them as a 'hampering influence' and wished to see them replaced. He had made the pointed remark which appeared in the *African Repository* that for the first time in the history of the College all eight students were Negroes,[31] and this had brought down on him the wrath of mulattoes. He seemed

[28] *West African Reporter*, VII, 19 Feb. 1881.   [29] Blyden to Coppinger, 4 July 1881, *A.C.S. Papers*, Vol. 20.   [30] Blyden to Coppinger, 25 March 1881, *ibid.* [31] *African Repository*, LVI, June 1881, 75.

to have regarded his appointment as President of Liberia College as the beginning of Negro ascendancy in Liberian education as well as in politics.

Blyden had further nullified his efforts on behalf of the College by assuming, while still retaining his presidency, the appointment of Minister of the Interior. His acceptance of this appointment was understandable. He himself was intensely interested in pushing Liberia's influence into its hinterland, but, nonetheless, it was an unwise and impolitic decision: his duties as Minister of the Interior took him away, not infrequently, from the College, at a time when he could easily have devoted all his energies to that institution. Besides, although he did not so regard it, his appointment to an especially controversial ministry made of him a political partisan, a characterization which was not likely to facilitate the carrying out of his duties as President of the College. The difficulty to which Blyden's combining of the two offices in himself gave rise, could be illustrated by the following incident: Blyden, as Minister of the Interior and Secretary of education wished to replace Arthur Barclay by R. B. Richardson as Principal of the Preparatory Department of Liberia College. By President Gardner's order this was done. But the Trustees of Liberia College denied that Gardner had the power to dismiss a member of the staff. They therefore upheld Barclay in office, even though Richardson was supposed to have assumed his duties. The impasse continued for three months, and although Blyden finally secured the appointment of Richardson, the incident had strained the relationship between him and the Board of Trustees.[32] This incident, too, illustrated the fact that it was not only with mulattoes that Blyden failed to get along. Barclay was a 'pure Negro' but because he did not share Blyden's dislike of the men of mixed blood, Blyden concluded that Barclay 'was a tool of mulattoes'. The fact was that Blyden was a difficult man to work with mainly because he regarded himself as a 'providential agent' working on behalf of the Negro race and was always convinced about the rightness of his ideas. He reacted to opposition by assuming a martyr-complex: he wrote to Coppinger that he was prepared to die for the cause of Liberia's advancement, and continued: 'I know God is at the helm and guiding the ship and if they (mulat-

[32] *Monrovia Observer*, IV, 12 Aug. 1881; Blyden to Coppinger, 3 Sept. 1881, *A.C.S. Papers*, Vol. 20.

toes) succeed in killing me they will have to utterly annihilate the
ashes, for out of them will arise a stronger influence than any they
have yet witnessed in Liberia for the right whose triumph they
dread.'[33] Blyden's bitter verbal opposition to mulattoes was all
the more pathetic because there is no evidence that he wished to
take concerted action against them.

But if Blyden was tactless, if he did not know how best to husband the resources at his command, he was, nonetheless, con-
scientious and with clear and strong views of what was good for
Liberia College. He reiterated these at every opportunity. One
such occasion was in his first annual report to the Board of Trustees, a duty which his predecessors in office had completely
neglected. It was a report of an 'unusual character' owing to
the 'peculiar circumstances of Liberia'. In it he made yet another
plea for greater support of Liberia College; he saw it as the key
to universal education in Liberia, and this in turn was 'essential
and indispensable' for 'healthful inward growth as a republican
constitutional government; and for healthful outward growth —
as we advance into the interior — safely to absorb and assimilate
the aboriginal elements'. Liberia College was also the only means
in the country of providing 'Culture which would not only give
mental strength, but wide views of duty in the country and for
the race'. 'We are a Negro nation, having a new and important
role to play in world history, and in the history of this great continent . . . That we have not had the advantage of culture will
furnish no excuse for us when we show incompetence in dealing
with great national questions.' He counselled that Liberians
should not despair unduly because Liberia College had passed
through 'great trials': it was by no means unique in this: all the
now 'great American Universities (Harvard, Yale, Dartmouth,
and Cornell)' had passed through similar difficulties. He pointed
to evidence which suggested that Liberia College was about to
leave its difficulties behind: the Government had taken a new
interest in the College; a respectable addition had been made to
the library as a result of the generosity of American donors;
Benjamin Anderson, the Liberian explorer, had been hired as
tutor in mathematics.[34]

[33] Blyden to Coppinger, 20 Aug. 1881, *ibid.*
[34] See *Report of the President of Liberia College to the Board of Trustees*, Cambridge,
Mass., 1882, 21 pp.

If looking back on his first full year in office, critics could point to his unwise involvement in Liberian politics, his tactless opposition to mulattoes, his censorship of 'modern history' in the curriculum of studies at Liberia College, they had to confess, too, that he had infused new life into the College and had stimulated new interest in the College in West Africa and abroad.

Early in the first term of the new academic year Blyden announced that the College had decided to award twelve honorary degrees. The list reflected Blyden's personal choice: it was comprised of two white men who had had an important influence on his early life, and ten men of colour (mainly 'pure Negroes') who had reflected credit upon their race. Blyden was very careful 'to guard the power of granting degrees against abuse'.[35] The degree of Doctor of Laws was conferred on nine persons: Rev. John P. Knox, Blyden's childhood mentor and friend; Rev. David Agnew Wilson, his teacher and friend in his first years in Liberia; the Rev. James W. Horne, a former principal of Monrovia Academy, a Baptist Secondary School; the Rev. Alexander Crummell, a former close associate of Blyden's in Liberia and a strenuous vindicator of the Negro race; John H. Smyth, United States Minister to Liberia and a strong supporter of Blyden's Negro policy; His Lordship, James T. Holly, Bishop of Haiti and an ardent lover of his race; Professor Richard Greener, a highly respected coloured American scholar; Professor W. S. Scarborough, the leading Negro classical scholar in America and a sympathizer of efforts to colonize American Negroes in Liberia; and H. R. W. Johnson, a leading Liberian and a former Professor at Liberia College. Three persons, all Liberians, received the degree of Doctor of Divinity: James S. Payne, a Presbyterian clergyman and ex-President of the Republic; Charles A. Pitman, an able Methodist minister; and Alfred B. King who had succeeded Blyden as Principal of Alexander High School.

Eight new students, two of them mulattoes, were admitted into the College for the new academic year. Blyden was pained that there were qualified Negro students whom he could not admit because scholarships were not available for their upkeep at the college; he himself had undertaken to support two new male students every year. As usual, he omitted no opportunity to create interest in the College among foreigners as well as Africans. Dis-

[35] Blyden to Coppinger, 20 Jan. 1882, *A.C.S. Papers*, Vol. 20.

tinguished visitors were taken on tours of the College and
acquainted with the new efforts to establish a thriving institution.
Sometimes they were surprised to find that a Negro was the
President: Blyden told the story of officers of the U.S. ship *Galena*
who were shown around the College by him and who, at the end
of the tour, asked to see the President.[36] Among Negro visitors to
whom Blyden was proud to show the College was Henry Highland Garnet, the new U.S. Minister to Liberia.

Despite criticisms, Blyden had continued as a Minister of the
Government, while remaining President of the College. Gardner
had been re-elected in 1881 and when he formed his new Cabinet
in January 1882, Blyden was confirmed in his position as Minister of the Interior. Once again Gardner had reaffirmed his intention of giving priority to opening up the interior. And once again
Blyden had congratulated and encouraged him in this decision.
As Minister of the Interior, he had once again to grapple with the
problem of the settlement of Liberia's north-western boundary.
The British, too, would have the dispute settled, but Liberians
were unhappy about the method which the Sierra Leone Government were employing: on 20 March 1882, Sir Arthur Havelock
went to Monrovia with four gun-boats, and demanded that the
Liberian Government consent to have its boundary delimited at
Marfur in the vicinity of Cape Mount. The British had by now
given up all pretence of protecting the rights of the Africans in the
disputed territory and were now seeking to annex it to Sierra
Leone. Governor Havelock made the contradictory claim that
Liberia had no rights to this territory while demanding that the
sum of £8,500 be paid to British traders as indemnity for attacks
of the Vai people on their property. President Gardner, overawed
by this show of British 'big-stick diplomacy', hastily appointed
Blyden and William M. Davis, Attorney-General, to treat with
the British Governor. After a conference lasting five days, the
Liberian commissioners practically capitulated: they agreed that
Liberia should abandon her claims to the territory west of the
Marfur River. President Gardner agreed to the decision of the
commission and the treaty was signed.[37]

This decision aroused fierce opposition in Liberia: meetings of
protest were held and threats made on the lives of members of the

---

[36] Blyden to Coppinger, 9 Jan. 1882, *ibid.*
[37] Johnston, *op. cit.*, 278–9.

Cabinet. The Liberian Senate, hurriedly summoned, refused to ratify the treaty. Blyden, of course, stood at the very centre of the controversy. It was he more than anyone else whom Liberians held responsible for so easily abdicating the rights of the Republic. Indeed, it was charged he had been bribed by the British to do so. While there is no evidence that this was so, Blyden and Davis had undoubtedly conceded territories which the Liberians had consistently claimed to be theirs. But Blyden's action could be reasonably explained if we remember that unlike other Liberians he regarded the boundary between Liberia and Sierra Leone as an artificial and temporary one: he was confident that Liberia would yet absorb Sierra Leone. He thus saw his task as Liberian Commissioner to bring the dispute to an end at any cost. Nonetheless the fury of the Liberians was understandable, and once again he had to flee from their wrath. As in his other moments of despair, Blyden saw himself as a martyr; he felt 'that God had honoured him to bear the cross and odium of helping to save Africa'.[38]

Blyden had sought refuge at Cape Palmas and, typically, he looked upon this visit as 'providential'. He found that the community here was without mulattoes, and being 'untrammelled by alien influences', possessed 'the power of race righteousness ... (and) ... the true germ and basis of nationality'. He was pleased to find 'intelligent educated natives' who 'adhered to native customs as to dress etc.' Thus, Cape Palmas had presented him with a new sign of Liberia's progress that he seemed always to be so desperately seeking.[39] He remained there for a month.

Blyden, of course, had been forced to resign from his ministerial position, and on his return to the College began full-time duties as President. But after only five weeks he left for the United States in an attempt to raise enough funds to remove the College into the interior, increase its facilities and add a female department. He spent nine months in the United States in this and other pursuits.

While in New York he sought to persuade the trustees of funds for the education of American youth who intended to work in Liberia to transfer these funds to Liberia College. He argued that these youths could best be educated on the scene of their future labours.[40] The New York Board of Trustees was sympathetic to

[38] Blyden to Coppinger, 26 April 1882, *A.C.S. Papers*, Vol. 20.
[39] Blyden to Coppinger, 18 April 1882, *ibid*.
[40] Blyden to Coppinger, 13 Oct. 1882, *ibid*.

this point of view and made an appropriation of money for him to visit those institutions where their beneficiaries were studying and report to them with a view to transfer of both students and funds to Liberia College.

Before leaving for the Southern Negro Colleges, Blyden visited Boston where he met members of the Liberia Board of Control. But he 'was astonished at their ignorance of Liberia College': he concluded that they could not have read his reports nor the news of the College which appeared in the *African Repository*: for instance, they still believed 'that only three or four students attended the College'.[41] Here he saw fully the disadvantage of foreign control of Liberia by well-meaning but ill-informed men. Blyden knew that the Boston Board of Trustees had rather reluctantly confirmed his appointment as President of Liberia College, and he now feared that they were looking upon Liberia College as an unnecessary rival to American Negro Colleges. But he was able to impress upon them with success that the College had an important part to play in the development of Liberia. The question of staff was discussed and three new appointments made: Hugh Mason Browne as Professor of Intellectual and Moral Philosophy, Thomas McCants Stewart as Professor of History and Law, and Jennie E. Davis to head the new Female department.

On leaving Boston, Blyden went South and spent some five weeks visiting Negro Colleges in Virginia, North Carolina and Georgia. During this tour twenty-six students including twelve from Hampton Institute, Virginia, agreed to transfer to Liberia College.

Blyden returned to Monrovia on 3 June 1883, after a long stay away from the College which must have provided further grounds on which his opponents could attack him. And yet his mission to America was successful, and with the staff, students and funds which were to follow him, his return might well have marked a new and progressive period for the College. But this was not to be so. The arrival of the two male Professors in Monrovia on 7 August, after fund-raising tours in the United States and England, inaugurated another era of dissension and discord in Liberia College and all Monrovia.[42] The two Professors were mulattoes

[41] Blyden to Coppinger, 28 Sept. 1882, *ibid.*

[42] Allen, *op. cit.*, 53–5; Blyden to Coppinger, 19 Sept. 1883, *A.C.S. Papers*, Vol. 21.

and on this ground Blyden had at first objected to their appointment but had given in when the American Boards of Trustees counselled him to judge a man on his merit rather than on his colour. But he could not overcome his almost automatic prejudice against mulattoes, and it must have been clear to the Professors even before they left the United States that Blyden did not consider them suitable for the appointments they held.

The rupture between Blyden and the two Professors took place so quickly that they taught not one day in the College. The Professors were, no doubt, encouraged to return Blyden's antipathy after finding out that he had powerful enemies in Monrovia. They rapidly grew audacious and before long recommended to the Boston Trustees that the College should be closed down: they maintained that there was nothing to do: the Professorships were sinecures. They found Blyden an easy target to hit. Blyden, for his part, charged the Professors with 'contempt for the College' and 'a desire to have management of things in their own hands'.[43]

The conflict reached a climax in January, 1884, at a meeting of the Liberia Board of Trustees where he found himself with very little support. Stewart and Browne 'attacked Blyden with unrestrained abuse'. H. R. W. Johnson, the new President of Liberia, was himself present at the meeting and sided with the Professors against Blyden. Following this meeting, Browne, changing his mind about closing the College, submitted a plan for its reorganization with Johnson as President.[44] Finding himself isolated and without support or sympathy, least of all from his mulatto wife, Blyden, to the chagrin of his friends and supporters everywhere, abandoned his post at Liberia College and sought solace in Sierra Leone.

The dispute in Liberia had initially caused a division in America, too. At first, the Boston Board had shown sympathy for Blyden, while the New York Board tended to believe the charges brought by the Professors against him. But his inability to bring the dispute to an end and make use of the new Professors at the College, and finally, his leaving the College for Sierra Leone had alienated whatever support he had had. In March, the Boston Board of Trustees had threatened to stop further appropriations

---

[43] Blyden to Coppinger, 13 March 1884, *ibid.*
[44] King to Coppinger, 19 Jan. 1884, *ibid.*

Blyden, circa age 40

Blyden as an old man
(circa 1910)

Bust of Blyden on Water
Street, Freetown, Sierra
Leone. This was erected at
the expense of some of his
European admirers.

of funds for the College unless the differences between the President and the Professors were reconciled. In April, Stewart returned to the United States and his report to both Board of Trustees had served further to undermine Blyden's position. At a meeting on 8 June the Boston Board of Trustees decided to suspend Blyden because of his long absence from the College. Faced with this censure, he tendered his resignation.[45]

The end of Blyden's Presidency, and particularly the manner of his end, had keenly disappointed his friends and admirers everywhere. By his intellectual ability, his initiative and industry, he had raised hopes that Liberia College would yet firmly establish itself; by his intolerance, lack of tact and his inclination to dilute his efforts by pursuing simultaneously too many activities, he had ensured that this would not be so under his Presidency. Ironically, not a single student graduated under his Presidency: the first graduation ceremony was due to take place in December, 1884: by March, all the Senior students, perturbed by the wrangling in Liberia College, left to seek employment; two months later Blyden's resignation officially ended his connection with the College.

PRESIDENTIAL CANDIDATE

Sierra Leone had now become the regular refuge of Blyden from the wrath of Monrovians, but his first loyalty remained to Liberia. With the loss of the Presidency of Liberia College, he pondered how best he could serve the Republic and reluctantly came to the conclusion that he could do this as its President. Ever since his return to Liberia in 1879, after serving as Liberia's ambassador to the Court of St. James, his friends both in Liberia and Sierra Leone had urged him to contest the Presidency of the Republic. But he had declined to do so partly because he thought that he could more effectively devote himself to education, partly because he felt that his plans for Liberia could only be executed under a revised constitution which, among other reforms, made the Presidential term at least four years. He had changed his mind and explained his new position thus to Coppinger: 'I have no desire to be President of Liberia—but I have a desire to take a position or do anything that will enable me to contribute effectively to the

[45] Allen, *op. cit.*, 55.

success of that Negro state.' He rationalized that if he deserved to be President it was to put 'educational matters on a more solid footing'.[46]

As much else in Blyden's career, it was ironical that it was the Republican Party—the one dominated by mulattoes and against which he had inveighed so hard and so long, that nominated him as a candidate for the Presidency. The party seemed to have made a special effort to win his allegiance by deciding on a programme which coincided with Blyden's known views. The party platform claimed that it desired that 'Liberia cut loose from its hampering prejudices and work for national prosperity on a line with the advanced ideas and forward movements of the present century'.[47] In accepting the nomination of the Republican party, an embarrassed Blyden sought to belittle the significance of party politics in Liberia: 'The phrases in the Liberian politics of "Whigs and Republicans" have no especial significance . . . but your platform indicates a desire . . . to take a new departure—to act upon lines so distinct and pronounced as to mark a new era in the political history of Liberia,' he wrote. But Blyden did fear that he might become the tool of a class of men that he despised. This, no doubt, was what prompted him to come to the unconvincing conclusion that, because the leading Republicans had agreed on his nomination, if he were elected President, he would not have owed his 'elevation to any clique in any section of the State'.[48] Because he felt that all Liberians should work together for the advancement of the Republic, he refused to acknowledge the reality and implications of party politics.

Blyden's main plans for Liberia were: attempting to attract foreign investment, while keeping it under judicious control; the inauguration of a comprehensive programme of education; alliance with the inland peoples and the extension of Liberia's jurisdiction interiorward; and finally, the extension of the President's term to at least four years. His plan for extension of Liberia's foreign and commercial relation was easily more extensive than that of any other Liberian Presidential candidate: they included sending representatives to Belgium, Germany and England to further stimulate the interest of these countries in commercial

---

[46] Blyden to Coppinger, 30 Sept. 1884, *A.C.S. Papers*, Vol. 21.
[47] *Methodist Herald*, III, 25 May 1885.
[48] *Ibid.*

activities in Liberia and at the same time to secure a pledge from these governments 'against aggressiveness from their subjects in case of large commercial privileges being granted to them'.[49]

In the election itself Blyden could hardly have had a more formidable opponent: Hilary R. W. Johnson, son of the illustrious Elijah Johnson, a haughty, hot-tempered, but able and politically astute man. He had already served one term as President, the first Liberian-born to do so, and he was now seeking re-election. The contest between these two able Liberians was bound to be as heated as they were bitter enemies. It had not always been so. As young men they had attended the same classes at Alexander High School and later had taught at Liberia College together. A rift first came between them over Liberia's relations with foreigners: Blyden was against the closed-door policy of the Republic, Johnson was one of its ardent supporters; Blyden favoured an active foreign policy for Liberia with the establishment of key embassies abroad, Johnson thought this unnecessary and had strongly disapproved of Blyden's appointment as Liberian ambassador to the Court of St. James. In 1882 he had criticized Blyden for easily conceding Liberia's rights to its north-west territories; and finally in Blyden's dispute with the new Professors at Liberia College, Johnson had supported the latter.

Now the duel between the two men was being carried on in the Presidential campaign. But here again Blyden was at a serious disadvantage: his frequent absences from the Republic made it easy for his opponents to charge him with being unstable; his pro-British inclinations were deemed unpatriotic; his wish to open Liberia's door to large-scale commercial activities by foreigners was seen as an unnecessary and dangerous step. Nor did Blyden possess the flair for politics: he was too forthright—he could never pander to the prejudices of the people—too idealistic, and lacking in organizing ability. The scholarly Blyden saw himself in the role of Plato's philosopher-king, owing allegiance to no one section of the community and expecting no criticisms from citizens who were not nearly so well-qualified as he for the vocation of governing. He had been accustomed to think of himself as a 'providential agent' and perhaps he believed that there might have been a Divine intervention on his behalf. At any rate, on the eve

[49] Blyden to Coppinger, 10 July 1885, *A.C.S. Papers*, Vol. 22.

of this hotly contested election he composed a poem in which he hoped that God would 'send salvation at the polls' and 'scatter the darkness of land' by electing him President.[50] But the Almighty did not answer his prayer; and Johnson won the election easily.[51]

Blyden expressed the view to Coppinger that had he been elected President, 'there would have been a flocking to Liberia of capital and intelligence from the various British settlements', as well as from the New World.[52] To support this contention he enclosed two letters which had been written to him. One was from Timothy Laing, a young Gold Coast lawyer and journalist and President of the Cape Coast Mutual Improvement Association and Debating Club, who under the mistaken impression that Blyden had been elected President had offered his services to help in developing 'the little Republic into something . . . more pretentious in character'. The other letter came from Francis Edmund Stuart, a 38-year-old Barbados-born schoolteacher in Jamaica, who assumed that Blyden, 'a profound scholar . . . far famed for his linguistic achievements' could easily get him a job teaching in a Government School. One would have been tempted to agree with Blyden's opinion that with him as President Liberia would have progressed, if in him an undoubted intellectual brilliance had been combined with qualities of able leadership, but as we have seen the latter qualities were largely absent in him. It is hardly a sign of leadership on Blyden's part that shortly after the election he retired to Sierra Leone and there consoled himself that all intelligent Liberians had voted for him.[53]

His contest of the Presidential election was his last foray into active politics. If Blyden had intended to stand again as a Liberian Presidential candidate, he gave up the idea altogether after a distasteful incident in 1886. In October of that year he returned to Monrovia from Sierra Leone after a fifteen-month stay there, and the City Councillors of the capital, determined to

[50] Poem by Blyden: 'Just Before the Battle', *ibid.*
[51] *Methodist Herald*, III, 10 June 1885; the final vote was 1438 to 873.
[52] Blyden to Coppinger, 26 Sept. 1885, enclosure: Francis Edmund Stuart to Blyden, 7 May 1885, and Timothy Laing to Blyden, 22 July 1885, *A.C.S. Papers*, Vol. 22; Laing later became an outstanding early Gold Coast nationalist: see J. Magnus Sampson, *Gold Coast Men of Affairs*, London 1937.
[53] *Methodist Herald*, III, 10 June 1885.

prove 'that Republics were not always ungrateful', passed 'resolutions of welcome and appreciation of his services to the nation and to the race'.[54] President Johnson regarded this as unnecessarily inciting Blyden to oppose him again in the next Presidential election and in an attempt to prevent this, instigated the calling of a public meeting in Monrovia at which a vote of censure was passed on the town council and threats were made to burn Blyden in effigy unless the resolutions were repealed.[55] Johnson's tactics were efficacious: Blyden, fearful of his safety, fled to Cape Palmas; on his return to Monrovia after a few weeks, he was, in fact, offered the Presidential nomination of the Republican Party but thought it advisable not to accept it. Again he returned to Sierra Leone. Yet he would have preferred to work for Liberia and was resentful that he was becoming identified with the British colony.[56]

If Blyden gave up the role of politician in Liberia in 1886, he had by then come to regard himself as its senior statesman and as such was always ready with gratuitous advice for the 'progress' of Liberia. He still hoped that Liberia would give the lead to the rest of Africa by creating 'new forms representing the African idea... African literature with the smell of Africa upon it... African freedom, African thought, and African theology'.[57] Such a state of creativity could be attained, according to Blyden, by the kind of education which would prompt the Liberian to 'amalgamate with his aboriginal brother' and carefully study his 'social organization, his religion, his politics' which, though they might be modified somewhat, must form the basis of a distinctive African culture. By the end of the 1880's he had concluded, theoretically at any rate, that the democratic form of government was unsuited to the needs and circumstances of Liberia and the rest of Africa. He asserted that historical evidence had shown that only the Anglo-Saxon people had been successful in making democracy work; France, Germany and Russia had all failed to manipulate

[54] 'Resolutions of Appreciation and Welcome Passed by the Common Council of Monrovia, 25 Oct. 1886, to Hon. E. W. Blyden, LL.D.', *A.C.S. Papers*, Vol. 23, No. 105.

[55] King to Coppinger, 13 Nov. 1886, *ibid*.

[56] See, for example, Blyden to Coppinger, 22 June 1885, *A.C.S. Papers*, Vol. 22, where he wrote: 'I am anxious to work for Liberia; my heart is there; all my plans for Africa's progress are connected with that Republic.' Also, Blyden to Coppinger, 2 June 1888, *A.C.S. Papers*, Vol. 25: 'I am jealous for Liberia's sake, of having to date my letters Sierra Leone.'

[57] *Liberia Bulletin*, No. 11, Nov. 1897, 40.

that form of government, and Liberia in attempting it was 'like David putting on Saul's armour'. He suggested that in politics 'the trained aborigine must take the lead to give the superstructure —the form which the untrammelled genius of the race will suggest and dictate'.[58] The implication here is that the 'evolved' African Government would be traditional government modified to meet changing economic and social conditions, and that paternal authoritarianism would be its most characteristic attribute. But Blyden himself did not forecast or make definite suggestions as to what the structure and machinery of such a government might be.

Because of his belief that educated natives were best qualified to suggest the new forms which African institutions should take, Blyden welcomed any evidence of their increasing participation in Liberia's national life. Thus, he regarded it as a 'sign of progress' that the Kru people had voted for the first time in the national election of 1887, and had returned a representative, S. W. Seton, to the legislature.[59] Moreover, he was pleased that Seton had displayed initiative based on intelligent independence of thought: in September 1887, Seton, a clergyman, together with his congregation, severed his connection from the Protestant Episcopal Mission at Cape Palmas so that he might preach 'the pure word of God under the sole authority and commission of none but Jesus'.[60] This was probably the first of several examples in West Africa of African congregations seceding from foreign missions, and it is conceivable that Seton, a friend and admirer of Blyden, was influenced by the latter's resignation from the Presbyterian Church in September 1886 to become an itinerant 'minister of truth'.[61]

Blyden was ever on the alert for evidence of Liberia's progress, and on a nine-month visit to the Republic in 1888/9, found this in a new public-spiritedness among wealthy Liberians as exemplified by the opening of a new Episcopal Church at Clay-Ashland built at the expense of William David Coleman, and the establishment on the St. Paul's River of Ricks Institute, a new secon-

[58] Blyden to Coppinger, 1 Oct. 1888, *A.C.S. Papers*, Vol. 25.
[59] Blyden to Coppinger, 14 July 1888, *ibid.*
[60] Blyden to Coppinger, 12 Sept. 1887, enclosure: Samuel W. Seton to Rev. S. D. Ferguson, D.D., 1 Sept. 1887; also Blyden to Coppinger, 3 Oct. 1887, *A.C.S. Papers*, Vol. 24.
[61] Blyden to Coppinger, 25 Jan. 1887, *ibid.*

dary school founded largely through the munificence of Moses
Ricks, a wealthy Baptist coffee-planter.[62] His friend, R. B.
Richardson, formerly Principal of the Preparatory Department
of Liberia College was Principal of the Institute, and among the
subjects taught were Arabic and West African languages. Blyden
himself was associated with Ricks Institute for five months as
Director of the Department of English Literature before leaving
Liberia in May 1889 for temporary work in the United States on
behalf of the American Colonization Society.

So that Liberia might get a new impetus, Blyden had continued
to attempt to persuade enterprising Africans from Sierra Leone to
emigrate to the Republic. But with the belief widespread in
Sierra Leone (primarily as a result of the 'Roye Revolution')
that 'life and property were not safe in Liberia, and that a man
could be shot or murdered with impunity',[63] few responded to
Blyden's urgings. Among the few who did, was Syble Boyle, son of
Moses Syble Boyle, a wealthy Aku Recaptive trader, who had
been one of the early African appointees to the Legislative Council of Sierra Leone. The younger Boyle had been Liberian Consul
in Sierra Leone from 1872 until 1888 when he settled in Liberia.
In that same year, Blyden was delighted to discover that another
Sierra Leone-born protégé of his, C. T. O. King, was being
seriously mentioned as a candidate for the next Liberian Presidential election. King was easily the most outstanding example of
a Sierra Leonean who had emigrated to Liberia and had pros-
pered. On Blyden's advice, he had emigrated to the Republic in
1871, and had worked as a Civil Servant in such capacities as
Clerk of the Courts, Justice of the Peace, Collector of Customs,
and Secretary to the Department of the Interior. In 1880, on
Blyden's recommendation, he was appointed Agent of the American Colonization Society in Liberia, and since 1884 had thrice
successively been elected Mayor of Monrovia. Hopefully, Blyden
wrote to a friend: 'I should not be surprised to see him (King)
President and lawyer (Samuel) Lewis, and other Sierra Leoneans
occupying prominent places in the Republic with a Negro representative in Europe trying to shape European policies for
Africa.'[64] But to Blyden's disappointment, King judged President

[62] Blyden to Coppinger, 8 Aug. and 1 Oct. 1888, *A.C.S. Papers*, Vol. 25.
[63] G. M. Macaulay to Blyden, 10 Sept. 1888, *ibid.*
[64] Blyden to Coppinger, 8 Aug. 1888, *ibid.*

Johnson, who intended to continue in office, to be too formidable an opponent and declined to contest the election.

Between 1888 and 1900 when he returned to help in the reorganization of Liberia College, Blyden made only short visits to Liberia during which he continued to urge the Government to adopt a policy which would make the indigenous peoples active participants in the Liberian state. On a visit in January 1897, Blyden was heartened to find that for the first tme in their history, Liberians had elected as President a man — William David Coleman — who had come from the rural interior; understandably, the new President was especially concerned with opening up and developing Liberia's interior.[65] 1897 was the year of Liberia's fiftieth anniversary of its independence, and Blyden took this opportunity of holding up to his countrymen his vision of the future: he was sure that the 'Liberian idea' was a 'divine' one, and that if the amalgamation between emigrants and indigenous peoples took place as was intended, then the nation would 'develop new sentiments, new ideas, new forms, representing the African idea' . . . which would be described and interpreted to the world by Liberian scholars, 'for the African is not always to be an intellectual pauper; a pensioner of other lands doing nothing but importing foreign ideas and quoting foreign expressions'.[66]

It was because he strongly believed that African scholars had a distinctive contribution to make to world knowledge that late in 1899 Blyden readily responded to the call of an old associate, and the new President of Liberia College, Garretson Wilmot Gibson, to return from Sierra Leone and help in the reorganization of Liberia College.[67] Since 1877 there had been no graduates from the College; as President, Blyden had temporarily revived it, but since his departure in 1884 it had been mostly in a dormant state. However, under an Act passed in 1893 the College was in future to be financed largely by the Liberian legislature, and its effective control no longer lay with the American Boards of Trustees.[68] The reorganized College was reopened on 21 February 1900 with a staff of seven, including the President and a librarian, and twelve students; there were forty-five students and two teachers in the Preparatory Department. As the leading Liberian intellectual,

---

[65] Johnston, *op. cit.*, 298.   [66] *Liberia Bulletin*, No. 11, Nov. 1897, 41.
[67] Blyden to Wilson, 1 June 1900, *A.C.S. Papers*, Vol. 28.
[68] Buell, *The Native Problem in Africa*, New York 1928, Vol. II, 754.

Blyden delivered the inaugural address in which he saw the role of the College as 'revolutionizing the thoughts not only of the citizens of the Republic about themselves, but of other Africans, and of foreigners with regard to Africans'.[69]

But Blyden's attempt to implement this role for the College met with strong opposition. In January 1901, he replaced Gibson, now President of the Republic, as President of the College, and in this capacity was charged by other members of his staff 'with teaching students . . . the principles of Mohammedanism and polygamy'.[70] Annoyed that his staff only wished to have the conventional subjects taught, Blyden impetuously quitted the College in March 1901, and a few months later took up the position of Director of Muslim Education in Sierra Leone.

Of course, Blyden continued to watch closely the fortune of Liberia, and noted with interest the ascendancy to the Presidency in 1904 of his West Indian-born compatriot, Arthur Barclay, whose administration turned out to be one of the most progressive in Liberia's history. Fifty-one when he was first inaugurated President, Barclay had already served the Republic impressively in the capacity of educator, journalist, administrator and Cabinet Minister, and was widely respected as being able, honest and hardworking. Spurred by the fact that European powers threatened the territorial integrity of Liberia, as well as by the example of British rule over the Sierra Leone Protectorate, Barclay set out to impress upon the peoples under Liberian jurisdiction that they were an integral part of the Republic and that they would be treated with fairness and justice.[71] Shortly after becoming President, Barclay summoned the chiefs of the interior to Monrovia and conferred with them; later in the year a similar meeting was held of Kru and Grebo chiefs, from the eastern part of Liberia. On Barclay's initiative, an Act was passed in 1905 for 'the Government of Districts inhabited by Aborigines'. The Act provided that District Commissioners appointed by the President should, in consultation with the Principal Chiefs and their Council, comprise the final arbiter in preserving order and settling disputes. These developments met with Blyden's full approval and in 1905 he obtained leave from his Sierra Leone job to give his

[69] *Liberia Bulletin*, No. 17, Nov. 1900, 14.
[70] J. C. Stevens to J. O. Wilson, 18 June 1901, *A.C.S. Papers*, Vol. 28.
[71] Johnston, *op. cit.*, 300–1.

support to the Barclay administration by taking up the position of Minister Plenipotentiary and Envoy Extraordinary to Paris in an attempt to finally delimit Liberia's northern boundary with French West African colonial territory. It is a further indication of the enlightened policy of Barclay's administration that in 1905 Blyden was voted a small pension by the Liberian legislature in recognition of his services on behalf of the Republic.

It was under Barclay's Presidency, too, that the reforms in the Constitution which Blyden had advocated since 1864 took place. In 1907 the revised constitution substituted the word 'Negro' for 'Colored', 'to put Liberia on a proper racial basis and make it an essentially African state'; lengthened the term of the Presidency to four years, and curtailed the four-year Naturalization Period for 'alien' Negroes to one year; Blyden hailed these amendments as 'triumphant'.[72]

And yet, ironically, this administration with which Blyden was so much in sympathy felt compelled in February 1909 to dis-continue his small pension on the grounds that he was party to a plot to put Liberia under a British protectorate. It is true that as early as 1905 Blyden had sought to use his influence to have Liberia placed either under a 'temporary' British or an Anglo-French protectorate, but this was because by then he had become convinced that the alternative for Liberia was dismemberment by the European imperialist powers.[73] And indeed, the British stake in Liberia had been increasing. In 1906 the Liberian Government granted a major concession to the British-controlled Liberian Development Chartered Company to exploit the natural resources of the Republic in return for a loan of £100,000.[74] The loan was secured against Liberia's custom receipts, and one of the condi-tions on which it was granted was that the Customs should be re-organized and controlled by British officers. In 1908 Liberia came further under British control when its Government con-sented to have a British Officer, Major Cadell, organize a Frontier Force. Cadell seemed to have worked swiftly and systematically to bring Liberia under British control. He employed large numbers of Sierra Leone Africans in the Frontier Force, took control of the

[72] Huberich, op. cit., Vol. II, 1033–4; also, Edward W. Blyden, The Three Needs of Liberia, London 1908, 27–9.
[73] C.O. 147/107, Blyden to Carter, 10 Nov. 1896; F.O. 403/363.
[74] R. L. Buell, Liberia: A Century of Survival, 1847–1947, Philadelphia 1947, 24.

Monrovia police, in which large numbers of Sierra Leone Africans were employed, and on the protest both of the Liberian Government and of the French Vice-Consul in Monrovia, seemed to have contemplated the overthrow of the Liberian Government.[75] On 1 February 1909 there was a mutiny among the troops and police loyal to Cadell, but decisive action by the Liberian Government supported by the American Resident Consul resulted in a quelling of the mutiny and the removal of Cadell. The Barclay Government was satisfied that Blyden had aided and abetted Cadell's attempted coup. This is likely and not at all surprising as Blyden feared that Liberia might yet fall victim to French or German intrigues; no doubt, he envisaged that as a British Protectorate, Liberia's future would be linked with Sierra Leone to produce ultimately a more viable state than either of them going their separate ways. Doubtless, this seemingly unpatriotic action stemmed from the highest racial loyalty, and was consistent with his long held view that the political destinies of Liberia and Sierra Leone were one. That Blyden's only penalty for alleged complicity in a plot to undermine the Liberian Government was a loss of his pension was recognition by the Barclay administration that his actions though perhaps misguided, were not malicious.

Of course, Blyden regarded the action against him as ingratitude on the part of the Liberian Government the more so as it knew that he was a desperately needy old man. But not even so severe a reprimand as the loss of a much-needed pension could serve to diminish his love or interest in the Republic. Significantly, even while recuperating from a serious illness, he journeyed to Liberia to witness the inauguration in January 1912 of Daniel E. Howard, a former pupil of his who succeeded Barclay.[76] His three-weeks' stay in Liberia after Howard's inauguration proved to be his last: he died two weeks after returning to Freetown.

As an educator, politician and statesman, Blyden had devoted much of his life and energies to Liberia because he believed its success would give much-needed prestige to his race, but his over-zealousness and restlessness combined with a lack of tact accounted for the fact that his actual contribution to the welfare and progress of the Republic was perhaps less than might be expected of a man of his towering prestige and intellectual stature.

[75] Buell, *Native Problem*, Vol. II, 787–8.
[76] *Sierra Leone Weekly News*, XXVIII, Feb. 10, 1912.

To the last he was dissatisfied and disappointed with Liberia's slow progress, but as a true race patriot he retained his fervent hope (and for him to hope was to believe) that a better future awaited Liberia, Africa and the Negro race. But to complete an assessment of his work on behalf of Liberia and his attempt to enhance the prestige of his race, it is necessary to examine his career as a diplomat.

8. Liberian Diplomat

As early as 1861 and 1862, Blyden had officially acted as Liberian Commissioner to Britain and the United States, in the former year to win support for the newly established Liberia College, and in the latter to invite 'oppressed' American Negroes to emigrate to an independent Negro Republic on their own 'fatherland'. And on subsequent visits abroad Blyden always regarded himself as an ambassador of Liberia, and indeed, of the entire Negro race. However, his first official diplomatic appointment came in 1877 when President Payne named him as Liberia's ambassador to the Court of St. James. But Liberia's first ambassador abroad assumed his appointment in rather inauspicious circumstances: the Liberian legislature was opposed to sending an ambassador abroad, and especially disapproved of Blyden whose pro-British proclivities they distrusted; however, Blyden was so glad of the opportunity to enhance the prestige of the Republic abroad, and to promote close relations between Liberia and Britain that he accepted the appointment directly from the President although this meant that he would receive no salary or allowance from the Liberian Government.[1] As an unsalaried official and the first ambassador in Europe from an African country Blyden was certainly unique in modern diplomatic history.

As Liberian ambassador in London, Blyden had the advantage of being well-known in influential British circles. He had visited Britain six times previously and had made firm friends in humanitarian, literary and academic circles. He had been grateful for the efforts of British humanitarians on behalf of the Negro and Africa, but he also sought to exploit the British reputation for humanitarianism by seeking to persuade the British Government to take a friendly and helpful interest in Liberia, and also increase its imperial responsibility in West Africa. Symptomatic of his gratitude to the British was an ebony walking-stick which as a young man on his first visit to England he gave to Lord Brougham in

---

[1] Blyden to Coppinger, 9 Aug. 1878, *A.C.S. Papers*, Vol. 18.

recognition of his services 'as a champion of Negro and African interests'.[2] In 1866, on his way to Lebanon, Blyden stayed in England for two and a half weeks and sought out his old acquaintances, Brougham and Gladstone, whose guest he was in the House of Lords and Commons, respectively.[3] He had corresponded irregularly with Gladstone and in 1869 wrote the new Prime Minister requesting him 'Not to forget my poor country and race in your extensive philanthropic operations'.[4] On a two-month visit to England in 1871, he greatly widened his contacts among scholars and clergymen.[5] Through the influence of Gladstone he obtained a ticket to read at the British Museum, and because of his interests in Arabic manuscripts, attracted the attention of Dr. C. Rieu, Keeper of the Oriental Manuscripts of Dr. William Wright, Professor of Arabic at Cambridge University, as also that of Professor Edward Owen, Superintendent of Natural History at the British Museum, who acquired the works of the Negro scholar for the Museum's library. In ecclesiastical circles, Blyden met Arthur Penrhyn Stanley, the affable, liberal and influential Dean of Westminster, through whom he met such outstanding clerics as Dr. James Fraser, Bishop of Manchester; Dr. William Thomson, Bishop of York; Dr. Frederick Temple, Bishop of Exeter; and Rev. Stopford A. Brooke, a biographer, and chaplain in ordinary to Queen Victoria. It was through Dean Stanley, too, that Blyden met R. B. Smith, the influential literary figure with whom later he enjoyed a close friendship. In 1876, on a six weeks' visit to England, Blyden spent much of his time at Smith's home at Harrow.

It was partly through the financial help of his English friends that Blyden was able to carry out his duties as Liberia's unsalaried diplomat. But perhaps his greatest help came from Edward S. Morris, a wealthy American Quaker businessman who had taken an interest in Liberia and had visited it several times. Morris, who was in London attempting to win support among British humanitarians for his scheme for the establishment in Liberia of a 'School for the Sons of Chiefs from all parts of Africa',[6] apparently volun-

[2] Blyden to Brougham, 29 May 1861, 5 Sept. 1863, and 11 June 1866, *Brougham Papers; Journal of African Society*, 11, 1912, 362.

[3] Blyden, *From West Africa to Palestine*, 46.

[4] Blyden to Gladstone, 11 May 1869, *British Museum Add. Mss.*, 44420/255.

[5] Blyden to Coppinger, 20 July 1871, *A.C.S. Papers*, Vol. 204.

[6] Edward S. Morris, *Africa's Call to America*, Philadelphia 1899, 13–4.

teered to be Blyden's Secretary, an arrangement which surprised and aroused the curiosity of Britons. Morris himself later told the following story in the *Philadelphia Evening Bulletin*:

As a foreign representative, Dr. Blyden was entitled to sit in the gallery of the House of Lords and as Secretary to Dr. Blyden, I was allowed to accompany him. We had no sooner taken our seats than the opera glasses in the hands of Lords, dukes, earls, peers and peeresses and duchesses were directed towards us.[7]

Blyden began his diplomatic career by making his second attempt to settle the boundary dispute between Liberia and Sierra Leone. On 22 August he was received in his official capacity by Lord Derby and later that same day wrote his first despatch to the Foreign Secretary. As in his first effort, Blyden did not rest Liberia's case solely on its legitimate claims. Again he sought to excite sympathy for the aspirations of the Negro Republic by reminding the British Foreign Secretary that Liberia 'owed its existences to philanthropists in the United States, and its continued national growth to the fostering care and kindness of Her Majesty's Government'. He pressed for an immediate settlement of the issue. He pointed out that the disputed territory was being used by traders to evade the custom duties of both Governments, and it was therefore as much in the interest of Sierra Leone as of Liberia to have the dispute settled. He opposed the British idea that a Commission should meet on the site of the disputed territory, correctly pointing out that the African chiefs who denied Liberia's claims were under the influence of foreign traders and were not likely to be impartial witnesses.[8]

But the Foreign Secretary was not moved by Blyden's plea for a tender consideration of the struggling Negro state. He insisted that there was need for a commission to visit the disputed territory and in addition, revived the question of claims against the Liberian Government of British subjects whose property had been seized or destroyed during a punitive expedition made by the Liberian Government against Prince Mannah in March 1871.[9]

To Lord Derby, Blyden replied that the pressing of the claim against Liberia was all the more reason why the dispute should be immediately settled. He pointed out that until this was done

---

[7] *West African Reporter*, VII, 23 July 1881.
[8] F.O. 403/9, Blyden to Derby, 22 Aug. 1877.
[9] *Ibid.*, Derby to Blyden, 12 Sept. 1877.

'Liberia was placed in the dilemma of either submitting to the reckless infractions of their laws by foreign traders, and to a consequent subversion of all order in their territory, or resisting by force such infractions so as to check the tendency towards widespread insubordination.'[10] To help his lobbying for the settlement of the dispute in favour of Liberia, Blyden sought help from influential public figures in London, among them, Sir Samuel Gurney, President of the Anti-slavery Society, whose father had contributed a £1000 for the purchase of the now disputed territory.[11]

Meeting with difficulty in settling the boundary dispute, Blyden concluded that the British Government, which was aware of the conflict between Negroes and mulattoes in Liberia,[12] had not shown more sympathy to the Negro Republic because it was governed by mulattoes. About two weeks after his first interview with Lord Derby he wrote to Coppinger that:

the Negro—pure and simple—has a large margin yet of the sympathies of the Christian world of which to avail himself. Lord Derby was no doubt surprised when I presented myself before him. He looked at me very hard during the whole interview. The feeling of the British Government and of the higher classes here is in favour of encouraging Liberia if it is to be a Negro state; but if it is to be mongrel, they think the sooner it falls into the hands of the European powers the better for the aborigines.[13]

It is probably more likely that the attitude of the British Government was dictated by its concern to protect the interests of British traders in the disputed territory.

Besides conducting negotiations for the settlement of the boundary dispute, Blyden attempted to unravel the financial entanglements which the Roye loan had created for Liberia. It is symptomatic of the gross mismanagement of Liberia's financial affairs in London that Blyden was on the one hand, faced with a claim that Liberia owed £400 to the British Post Office, while, on the other hand, he had to seek legal means to secure £1,000 of the Republic's money from its Consul-General, Jackson, whom Roberts had appointed to succeed Chinery, the man who had

[10] Ibid., Blyden to Derby, 3 Nov. 1877.
[11] Blyden to Sir Samuel Gurney, 14 Aug. 1877, Anti-Slavery Papers.
[12] F.O. 403/6, Kennedy to Granville, 20 March 1869.
[13] Blyden to Coppinger, 3 Sept. 1877, A.C.S. Papers, Vol. 18.

negotiated the loan. The Negro diplomat was perturbed by the 'disagreeable' newspaper attacks on Liberia arising out of the Roye loan.[14]

But he was heartened by his own reception and by the interest the British had in Liberia. He was pleased with the personal attention Lord Derby had shown to him. He was frequently the guest of important individuals, organizations and institutions, and welcomed those opportunities to create or increase interest in Liberia. Two weeks after his arrival in England a big reception was given him in Brighton and here he expressed the wish that his stay in England would help to promote friendly relations between Britain and the Negro Republic.[15] On 9 November, at the invitation of the Lord Mayor of London, he attended the great annual banquet at Guildhall sitting 'at the Principal Table with the Ministers of the [British] Cabinet and Foreign Ambassadors.'[16] On 13 November, he was the guest in London of 'the Worshipful Company of Plumbers'. 'As the representative not only of Liberia . . . but . . . of the Negro race and of the great continent', he spoke hopefully of Africa as 'the continent of the future' and of Liberia 'as one of the brightest and most promising spots in the continent'.[17]

But amid the whirl of pleasant social life in London, Blyden did not neglect his duties. During his stay in London Liberian coffee was in vogue. To further increase its production, he managed to persuade English capitalists to form a company. During his two years' stay at Harrisburg he had found that poverty among the people there had prevented them from fully availing themselves of the educational facilities, and he became convinced that large-scale agricultural enterprises could solve this problem. His plan aimed at giving greater security to farmers by eliminating their dependence on unscrupulous traders: the English company was to provide the capital, the machinery, provisions and goods at a cheaper rate than could ordinarily be obtained, as well as ready cash to farmers so that they could expand the area of their operation and hire more labourers. The entire crops of the farmers who participated in the scheme were to be shipped to

[14] Blyden to Coppinger, 15 Nov. 1877, *ibid.*
[15] *Sussex Daily News*, 1 Sept. 1887; *West African Reporter*, IV, 3 Oct. 1877.
[16] Blyden to Coppinger, 15 Nov. 1877, *op. cit.*
[17] *West African Reporter*, IV, 19 Dec. 1877.

England. In organizing the scheme, he also had in mind new emigrants from America: if the scheme were successfully operated, it would provide employment for them and prevent the discouragement and dissillusionment which many of them suffered in their first few months in the Republic. He had held high hopes that this agricultural scheme would be the means by which Liberia would 'cease depending upon America for her religious and educational institutions'.[18]

Before leaving to assume the duties of his special appointment in London, Blyden had 'to the great disgust of the traders', persuaded seven farmers to participate in the agricultural scheme. And despite the poor publicity Liberia was receiving in the London press, he was able to persuade 'some of the friends of Africa' to organize a company to carry out his plans. The company was called the Liberia Coffee Estates Ltd., its London agents were Malcolm, Brunner and Company; and Blyden was named its General Superintendent in Liberia.[19]

After four months in London, Blyden had to return to Liberia to see if the new President, Anthony William Gardner, or the new Liberian Government would confirm his appointment. But before leaving London he decided to ensure that Gardner's administration, which was to start on 1 January 1878, would 'enter into its work with some dignity'. Hitherto every Liberian administration had 'found itself destitute of stationery and everything with which to carry on the Government'. Now, he had 'paper and envelopes prepared for the various departments—stamped and headed so that they may be used only for office purposes'.[20]

In Liberia Blyden's efforts in London had not been appreciated. There was widespread feeling that the Republic should not have taken the initiative in reopening the question of Liberia's boundary with Sierra Leone. The majority in Gardner's Cabinet as well as in the House of Representatives was against Blyden's reappointment. But the President was satisfied that Blyden could do much to promote the welfare of the Republic in Britain, and so confirmed his appointment. In protest, H. R. W. Johnson, Secretary of State, resigned from the Cabinet: he felt that it was 'an absurdity' for Liberia to have an ambassador abroad, and

[18] Blyden to Coppinger, 3 Sept. 1877, *op. cit.*
[19] *West African Reporter*, IV, 19 Dec. 1877.
[20] Blyden to Coppinger, 15 Nov. 1877, *op. cit.*

that Blyden in that position was the first step towards 'the dismemberment of the Republic'.[21] Blyden's partiality towards the British had caused misgivings among leading Liberians.

Returned to London in late May 1878, Blyden had four major diplomatic goals in mind: to try again for a settlement of the boundary dispute in favour of the Republic; to make clear Liberia's willingness to honour its debts and to arrange for the payment of at least the interest; to endeavour to secure for his government a small vessel as a revenue cutter to prevent violation of custom laws by foreign vessels along the Liberian coast; and finally, to secure the investment of foreign capital in a railway from Monrovia or the St. Paul's River 'to the populous regions of the interior plateau'.[22]

With regard to the boundary dispute, the Liberian Government had failed to name its members for the proposed joint commission which was scheduled to meet in the earlier and drier months of 1878. In the interim, Sir Samuel Rowe, Governor of Sierra Leone, recommended that the British Government take a hard line against Liberia; he suggested that Liberia should be made to pay the indemnity assessed against it for damages done to British traders and he himself revived the claim of the British Government to extend its protectorate along the coast as far as the Mano River, partly on the pretext that the Liberian Government was unable to keep order among the tribes west of that river.[23] But with a boundary commission due to meet in 1879 there was nothing further Blyden could do towards settlement of the dispute.

In his objective of having a railway constructed from the coast to the interior of Liberia, Blyden felt that his best chance of obtaining aid was from the Government of the United States. He had cultivated the friendship of the American ambassador in London, John Welsh, and sought to persuade him of 'the paramount importance to Liberia' of a railroad into the interior. Welsh was doubtful that such aid could be constitutionally given but nonetheless forwarded his correspondence with Blyden to William H. Seward, Acting Secretary of State for the U.S., who noted that Blyden's suggestion had been received 'with great

[21] Cited in Blyden to Coppinger, 9 Aug. 1877, *A.C.S. Papers*, Vol. 18.
[22] Blyden to G. W. Gibson, 30 Aug. 1878, *ibid.*
[23] Johnston, *op. cit.*, 268.

interest' and would be duly considered. Blyden interpreted this reply as 'encouraging' and wrote to the executive members of the American Colonization Society urging them to lobby on behalf of the project. Blyden's idea of a railroad into the interior was linked up with that of American Negro 'repatriation'. With a character-istic flight of visionary fancy, he envisaged that the proposed rail-way would facilitate 'black Americans . . . moving eastward from California to the banks of the Niger and farther still even to the highlands of Abyssinia'.[24] But Blyden's ambitious project was never seriously entertained by the United States Government.

Blyden found it especially arduous and irksome working for a bankrupt government. Moreover, the lack of the support of the Liberian Government had diminished his bargaining powers. Clamorous bondholders were not satisfied with his pledge that the Government intended to redeem its debts. He had failed to obtain a vessel as revenue cutter because he was unable to negotiate the necessary loan solely on Presidential orders and without the authority of the Liberian Government. Of his coffee enterprise, the result of the first year had fully justified his confidence in it: there had been a marked increase in the yield of coffee in the St. Paul's River, but the economic depres-sion of 1878 gave the Liberian Coffee Company a major set-back.[25]

But for a man of Blyden's tastes and predilections, life in Lon-don had ample compensations. His growing literary reputation combined with the sympathy and respect which was commonly offered to outstanding Negroes by the British upper class of the nineteenth century, brought him an increasingly larger number of influential friends and acquaintances; and in all these encoun-ters Blyden thought of himself primarily as a representative and ambassador of the Negro race. He maintained contact with Gurney and Sir Thomas Foxwell Buxton and encouraged their efforts to protect the interest of Africans.[26] He was frequently the guest of Gladstone at the House of Commons and was regularly entertained at the home of Dean Stanley. One such occasion was the evening of 24 July 1878, when Blyden and three other Negroes, King George of Bonny, John H. Smyth, and James T.

[24] Blyden to Coppinger, 9 Aug. 1878, *A.C.S. Papers*, Vol. 18.
[25] Blyden to Coppinger, 7 Sept. 1878; also Blyden to Gibson, 30 Aug. 1878, *ibid.*
[26] See, for instance, Blyden to Buxton, 22 June 1878, *Anti-Slavery Papers*.

Holly, Bishop of Haiti, were among a large number of distinguished guests entertained by the Dean. This kind of social intercourse was very much to his liking: he wrote proudly to Coppinger: 'For the first time, I believe, in the history of English Society have four persons of purely African descent so freely mingled with the elite.'[27]

He was also frequently the guest of friends at such literary and social rendezvous as the Athenaeum, and the Russell and Sunbeam Clubs, where he made the acquaintance of outstanding litterateurs and scholars. For instance, it was at the Athenaeum that he first met Herbert Spencer, the British philosopher and sociologist. Blyden reported the story of their meeting thus: 'By a curious coincidence when he came in I had before me Coussin de Perceval's *Histoire des Arabes* in which I was trying to verify a quotation made from that work in Spencer's *Principles of Sociology* which also lay before me.' This gave them a good starting-point for conversation which seemed to have centred on the interior tribes of Africa and of the 'wonderful coffee' that was indigenous to Liberia. Spencer then mentioned that he had read Blyden's recent article, 'Africa and the Africans' in *Fraser's Magazine* and added: 'It is quite a new thing to find members of your race writing as you have done on questions of race, and I consider it very useful.' Blyden was extremely gratified by this remark and received it 'as in the highest degree complimentary'; to him it was 'no small encouragement to have the imprimatur of one of the leading thinkers of Europe'. Herbert Spencer was the type of Englishman with whom Blyden was most impressed. Of him he wrote: 'He has the quiet and refined manner of a gentleman, nothing self-assertive or dogmatic, apparently carries on conversation on his part in a sort of interrogatory yet suggestive manner. It is so charming to meet such persons. They make you feel at home at once—and you learn so much while appearing to teach.'[28]

Two of Blyden's most gratifying experiences during his stay in London in 1878 were his audience before Queen Victoria and his election as an honorary member of the Athenaeum Club. He was received by the Queen on 30 July, an event to which he attached the highest significance: he felt that this formal recognition of

---

[27] Blyden to Coppinger, 6 Aug. 1878, *A.C.S. Papers*, Vol. 18.
[28] Blyden to Coppinger, 7 Sept. 1878, *ibid.*

Liberia's representative at the Court of St. James was 'of immense service to Liberia' who had now 'in the eyes of the British people made a step in advance'. He requested Coppinger to publish the news of his reception by the Queen in the *African Repository* so that it 'might serve to encourage Negro youth in America'.[29] Dean Stanley had proposed Blyden for honorary membership of the Athenaeum and his election to 'one of the most aristocratic and exclusive clubs in London', Blyden regarded as 'one of the chief triumphs of his literary life'.[30]

Because Blyden believed that a Liberian Legation in London would help to give Liberia the prestige that it so badly needed, he was all the more perturbed that there was strenuous opposition in Liberia to this, and that the Legation was likely to be discontinued. He took what little measures he could to avoid this. He pleaded with Coppinger to insert the news of the opening of the Legation in the *African Repository* and to send a copy to each member of the Liberian legislature to encourage them to keep it up. Blyden was heartened when Rev. G. W. Gibson, who had replaced Hilary Johnson as Secretary of State pledged his support to him and 'others who were so inclined to affect some good for the nation and the race'.[31] Blyden wrote to him expressing his 'gratification ... that the Legation will have your able and efficient support at the Department of State of Monrovia'. He wanted Gibson to have no doubt whatever of the importance to Liberia of the London legation: he wrote:

The residence of a Liberian Minister with full diplomatic powers at the Court of St. James and recognized personally in the highest social and literary circles gives the whole national character of the Republic a new aspect and a fresh significance in the eyes of the world. . . .
The importance of the step on the part of Liberia of establishing a Legation here cannot be exaggerated and I am endeavouring to make its influence felt not only here but on the continent of Europe and America.[32]

But the view of the majority of articulate Liberians was to prevail: Blyden was recalled and the temporary legation closed down.

[29] Blyden to Coppinger, 9 Aug. 1878, *ibid.*
[30] *Monrovia Observer*, III, 8 Jan. 1880; *West African Reporter*, VII, 23 July 1881.
[31] Quoted in Blyden to Coppinger, 6 Aug. 1878, *op. cit.*
[32] Blyden to Gibson, 31 July 1878, *A.C.S. Papers*, Vol. 18.

Blyden left England on 19 December 1878 for Sierra Leone where the Anglo-Liberian Commission was due to meet and he hoped to work together with the Liberian commissioners in an attempt finally to bring the dispute to an end. There had been some hope of this as both parties had agreed to have the American naval captain, Commodore R. W. Shufeldt, as an arbiter. But on arriving in Freetown, Blyden found that Secretary of State Gibson, who was to be the main Liberian commissioner was not there because of illness, and that the two commissioners from the Republic, James S. Smith, an ex-Vice-President,[33] and Attorney-General Hilton, were mulattoes who had opposed his appointment to London. He did not hide his aversion to them. He complained to Coppinger that 'Their very appearance as being more white than black and their constitutional vanity and self-importance prejudices the question in the mind of Europeans...'[34] Thus, while it was in the interest of Liberia that the ex-ambassador and the two commissioners should co-operate, they studiously avoided each other. And when Commodore Shufeldt tactfully brought them together as his breakfast guests, the meeting was a strained and useless one. At any rate, the commission on the disputed territory did not arrive at a solution.

It was not until 1892 that Blyden again served Liberia in a diplomatic capacity. In the intervening years the growth of European imperialism in Africa had threatened the sovereignty and territorial integrity of the weak but potentially rich Negro Republic. As early as 1879 France had offered to liquidate Liberia's debts if the Republic would place itself under its protection, and when this offer was rejected, made an extravagant and unfounded claim for ninety miles of the Republic's eastern boundary.[35] In 1885 the British Government had decided to bring the Anglo-Liberian boundary dispute to an end by bringing pressure upon the Liberian Government to sign a treaty accepting the very terms which the Liberian Senate had repudiated in 1882: the Mano River was named as the new boundary between Sierra Leone and Liberia, and the Negro Republic thus lost about fifty miles of coastline with its hinterland, rich in oil palms and cola

[33] Smith had been Vice-President under Roye but had strongly supported the Roberts' faction when the 'Roye Affair' broke: see Banks Henries, *Presidents of the First African Republic*, 59.
[34] Blyden to Coppinger, 2 Feb. 1879, *A.C.S. Papers*, Vol. 19.
[35] Buell, *Liberia*, 24.

nuts to which she had legitimate claims.[36] In that same year Spain seemed to have entertained the possibility of eventually forcing Liberia to accept its protection when it expressed willingness to give a sizeable loan to the Republic provided it put 5000 acres in each of its three countries under her 'absolute control'.[37] In the following year, the German Government, too, offered to pay off Liberia's foreign debts provided it would become a German Protectorate.[38] In 1892, France followed the British example of 1885 by unilaterally declaring the Cavalla River to be the boundary between Liberia and the Ivory Coast, and forcing Liberia to give to the French West African colony a sizeable portion of the former Maryland colony which Liberia had incorporated in 1857.[39]

With the European powers seeking to dismember Liberia, Blyden regarded it as imperative for the Republic to have a diplomatic representative in Europe. But President Johnson (1884–92) had remained consistently opposed to such an appointment. In the interim Blyden saw the best chance of Liberia's survival in getting the British to extend their economic interest in the Republic so that they would be loathe to see it fall into the hands of other European powers, and it is noteworthy that in 1890 he took part in the negotiations which led British holders of Liberian bonds and other capitalists to form the Liberian Concessions Company 'with the exclusive rights of exploiting all the rubber in the forests and public lands of Liberia subject to royalty payable to the Liberian Government'.[40] Since the 1850's the main European exploiters of Liberia were the German firms of Woermann and Weichers and Helm, and the Dutch firm—Oost Afrikaansche Compagnie. The Dutch had no imperialist aims but Liberians were afraid of German designs on the Republic through the operations of the two German commercial firms.[41]

When in 1892 Joseph James Cheeseman replaced Johnson as President, Blyden persuaded the new incumbent to let him re-

---

[36] Johnston, *op. cit.*, 279.

[37] Blyden to Coppinger, 4 July 1885, *A.C.S. Papers*, Vol. 22.

[38] King to Coppinger, 13 Nov. 1886, *A.C.S. Papers*, Vol. 23. As early as 1870 there had been a rumour that Germany had offered Liberia its protection; C.O. 267/307, Kennedy to Kimberley, Confidential, 28 Dec. 1870.

[39] Johnston, *op. cit.*, 283; Buell, *Native Problem*, Vol. 11, 789–90.

[40] F.O. 403/363, Memo. by Sir Harry Johnston, 29 May 1905.

[41] Johnston, *op. cit.*, 290.

sume his appointment as ambassador to the Court of St. James. His major diplomatic objective was to get a commitment, or at least a tacit agreement, from the British Government that it would not countenance the dismemberment of Liberia.[42] He was also authorized to attempt to give the British a greater economic stake in Liberia by granting further concessions to any interested British companies. On 14 May, accompanied by the British Foreign Secretary, Lord Salisbury, Blyden presented his credentials as Envoy Extraordinary and Minister Plenipoteniary from the Republic of Liberia to Queen Victoria. Blyden spent four months in Europe including a week's visit (August 11–18) to Belgium to ratify a treaty of friendship and commerce between the Congo Independent State and Liberia during which he was the guest of King Leopold at his summer palace at Ostend, and also of the Liberian Consular representatives at Brussels and Antwerp.[43] On his return to London he spent another month before leaving for Liberia.

As a diplomat for Liberia, Blyden had made no tangible gains, but as an ambassador for the Negro race, once again, he had been a great success: he had been a much sought after guest in Britain's highest circles because of his social graces and intellectual ability, thereby vindicating his much maligned race. The West African newspapers, particularly the *Sierra Leone Weekly News* and the *Lagos Weekly Record* proudly reported Blyden's social activities. Their readers were told that he attended dinners and receptions at Buckingham Palace, and at the Foreign Office; that he was the guest of the Mayor of London; that he renewed his acquaintance with such old literary friends as R. B. Smith and Stopford Brooke; that he made distinguished new acquaintances in Dr. J. H. Bridges and Frederick Harrison, two of Britain's leading Positivist philosophers, and in Professor John Westlake of Oxford University, an authority on international law; that he accepted an invitation to renew his honorary membership at the Athenaeum Club, as also a new offer to enjoy similar privileges at the 'exclusive' St. George's Club, Hanover Square; and that he was in great demand as a lecturer. Many of these reports in the West African newspapers were reprints from British newspapers. Thus

[42] C.O. 267/398, Blyden to Salisbury, 2 June 1892; enclosure: Resolutions of the Liberian Government for closer relations with England; *Lagos Weekly Record*, III, 24 Sept, 1892.

[43] *Sierra Leone Weekly News*, VIII, 13 Aug. 1892.

the *Sierra Leone Weekly News* carried a story from the *London Star*, which reported that at a private party given on 18 May by a well-known London hostess, Blyden received the full attention of 'the fairer portion of the company' with the report going on to predict that he would be 'one of the social lions of the season'.[44] The *Lagos Weekly Record* reprinted an interview with Blyden from the *Liverpool Courier* in which the reporter expressed his amazement at Blyden's breadth of knowledge and his conversancy with contemporary events and thought.[45]

Indeed, in the summer of 1892 West Africans attracted more than the usual attention in the British press. Apart from Blyden, the person most responsible for this was 'Aunt' Martha Ricks, a 76-year-old Liberian, who through the generosity and influence of Sir Alfred Jones, was able to satisfy her wish to meet Queen Victoria.[46] Accompanied by Blyden and his wife, Mrs. Ricks lunched with the Queen and members of the Royal family at Windsor Castle on 20 July. The grand old Liberian lady had a busy schedule, and was often accompanied by Blyden, his wife, and other prominent West Africans then in London, among them the Hon. J. A. McCarthy, the Queen's advocate of Sierra Leone; Arthur E. Boyle, the Liberian Consul in Sierra Leone, and R. B. Blaize, the wealthy Lagos merchant. The 'summer season' for West Africans in London came to an end in late August at 'a grand farewell party' for Mrs. Ricks and Blyden given by Blaize at the 'fashionable' Holborn restaurant.[47]

It was not until 1905 that Blyden, then an old man of seventy-three, was called upon for the last time to be of diplomatic service to Liberia: he was appointed by President Arthur Barclay as Envoy Extraordinary and Minister Plenipotentiary to Britain and France with the special mission of negotiating a settlement of the boundary dispute between Liberia and French West Africa. Liberia was especially vulnerable to French encroachment on her northern hinterland which was as yet largely unexplored by and unknown to Liberians with the result that the claim of the Liberian Government in this area was vague. In contrast, the French had made an extensive exploration of the Liberian hinterland in 1899 after which France laid claim to

[44] *Ibid.*, 11 June 1892; *London Star*, 19 May 1892.
[45] *Lagos Weekly Record*, III, 10 Sept. 1892; *Liverpool Courier*, 5 Aug. 1892.
[46] *Lagos Weekly Record*, III, 20 Aug. 1892.   [47] *Ibid.*, III, 27 Aug. 1892.

2,000 square miles of territory which the Liberian Government believed to belong to the Republic.[48]

But Blyden did not view the problem of the settlement of Liberia's northern boundary in isolation. To him Liberian diplomacy was to be primarily directed towards the central problems of preserving the Republic as a political unit from the machinations of the European imperialist powers, as well as of getting the Negro nation out of its desperate economic plight, aggravated by its inability to repay the Roye loan,[49] and into a programme of economic development. And indeed when Blyden was appointed on his diplomatic mission, negotiations were already far advanced for the establishment of the British-controlled but largely French-financed Liberian Development Company which had promised the Republic £100,000 against the receipts of the Liberian customs which were to be placed under British controllers.[50] With the Germans, British and French having large economic stakes in the country, Blyden correctly saw that Liberia's sovereignty and territorial integrity was imperilled. He thus sought a solution which would at once settle Liberia's boundary dispute as well as guarantee its survival and its economic development. The solution he advocated was that the British and French Governments should 'enter into an engagement' to introduce administrative and economic reforms in the Republic while upholding it in its sovereign independence'.[51] Blyden was in fact recommending 'an Anglo-French Protectorate over Liberia in all but name', and despite his assertion to the contrary, he must have realized that such a protectorate would have been incompatible with Liberia's retention of its sovereign independence. But he might have reasoned that Liberia was in danger of losing its sovereignty anyway, and such sovereignty if forcibly taken away rather than voluntarily relinquished might be impossible to regain. The possible advantages of his scheme if it were accepted by all parties were as follows: France was likely

[48] Buell, *Native Problem*, Vol. II, 785.
[49] The Government had at first assumed full responsibility for the loan, but in 1874 it stopped paying the exorbitant interests. After long negotiation the Liberian Government agreed in 1898 to pay off the principal at a progressive interest rate of 3 to 5 per cent. This was done until 1913 after the 1871 loan had been refunded by a new loan of 1912. See Buell, *Native Problem*, Vol. II, 802.
[50] Buell, *Liberia*, 24.
[51] F.O. 403/363, 'Memo. by Dr. Blyden on the Liberian Situation.'

to be reasonable and perhaps even generous to Liberia in the settlement of its northern boundary; it would nullify the German threat on Liberia posed by meddling commercial houses, and might altogether obviate the danger that Liberia might fall victim to a 'deal' between the three major European powers.

On 23 May in an interview with officials at the British Foreign Office, Blyden disclosed his 'novel plan' and on the following day met with Lord Lansdowne, the British Foreign Minister for whom he had prepared a memorandum on the subject. But aware that he was unauthorized to make so far-reaching a suggestion affecting Liberia's future, Blyden advised that the tone of the note to Liberia should not be 'peremptory' but 'advisory' and 'sympathetic', and that the note itself should make unmistakably clear that the projected Anglo-French 'assistance' would be 'a purely temporary and provisional solution of the Liberian crisis'.[52]

Lord Lansdowne viewed 'with favour' Blyden's proposal for an Anglo-French protectorate over Liberia.[53] Indeed, a few months before, in December 1904, the British Government had indicated its willingness to put the Republic under its protection,[54] a proposal which the Liberian Government rejected confident that both Germany and France would have opposed any British attempt forcibly to impose a protectorate upon it. But in the case of a joint protectorate, it was felt that Britain and France together could meet Germany's objection by assuring it that no restrictions or handicaps would be placed on German economic activities in Liberia. Before proceeding further, the British Government wished to ascertain whether the Liberian Government was amenable to the idea, but an indignant President Barclay firmly repudiated Blyden's unauthorized suggestion.[55]

The French Government's knowledge of Barclay's repudiation of Blyden's plan hardly served to deflect it from its determination to seize a large area in Liberia's hinterland. But the French were in no hurry to settle the boundary dispute for fear that Liberia might invoke the protection and aid of Britain and, perhaps of Germany, should it consider the delimitation of the boundary unfair. The British Government, for its part, was concerned lest

---

[52] *Ibid.*
[53] *Ibid.*, Lansdowne to Wallis, 15 June 1905.
[54] *Ibid.*, F.O. to Treasury, 5 June 1905.
[55] *Ibid.*, Wallis to Lansdowne, 1 and 12 July 1905; Barclay to Johnston, 16 Sept. 1905.

the French in seizing a huge section of Liberia's hinterland, should adversely affect the interest of the two British Companies, the Liberian Development Company and the Liberian Rubber Company. Sir Harry Johnston who was a large shareholder in both Companies, and familiar with Liberia's hinterland, persuaded the Foreign Office to give him private official backing to visit Paris 'partly to watch over the interest of the two British companies', 'partly to assist Dr. Blyden with matters of geographical details'. Johnston suggested that the British line of diplomacy in Paris, should be as follows: 'we don't want to annex Liberia, we assume you don't, but neither of us want to see Liberia come under undue German influence or fall altogether into German hands. Nor is there any need for you to seize Liberia's hinterland; instead your Government could interest your capitalists in investing in the Liberian Chartered Company, and through this means your country could gain from the exploitation of that country.'[56] Through the Company, too, the British and French could control Liberia politically as 'it would be tacitly understood that the Company would have the support of both Governments in case of trouble with the Liberian politicians'. The Foreign Office agreed with Johnston's diplomatic line, and he left for Paris at the end of July. In Paris Johnston and Blyden worked together but they were not successful in engaging the French Government in serious negotiations.[57] A Franco-Liberian treaty was finally signed on 18 September 1907, under the terms of which Liberia lost 2,000 square miles of hinterland to which it had laid claims.[58]

Blyden had remained in Paris until mid-September, and if through the evasion of the French Government he had failed in his mission, he had been a great social success, and characteristically had used the opportunity to disseminate information about Liberia and West Africa.[59] He had exchanged courtesies and visits with foreign ambassadors, and held interviews with Oriental magnates among them the Shah of Persia 'with his numerous retinue'. He had been a magnet attracting to him Negro and African visitors to Paris, among them Miss Portia Washington, daughter of the American Negro leader, Booker T. Washington.

[56] *Ibid.*, Memo. by Johnston to Sir F. Bertie, 29 May 1905.
[57] *Ibid.*, Johnston to F.O., 2 and 11 Aug. 1905.
[58] Buell, *Native Problem*, Vol. II, 790.
[59] *West African Mail*, III, 21 and 28 July, 4 and 11 Aug. 1905.

His official reception at Elysée Palace by President Loubet on 14 July was a grand affair. He was driven to the Elysée Palace in a state carriage, attended by a guard of honour consisting of thirty cuiraissers with their officers. He himself wore evening dress with his many decorations of honour. The neat, dignified, silver-haired Liberian of 73 — the only Negro ambassador in Paris — cut a resplendent figure, drawing the attention of gawking Parisians. For despite his romantic and sincere effusions about rural traditional Africa, he enjoyed the pomp and circumstance accorded him in foreign capitals; he saw himself then as a symbol of the Negro race, as an advertisement of Negro ability, as a forerunner of ambassadors from black Africa which in time would be found the world over.

9. Europe and the Pan-Negro Goal

If initially Blyden assigned primarily to New World Negroes the task of helping to project the 'African Personality' on the world stage, he came later to believe that it was Europe which could successfully (if perhaps unwittingly) bring about that result. He had especially wished the British to extend their influence and jurisdiction in West Africa, and, as we have seen during his stay in Sierra Leone in 1871–3, had sought unsuccessfully to persuade the Government to do so. But so reluctant was he to relinquish his grand vision of a West African 'empire' created through British imperialism, he continued to badger and cajole the British in the vain hope that they would execute his plan.

In February 1874, when a new and more imperial-minded British Government under Benjamin Disraeli came into power, exactly a week after British troops had defeated the Ashanti, and there seemed a possibility of reversing the recommended policy of territorial non-extension in West Africa, Blyden again felt compelled to let his views be known at the Colonial Office.[1] He pointed out to the new Colonial Secretary, Lord Carnarvon, 'the fundamental error' of the British that it was 'necessary in order to develop trade to encourage the feeble and demoralised natives on the coast in hostility to the more industrous, more intelligent, and better organized races of the interior'. He hoped that as a result of the experience and expense of the Ashanti war, the British would adopt a policy of establishing 'amicable relations . . . with the superior natives of the interior to be perpetuated by sympathetic intercourse which will be at once more rational, satisfactory and profitable.' But such a policy would be successful or effective only if the British discarded their ethnocentric belief 'that the natives of this country cannot grow up and become prosperous and happy without having suddenly imposed upon them European institutions'; he emphasized that 'to mould African institutions after the English model would be to give the people

[1] C.O. 879/8, African No. 82. Blyden to Berkeley, 12 Feb. 1874.

a garment which not having been made for them, and of which they do not feel the necessity, would not only not fit them, but would hang extremely awkward upon them'. Again using the recommendations of the 1865 Parliamentary Committee as a pretext, Blyden suggested as a 'pressing necessity' for the development of the West African colonies, the implementation of the following programme:

1. A system of compulsory elementary education for the masses, and a provision for the higher intellectual wants of the natives, to fit them gradually to fill, without discredit, offices which in the civil, ecclesiastical and commercial operations of the country must more and more devolve upon them.

No doubt, with the thought of his recent disillusioning experiences in Sierra Leone in mind, he further remarked that even 'the most cursory observer' of that colony 'must see that education will have a great deal to accomplish, before the masses will be prepared for the responsibilities of self-government'.

2. The securing of regular interviews by the Colonial Government by means of suitable Agents, with the powerful interior Chiefs and the affording of facilities for multiplying the friendly intercourse between the coast and central Negroland.

This step, he argued, would 'enable the Government to know more of the people whom they indirectly govern, to understand their feelings, sympathize with their aspirations, and make allowances for their prejudices'.

3. 'A regular and persistent colonial policy . . . which did not depend on the individual views of Governors.'

If such a programme were implemented, 'leaving the people otherwise, as far as possible to themselves', it was Blyden's view that 'a few years only would suffice to make it safe for the Government . . . to "withdraw" from the coast'. But not even the imperial-minded Disraeli Government was prepared to expend money for the systematic development of the West African colonies or take steps to ensure 'a regular and persistent policy' in governing them.

Six months later Blyden reinforced his plea for an extension of British power in West Africa by a direct appeal to the British public. In a speech delivered in Middlesex in July 1874, he advised his audience that 'England had it in her power to determine to a great extent what the condition of West and Central Africa should be in ten or twenty years'. 'A great deal had been done', he continued, 'but a great deal still remained to be done before England in keeping with her philanthropic antecedents could honorably withdraw from the coast.'[2] On subsequent visits to England, and particularly during his ambassadorship to the Court of St. James (1877–9) Blyden made similar pleas. Thus, writing in an influential British quarterly in 1878, Blyden appealed for 'wholesome British influence' in Africa: the British should go to Africa as teachers and guides but should first 'study the people so as to be able to deal with them scientifically'.[3]

It is interesting to note that when in 1882 Britain, to protect its vast empire and commercial interests in the East, sent a military expedition to crush the Egyptian nationalists led by Arabi Pasha, whom the British Government had regarded as a threat to its vital interest in the Suez Canal, and afterwards practically assumed control of Egypt, Blyden fully approved of this development. He wrote: 'England's interest in Egypt is such that she must see that order is entirely restored and peace placed on a permanent basis ... The disbanding of the Egyptian army, the punishment of its leaders, and the establishment of an efficient government at Cairo, are the indispensable conditions of any settlement which England will accept.' One immediate beneficial result Blyden hoped for in the British intervention was the stoppage of the enormous Arab slave trade in Negroes from the Sudan and Egypt to the Middle East. Typically, and this time prophetically, he expressed the view that the occupation of Egypt would be the beginning of a vastly increased British territorial expansion in Africa, but he was disappointed that this expansion did not take place nearly as much in West as in East Africa.[4]

Blyden's next direct appeal to the British Government to extend its jurisdiction in West Africa came eight months after the end of

---

[2] *African Repository*, L, Oct. 1874, 300.
[3] Blyden, 'Africa and the Africans', *Fraser's Magazine*, Aug. 1878, 194; also *Christianity, Islam and the Negro Race*, 321.
[4] *West African Reporter*, IX, 25 Nov. 1882. For a detailed discussion of the events and circumstances leading up to British military intervention in Egypt, see Ronald Robinson and John Gallagher, *Africa and the Victorians*, London 1961, chaps. IV and V.

the Berlin West Africa Conference (15 November, 1884–26 February 1885).

Blyden was in Sierra Leone during this time, and here the combination of an economic depression and the fear that French territorial expansion would circumscribe Sierra Leone prompted the traders, both Europeans and Africans, to form the Sierra Leone Association to lobby for a British protectorate over the hinterland of the colony. Between August and October 1885 a series of public meetings was held urging this step, and in addition, a petition was sent to the Colonial Office advising urgent action.[5] Blyden himself gave strong support to the traders.

But if he supported the attempts of the traders to persuade the British to annex the hinterland of Sierra Leone, it was as much, if not more, for political as for economic reasons: he wanted to see the influence of the French curbed and he hoped that a British protectorate over a large area of West Africa would ultimately result in the creation of a major West African state. He was against French territorial extension in Africa not only because he believed English to be the most suitable European language for uniting West Africans, but because he feared that, unlike the British, the French would regard African territory as an integral part of France, and in attempting to impose French civilization upon Africans would 'destroy the native rule and authority, overthrow the native dynasties, and turn the whole country into a French province'.[6] He urged the British to annex immediately the hinterland of Sierra Leone to forestall vigorous French expansion in the Western Sudan. He recalled the long and persistent efforts of African merchants, led by such well-known public figures as William Grant and Samuel Lewis, for a British protectorate in the interior which would ensure uninterrupted trade between it and the colony. He quoted Sir Samuel Rowe, the Governor of Sierra Leone, as being in favour of such a policy. He noted that the tribes in the hinterland had 'a positive feeling of friendship for the British', and since the widespread conquest of the Muslim warrior, Samori, were all the more anxious to 'find refuge under

[5] *Methodist Herald*, III, 26 Aug. 1885; *Sierra Leone Weekly News*, II, 14 Oct. 1885; Fyfe, *History of Sierra Leone*, 45–52.

[6] Blyden, *Christianity, Islam and the Negro Race*, 244. Cf. Blyden to Coppinger, 16 May 1888, *A.C.S. Papers*, Vol. 25, where he wrote: 'The French language will never spread in Africa and French literature to which it will give access is not adapted to the elevation of the Negro.'

a strong and regular Government'. He reminded the Colonial Secretary that Samori himself, in need of support against the French, had volunteered to place his conquests under a British protectorate, and that the King of Segu had requested closer commercial links between Sierra Leone and his Kingdom. The hinterland, Blyden continued his argument, contained rich agricultural lands which could be developed by the British Government, in co-operation with the American Colonization Society, colonizing the area with about 700,000 American Negroes. The new society which would be created would provide 'safe and permanent markets' for British manufactures and would 'in a short time take from the British Government the whole burden of local expenditure'. Remembering the cool reception he had received in the past from the Colonial Office to such schemes, Blyden proposed that 'If in the opinion of Her Majesty's Government the time has not yet come for Government action in the matter, that the attention of philanthropists and capitalists be called to it.'[7]

Blyden's scheme won the sympathy of A. W. L. Hemming, Principal Clerk at the Colonial Office, who had been a member of the British delegation at the Berlin Conference. Hemming felt there 'was a great deal in his (Blyden's) ideas', and envisaged no difficulty in colonizing American Negroes in the hinterland of Sierra Leone. He noted, caustically, that Liberia had failed because 'American Negroes were not fit to govern themselves' but that 'under a settled Government, such as of this country, the drawbacks and mistakes which have so hampered the progress of Liberia, would not be felt'. He confessed, though, that the preliminary step of annexation was too expensive to contemplate. He regretted this because he believed that British hesitation to act would 'end in our being cut off by the French and Germans from the interior and therefore losing our trade and revenue'. R. H. Meade, Assistant Under-Secretary of State, summed up the attitude of the Government when he succinctly commented: 'Annexation is out of the question, we have neither the armed forces nor the means that would be required'.[8] As Blyden had feared, the French were to circumscribe Sierra Leone by seizing its potentially rich hinterland.

Indeed, the Berlin Conference had been, in effect, the signal for

---

[7] C.O. 267/362, Blyden to Rowe, 22 Oct. 1885.
[8] *Ibid.*, Colonial Office Minutes.

the scramble for Africa. Even while the conference was in progress, German officials were securing by hastily made treaties what was to become the German colonies of Togoland and Cameroons. France, with a grand design for African empire systematically executed, was easily the greatest gainer, territorially. First, consolidating her old claims on the West African coast and adding as much as she could by treaties made with African chiefs, she went on by a series of sustained military campaigns to conquer and control the Sudan from the Senegal to Lake Chad. The British Government, long opposed to a policy of territorial expansion was stirred by the bustling activities of the French and the Germans, and itself became an aggressive imperial agent, when the energetic and powerful Joseph Chamberlain became Colonial Secretary in 1895.[9] The keen colonial ambitions of the British and French had led to a serious dispute over the Ilo-Bussa region on the banks of the Niger which almost precipitated war. By the end of the century the partition of West Africa was complete. And despite the platitudes uttered at the Berlin Conference (1885) and the Brussels Conference (1890), and the propaganda emanating from the European capitals about the humanitarian motives for European intervention in Africa these powers were there primarily to promote their own interests.

But even while the scramble was on, Blyden still vainly entertained the hope that Britain would yet emerge as the dominant imperialist power in West Africa. In London in April 1890 as the dinner guest of the newly-formed British-controlled Liberian Concessions Company, he sought to stir the Government to imperialistic exploits in West Africa when he told his audience, flatteringly, that Britain was the only European power which protected the interest of Africans and introduced constructive agencies among them.[10] He continued his cajolery by expressing the view that 'the costly French and German experiments' in West Africa 'were bound to fail', and 'the result would be that they would withdraw in a few years, and the whole thing would be left in the hands of the English people'. As ambassador in London in 1892 Blyden continued to express hope for British ascendancy in West Africa, and as late as 1896 was still asserting

[9] Julian Amery, *Life of Joseph Chamberlain, 1901–3*, London 1951, Vol. IV, 222–31.
[10] *The Times*, 11 April 1890.

that Britain 'ought to have unquestioned precedence in respect of territory and political influence in West Africa'.[11]

But with the partition of Africa a *fait accompli*; and despite the fact that the British Government had not staked out the large territorial claims that he wished it would, Blyden chose to believe that the partition was 'an act of Providence' and was ultimately for the good of Africans. He stated this view most explicitly in 1903: 'Our country has been partitioned, in the order ... of Providence, by the European powers, and I am sure that, in spite of what has happened, or is now happening or may yet happen, this partition has been permitted for the ultimate good of the people, and for the benefit of humanity.' It was not that he naïvely believed in the altruism of Europe. He recognized that Europe was attempting 'to utilize Africa for her own purpose', but he clung to the transcendental belief that 'Providence used men and nations for higher purpose than they themselves conceived.'[12]

Yet, despite his vaunted belief that European rule in Africa was ultimately for the good of that continent, he realized that that rule carried hazards with it. One of his secret fears was that the European nations, particularly the French and the Belgians, would attempt to colonize Africa with large numbers of white settlers.[13] He constantly reiterated the hope that, because the African climate and diseases were so dangerous to health of Europeans that they would never be able to colonize successfully in tropical Africa, but his fear that Europeans might seriously make this attempt was never completely stilled. Indeed by the turn of the century preventatives and cures were being found for tropical disease, mainly as a result of research conducted at the Schools of Tropical Medicine in London and Liverpool, which had been founded through the influence and encouragement of Joseph Chamberlain and Alfred Lewis Jones, the shipping magnate who

[11] *Lagos Weekly Record*, VIII, 11 April 1896.
[12] Blyden, *Africa and the Africans*, 34.
[13] Blyden to Coppinger, 2 July 1886, *A.C.S. Papers*, Vol. 23; Blyden to C. T. O. King, Feb. 1887, *A.C.S. Papers*, Vol. 24. There seemed to have been some basis for this fear; in 1893 a French syndicate, L'Union Coloniale Francaise, composed of leading French industrialists and bankers were formed and had as one of its principal aims encouraging emigration to the colonies; see Philip Neres, *French-speaking West Africa*, London 1962, 16; the Belgian Mouvement Geographique had similarly sought to encourage European colonization of the interior of the Congo, see Ruth Slade, *King Leopold's Congo*, London 1962, 71.

was President of the Liverpool Chamber of Commerce. Blyden feared that this comparative new immunity to tropical diseases might result in 'an increase in the European population, and as had happened in South Africa, a subjugation of native Africans'. But despite these private fears, Blyden continued to maintain publicly that no foreign race could supersede Negroes in tropical Africa. Blyden had feared, too, that the rivalry among European nations which the scramble for Africa had at times exacerbated might lead to a war partly fought out in Africa; it was with relief that he witnessed the Niger Agreement settling Anglo-French rivalry in West Africa in 1898.[14] He deprecated the fact that in staking out their claims Europeans had shown little regard for African peoples on whom too often unnecessary and ruthless wars had been waged, and African rulers were tricked, humiliated, deposed and deported. Blyden had wished to see the European powers govern through the natural rulers and envisaged a gradual change-over to a more enlightened and progressive system as the rulers themselves, their advisers and the people generally came to select and utilize the most useful elements of western culture.

It was because he regarded the European power as a necessary evil in Africa, that Blyden had wished that the United States had created an official colony for its black citizens on that continent. He had hoped that the United States would act as a disinterested imperial agency curbing and restraining European powers from excesses. Indeed, shortly after the Berlin Conference, Blyden attempted, through the influence of the American Colonization Society to persuade the United States Government to appoint him as a roving agent in West Africa to report on the activities of the European powers so that the American Government could intervene on the part of Africans whenever necessary.[15]

If he privately expressed misgivings about European rule in Africa, his public pronouncements, for the most part, continued to be optimistic. In 1895 writing in the *North American Review*, at the request of its editor, Blyden represented the European powers in Africa as 'gradually repairing the waste places and teaching the natives to make the best possible use of their own country, by fitting it for exiles in distant lands who may desire

<hr>

[14] Edward W. Blyden, *West Africa before Europe and Other Addresses*, London, 1905, 117.

[15] Blyden to Coppinger, 2 Oct. and 25 Nov. 1885, *A.C.S. Papers*, Vol. 22.

to return to the ancestral home'.[16] Discarding his former distrust
of the French, he commended them for 'exploiting and developing' the territories in their sphere of influence, and in particular
for their conquest of Dahomey (1893) and the freeing of such 'a
great country from the cruel savagery of ages and throwing it
open to the regenerating influences of an enlightened nation'. He
applauded the fact that the 'sons of powerful chiefs whom they
conquered in the French Soudan were sent to France or North
Africa for education', and saw this as 'fitting them to take charge
of their respective countries and govern them under French supervision in the interest of order and progress'.

He thought that Germany, 'considering her inexperience in
colonial matters was developing astounding ability and resources'.
He knew of the great public scandal caused by the brutality and
immorality of Herr Leist in the Cameroons[17] but felt that his
punishment was a 'decided step in behalf of native protection'.

Blyden lavished his fulsome praise on the British, too. He
especially commended them for having declared a protectorate
over the Niger Delta. He had not 'the slightest doubt, now that
British enterprise under government protection had access to that
region, that in the course of time those forests will be levelled,
those swamps drained, and the soil covered with luxuriant har-
vests'. He had praise for Sir Claude Macdonald, Britain's Commissioner and Consul-General of the Niger Coast Protectorate,
whom he thought genuinely actuated by the interests of Africans.[18] Of him and his activities, Blyden wrote:

He has created a revenue which more than suffices for the work of
administration. He has abolished barbarous customs and suppressed
marauding practices. The natives . . . are encouraged to spontaneous
activity, and to a love of achievement from which important results
must before long accrue. The progress has been rapid as well as
steady; and may be measured from month to month, almost from
day to day.

He expressed gratitude to the Liverpool commercial interests
which he regarded as 'the most potent of the European agencies

[16] Edward W. Blyden, 'The African Problem', *North American Review*, CLXI,
Sept. 1895, 307–39. The material in the following four paragraphs is from this
source.

[17] Cf. Harry R. Rudin, *The Germans in the Cameroon*, London 1938, 210–12.

[18] Cf. John E. Flint, *Sir George Goldie and the Making of Nigeria*, London 1960,
chap. 7.

in the work of African regeneration'. The only critical note he sounded was that against the Royal Niger Company which, contrary to its charter, had set up a commercial monopoly and was ruthlessly eliminating the African middleman. He complained that under Company rule the welfare of Africans was being sacrificed to the interest of the shareholders, and expressed the hope that the territory controlled by the Company would be taken over by the British Government. This was actually done in 1899.

Blyden's extravagant praise of European imperialism in Africa might partly be explained by the fact that he was writing for an American audience and did not want to impart information which would discourage American Negro emigration to that continent. It is significant that in this article he emphasized that Europeans could not and did not intend to colonize Africa:

> None of these powers has any idea of making Africa a home for its citizens. They know that European colonists cannot live in that country. Nature has marked off tropical Africa as the abiding home of the black races . . . All that Europe can do is keep the peace amo.ng the tribes, giving them the order and security necessary to progress; while the emissaries of religion, industry and trade teach lessons of spiritual and secular life.

Ironically, after the establishment of European rule in West Africa, it was, in Blyden's view, the French of all the imperial powers whose rule came closest to conforming with the interests of Africans. In early 1901 Blyden visited regions of the Ivory Coast that had been, prior to the Franco-Liberian treaty of 8 December 1892, Liberian territory, and so satisfied was he with 'French administration upon the life and prospect of the natives', that he did not censure France for taking territory to which Liberia had strong claims. In an address before the Liverpool Chamber of Commerce in September 1901, Blyden briefly reviewed European imperialism in Africa, praising the French and being critical of the British.[19] Of the French he remarked:

> France has a peculiar work to do in West Africa—a work much needed, and suited to the genius of the Celtic race . . . France is doing her part to pacify West Africa, to improve her material conditions, and to give an opportunity for permanent progress to the sons of the soil . . . Africans would gladly co-operate with each nation accord-

[19] Blyden, *West Africa Before Europe*, 1–36.

ing to the measure in which their systems accord with native ideas and native customs and traditions. And there seems to be more of this conformity in the French methods than in the more rigid and unimaginative system of the Anglo-Saxon.

He also had kind words for the Germans:

The Germans have only recently entered the field, but, as apt pupils, have already mastered the situation. They are taking their part with intelligence, energy and capital. In commercial thoroughness and success only the English are their superiors. Their steamers are found in every inlet and outlet along the Coast. Their settlements in Togoland ... are becoming centres of trade ... Germany is in West Africa ... to give her desirable quota to its development and prosperity.

But Blyden was disappointed that the British, whose influence he still hoped to see predominate in West Africa, had been ruthless, and even treacherous in their dealings with African rulers, as exemplified by Governor Maxwell's unnecessary humiliation and deposition of Prempeh, the Asantehene in 1896, and Consul Phillips's destruction of Benin and deportation of Oba Ovonramwen.[20] He advised that Britain could still rise to 'the full height of her magnificent Imperial destiny' without the use of 'Maxim guns and Marini rifles.'

In March 1902, Blyden visited Senegal and his good impression of French rule in West Africa was again confirmed. He wrote to his friend, E. D. Morel, the British journalist and reformer, praising the continuity of French administrative policy and their fostering of native agriculture.[21] Blyden was impressed, too, with the French scheme of training and using Muslim Negroes as officials. He reported that his guide during his stay in Senegal was Al Hajj Ahmed Sek, a Jolof, 'thoroughly educated in French and Arabic, and who has performed the pilgrimage to Mecca'. Sek took him to a Muslim Court presided over by Alkadi (Judge) Bakai Ba, by Blyden's account, a dignified, physically impressive and learned African, whose decisions in all civil and religious cases affecting his co-religionists, were final.[22]

[20] David Kimble, *A Political History of Ghana*, London 1963, 296; Michael Crowder, *The Story of Nigeria*, London 1962, 184.

[21] Blyden to Morel, 15 Sept. 1902, *Morel Collection*, Misc.

[22] Edward W. Blyden, 'Islam in the Western Soudan', *Journal of African Society*, 1 Oct. 1902, 30.

Speaking before the African section of the Liverpool Chamber of Commerce on 16 June, 1903, Blyden told of his visit to Senegal and praised French imperialism. He applauded their lead in building railroads, docks and wharves, and in fostering agriculture, all as part of an integrated plan for the economic development of French West Africa. 'While England hesitated', he chided, 'France was covering her West African possessions with a network of high roads . . . and now she is extending her railways in every direction, linking together French Guinea and Dahomey and the Ivory Coast.' He praised the French plan of educating the sons of the African élite as leaders. He declared that the French were 'far ahead in the necessary task of training co-workers and leaders' from among the Muslims. 'These are the high-minded uses which the French in that part of Africa are making of Imperial power, so that whatever their faults they must command the respect and confidence of their Mohammedan subjects,' he eulogized.[23]

Ideally, Blyden wished to see France and England co-operate in 'impressing a wholesome direction upon what must be regarded as the most critical period in the modern history of Africa'. And in a fit of wishful hyperbole he believed that 'the most important railway yet to be constructed in the cause of Africa and humanity, is that to be built by Great Britain and France conjointly, from Algiers to the Cape of Good Hope, the terminus on one side being in French territory, and on the other in English'.[24]

But in his realistic mood Blyden knew that close co-operation between France and Britain in Africa was not likely. And although he had the highest praise for French rule in West Africa, he still believed that from his pan-Negro point of view the British influence was potentially the most useful and wholesome. He advised the British Government to assume direct responsibility for the territory under the control of the Royal Niger Company, to make an honest attempt to win the confidence of its Muslim population and to give an English training to a corps of them and use them in the British imperial service. Blyden himself had done what he could to prepare Muslims to co-operate with the British. Between 1887 and 1895 much of the time he spent in

[23] Blyden, *West Africa Before Europe*, 106. For a discussion of this French economic programme and development, see Roberts, *op. cit.*, 318–36.
[24] Blyden, *West Africa Before Europe*, 118.

Sierra Leone was devoted to privately teaching English to select Muslim students. In 1896, as Agent of Native Affairs in Lagos, he had been permitted to start a school at which Muslim youths were sent for 'western training'. In 1899 he urged the Colonial Secretary to set up a major educational centre for Muslims in West Africa, so as to provide an 'intelligent and efficient corps of co-workers' in the British administration of Northern Nigeria.[25] Impressed with the facility with which Muslims travelled about Blyden suggested that Muslims trained in English would spread British influence even beyond the sphere of the Government— a factor that interested him more than it did the British Government. He had been perturbed by the war waged by the Royal Niger Company against the Emirates of Nupe and Ilorin in the early months of 1897,[26] but he assured the Colonial Secretary that in spite of this:

The Negro Mohammedans have deep reverence and abiding confidence in the intention and ability of the British Government to give them every possible assistance. They are not to be most effectually conquered or ruled by arms. Money and books, trade and literature, will do more to win them to allegiance and devotion than any other agency.[27]

Shrewdly, Blyden emphasized that his educational scheme was 'in close harmony' with Joseph Chamberlain's plan for the development of the British colonies. He offered his services as Director of the educational centre he had recommended.

Officials in the Colonial Office were impressed by Blyden's letter and sympathetic to his suggestion. Sir C. P. Lucas, Assistant Under-Secretary of State, thought Blyden 'a man of high ideals but withal of sound and moderate views and that his proposal was a good one' but he had two reservations: first he wondered 'whether the Mohammedans of the different colonies were sufficiently in touch with one another and with Sierra Leone in particular to make it a success', and secondly he feared 'that whatever good results Dr. Blyden's personal force may be able to achieve it will be very difficult to provide a successor to him'.[28] Despatches were sent out to West African Governors in which the

[25] C.O. 147/142, Blyden to Denton, 10 April 1899.
[26] Cf. Flint, *Sir George Goldie*, 243–63.
[27] C.O. 147/142, Blyden to Denton, 10 April 1899.
[28] *Ibid.*, Colonial Office Minutes.

Colonial Office expressed its 'appreciation of the importance of
the object in view', and sought the opinion about the feasibility
of the scheme. Blyden's plea did finally result in his appointment
in 1901 as Director of Mohammedan Education in Sierra Leone
but the educational scheme which he supervised was a very
limited one and was certainly not intended for all West Africa.
The entire department which engaged twelve teachers, not including Blyden himself, was run on £600 a year. It was not surprising that Blyden remonstrated against the meagreness of the
budget allowed to a department which he considered 'one of the
most important elements in the future of British administration in
West Africa'. He made a second plea in 1903 for a West African
Institution in Sierra Leone 'for the secondary education of
Mohammedans . . . in Western ideas'.[29] But nothing was done
about this.

In order to emphasize the importance of this theme Blyden
wrote an article on 'Islam in the Western Soudan' which appeared in the *Journal of the African Society* for September 1902.
In it, he contended that there was then 'no question of deeper
practical interest to European powers'. In Britain 'Public opinion
to a most remarkable degree, had been attracted to that important
region, recently brought within the British Empire.' Yet, he
claimed truthfully, that Islam in the Sudan had not been studied
by foreigners 'with anything like insight or thoroughness'.[30]

In another article, 'The Koran in Africa', published in the
same journal, in January 1905, Blyden again argued that West
African Muslims would be glad to co-operate with the British if
the imperialists were to remember that the Muslims strongly
objected to 'the desocialising influence of the missionary method
which breaks up family ties and disintegrates communities',
'caste arrangements which separate the missionary from the
people', and the connivance of Christians to the liquor traffic
and liquor drinking.[31] In his lectures during his visits to England,
Blyden did not neglect to plead for British understanding of the
Muslims and co-operation with them. In an address before the
African section of the Liverpool Chamber of Commerce de-

[29] C.O. 267/471, Blyden to Antrobus, 4 July 1903.
[30] Blyden, *Islam in the Western Soudan*, 37.
[31] Edward W. Blyden, 'The Koran in Africa', *Journal of the African Society*, No.
XIV, Jan. 1905, 168-9.

livered on 26 June 1903, he again recommended 'the establishment of a Central Institution on the highlands of Sierra Leone
for the education in English and Arabic of Mohammedan youth
from Northern Nigeria and the colonies on the coast'.[32] Blyden
also attempted to get Sir Frederick Lugard, the first High Commissioner of Northern Nigeria, who had occasionally sought his
advice on problems relating to administration, to exert his influence to have a major West African institution for Muslim education established. But these pleas were in vain.

Blyden's praise for French colonial policy and his campaign to
get the British to understand and co-operate with the Muslims
was in reality part of a greater campaign in which he sought to
impress upon European powers in Africa the need for a careful
study of African social systems if they were to rule wisely and to
mutual advantage. Blyden had long maintained that Europeans
could be useful in Africa only if they attempted to understand and
respect African customs and institutions: he had admitted that
there were some aspects of African life that needed reform, some
customs that needed excision, but had pleaded that the basic
African social system should remain intact. With European partition of Africa Blyden wrote more insistently, explicitly and urgently on the theme.

For long his almost solitary pleas that the African social system
suited its inhabitants best under their own circumstances and was
deserving of careful study met with very little favourable response.
The belief prevailed among Europeans that African culture was
worthless or non-existent and should be replaced by a European
one. But after the European partition of Africa, and with more
serious thought being given to the question of how best to rule
the Africans a few British writers began to espouse Blyden's point
of view.[33] Perhaps the most outstanding of these was that un-
conventional Victorian Englishwoman, Mary Kingsley, scion of
the literary, wanderlust Kingsley family, and herself a restless
spinster who made two trips to French West Africa between 1893

[32] Blyden, West Africa Before Europe, 107.
[33] The most important of them were R. E. Dennet, Notes on the Folklore of the
Fjort, with an Introduction by Mary H. Kingsley, London, 1898, and At the Back of the
Black Man's Mind, London, 1906; Major Arthur Glyn Leonard, The Lower Niger
and its Tribes, London, 1906; Dudley Kidd, The Essential Kafir, London, 1904,
Savage Childhood, London, 1906 and Kafir Socialism, London 1908; and Lady Lugard,
A Tropical Dependency, London, 1904.

and 1895. This intrepid feat deservedly brought her much attention, and from 1896 until her death in 1900, through her lectures and writings, she, more than any other person, commanded
the attention of all associated with West Africa.[34] A powerful and
indefatigable propagandist she brought West Africa very sharply
to the attention of the British people.

Thus Miss Kingsley became a powerful ally of Blyden in the
task of getting Europeans to understand and appreciate the
African social system. It is true that their views differed in two
essential respects: whereas Mary Kingsley was a fierce champion
of the rule of commercial companies in Africa, Blyden was opposed to these and thought that the interests of Africans were
better safeguarded under Government rule. Neither did he agree
with Miss Kingsley's low estimate of the Negro contribution to
world civilization, otherwise there was much common ground
between the influential agnostic Englishwoman and the African
patriot: like Blyden, Miss Kingsley believed that the Negro had
his own peculiar aptitudes; that his customs, laws and institutions
were essentially sound and wholesome and that foreigners in
Africa should attempt to understand and respect these; she castigated both the Colonial Office and missionary societies for their
smug disregard of these factors. Like Blyden she contended that
the 'true African' was found only away from the coast; that
Islam had had a more beneficial effect on Negroes than Christianity: she contrasted the 'courtesy and self-confidence' of the Muslim Negro with the 'brashness and insecurity' of the African
Christian. Like Blyden, Mary Kingsley believed that Britain had
every right to extend the sphere of her imperial influence in Africa
but this was to be done without jingoism or nauseating sentimen-
tality. She wanted a relationship in which both sides would stand
to gain; Britain, in material prosperity and the Africans in a
generally improved mode of living. This was enough justification for British imperialism. And in this relationship there was
no need to destroy African laws, customs and institutions; but
there was every need to give the African the 'fullest opportunity
for self-development and self-advancement'.

[34] See C. Howard, *Mary Kingsley*, London 1957; Stephen Gwynn, *Life of Mary
Kingsley*, London 1933; J. E. Flint, 'Mary Kingsley—A Reassessment', *Journal of
African History*, IV, 1, 1963, 95–104. Miss Kingsley's own major works are *Travels
in West Africa*, London 1897, and *West African Studies*, London 1900.

Blyden had met Mary Kingsley in London in 1898, and in a letter written to the editor of the *New Africa*, A. P. Camphor, on her sea voyage to South Africa in 1900, just before she died, she commended herself 'to my dear friend, Dr. Blyden'. In that letter she pleaded with educated Africans to 'place before the English statesmen the true African and destroy the fancy African made by exaggeration ... to forward and demonstrate that African nationalism is a good thing, and that it is not a welter of barbarism, cannibalism and cruelty.'[35]

By her vigorous campaign, Mary Kingsley had stimulated others to attempt to take a scientific view of African society. And her influence continued beyond her death. For, to commemorate her memory and to continue the work she had begun, the African Society was founded in London in June 1901. The Society received strong support not only from the commercial section she had championed but also from the Colonial Office and the missionaries—two of the main butts of her criticisms. Blyden, an enthusiastic admirer of Mary Kingsley, welcomed the founding of the African Society, of which he was an original member and one of its first Vice-Presidents. Blyden paid several public tributes to Mary Kingsley, and described her as 'the greatest missionary to Africa ... in the nineteenth century'.[36] The African Society, he saw, hopefully as

the harbinger of a great future for Africa. It is like the song of a nightingale after the long and dreary winter of misconception on the part of the foreigner, of woes innumerable on the part of the native. It is as yet on the threshold of the work to be done, and ought to be instrumental in exploding the fallacies which during the ages have hindered effective and beneficient results.[37]

In a speech before the Liverpool Chamber of Commerce in 1903, Blyden gave advice on the 'two principles that should guide the policy of the Imperial Powers'. First, 'encourage the development of the natives along the lines of their own idiosyncracies as revealed in their institutions'. Secondly,

... give to the African ... all the advantages, in their spirit and effect, which as individuals or communities, as rulers or people,

---

[35] Quoted in Gwynn, *op. cit.*, 263; also John Mensah Sarbah, *Fanti National Constitution*, London 1906, Appendix 3.
[36] Blyden, *West Africa Before Europe*, 3–4; cf. Blyden, 'Islam in the Western Soudan', 38.   [37] Blyden, *West Africa Before Europe*, 130.

they would have enjoyed under native conditions. Do not deprive them of rights and advantages which they valued and enjoyed before you came, and which were in accordance with justice and equity, without making it clear to them that you give them their equivalent. The sense of justice is as keen in the African as in any one else.[38]

A serious problem faced by Europeans in Africa was the reluctance of Africans, in the early stages of colonial administration to work for wages. To the African with land plentifully available under the system of communal tenure, there seemed little inducement to labour for others, a procedure which smacked to him of servility and indeed of slavery. The badge of a freeman was that he worked for himself. Hence there occurred an apparent 'shortage of labour' and the result was that European administrators resorted to forced labour either openly, or by using disguised compulsion. Blyden deprecated this compulsory labour. Writing in 1901 he pointed out that the use of forced labour in South Africa had had disastrous results for the natives and expressed the hope that 'the conditions in South Africa should furnish no encouragement for the adoption in West Africa of any of the methods adopted by the enterprise of Europe towards the natives of that counry'. And when the British Cotton Growing Association in 1903 announced plans for large-scale cotton production in West Africa, Blyden advised it 'to uphold native authority in the country', and work through that authority to carry out its scheme.[39]

As an articulate exponent of African interest, it might have been expected that Blyden would strongly and publicly condemn the well-known atrocities which were being perpetrated in King Leopold's Congo. And yet this was not the case. He first referred to the Congo in his published writings in 1895. And despite the fact that he certainly did have knowledge of Belgian atrocities in the Congo,[40] Blyden gave as his opinion that 'everyone has confidence in the philanthropic aims and the practical and commercial efforts of the King of the Belgians in the arduous and expensive enterprise he has undertaken in the Congo'.[41] His one public attempt at a protest was at a dinner given in his honour by fellow Africans in London on 15 August 1903. But this was a mild

[38] *Ibid.*, 140.   [39] *West African Mail*, II, 8 April 1904.
[40] Blyden to Coppinger, 24 May and 20 June 1888, *A.C.S. Papers*, Vol. 25.
[41] Blyden, *The African Problem*, 331.

protest which merely referred to the 'melancholy rumours of the treatment accorded to our people at the Congo by alien rulers'. He immediately went on to defend the Belgians whom he thought were 'neither by taste nor by temperament ... inhuman or cruel'.[42] He thought the intentions of the Belgians good, their methods bad.

Why did Blyden not more strongly castigate the Belgian regime? As Liberian Ambassador to London in 1892 Blyden had spent a week in Belgium where he had been lavishly entertained and had been the luncheon guest of King Leopold himself.[43] In addition, Blyden was a close friend of Alfred Lewis Jones, the West African trader and shipping magnate, of whose generosity Blyden had often been the recipient; but Jones was the consul in Liverpool for the Congo state, had large commercial interests in the Congo and was well-known as a defender and apologist of the Belgian regime in the Congo.[44] It might be that Blyden's acquaintance of the Belgian monarch and his friendship with Jones had deterred him from a more outspoken condemnation of the Belgian Congo. But perhaps the main reason for his reticence was his oft repeated article of faith that European nations were Providential Agents working for the regeneration of Africa and that, 'retribution for their misdeeds will come from God'.[45]

Blyden had consistently maintained and acted on the assumption that European nations were agents working to make Africa a progressive continent. Yet he did not want Africa to be a black replica of Europe: he wanted it to be culturally distinctive—retaining as much of its customs and institutions as was compatible with the adoption of the best elements of Western Culture. He expected educated Africans to take the lead in understanding and explaining African culture and in attempting, idealistically, to bring about a happy amalgam between it and an aggressive western culture which tended to overwhelm all before it. Blyden had also maintained that European rule in tropical Africa would be temporary. His optimism was based on the belief that Europeans could not settle permanently there, and that this fact would facilitate the withdrawal of Europeans as political overlords when they were no longer needed. In this history has proved him right.

[42] Blyden, *Africa and the Africans*, 34.
[43] *Sierra Leone Weekly News*, VIII, 13 Aug. 1892.
[44] *West African Mail*, I, 1 Jan. 1904.   [45] Blyden, *Africa and the Africans*, 45.

10. Towards a West African Community

Although Blyden talked and wrote of all black Africa, his influence on that continent was confined mainly to West Africa. By 1871 he had become the intellectual focus of English-speaking West Africa and was to work for the creation of a united West Africa. This chapter will discuss his attempts after 1874 to create among West Africans the consciousness of a West African community.

Blyden had realized that the newspaper was an indispensable medium for the creation of a community spirit among English-speaking West Africans, and it is noteworthy that he either helped to found or wrote for the most important contemporary West African newspapers. In 1874, the year in which the *Negro* was discontinued, Blyden helped one of its former proprietors, William Grant, to found the *West African Reporter*, the declared aim of which was to forge a bond of unity among English-speaking West Africans, and in particular to bring about a close relationship between Sierra Leone and Liberia.[1]

In fact, the relationship of the two territories had been less than cordial because of trade and boundary disputes between them. Moreover, despite the physical proximity of the two territories, there had been surprisingly little social intercourse between their educated classes. Instead the Liberian elite feared competition from enterprising Africans from British West Africa and had sought to discourage them.[2] It was with this view that the Naturalization Act of 27 January 1876, was passed: under it 'alien' Africans were required to spend a minimum of four years before citizenship could be granted.[3] Blyden, who viewed Liberia as the focus and centre of a West African territorial entity, had been strongly opposed to the measure, and he and Grant were

[1] *West African Reporter*, III, 26 Dec. 1876.
[2] See, for instance, C.O. 267/313, W. W. Reade to Granvelle, 3 Feb. 1870.
[3] Huberich, *op. cit.*, Vol. II, 1033; this Act was repealed in 1907: See below, p. 170.

determined to bring Liberia and Sierra Leone together. Significantly, it was on Blyden's invitation and as his guest that Grant
first visited Liberia in December 1876 and spent a week there. At
a tea party which Blyden gave for Grant and which was attended
by several prominent Liberians, it was resolved 'that the time has
arrived, when there ought to be a contribution of negro talents
and ability on the West Coast of Africa ... for the elevation of
our race morally, socially, politically ...'[4] At a dinner party at the
President's mansion on the following evening, Grant urged 'the
importance of better understanding and closer connection between Sierra Leone and Liberia'. On his return to Sierra Leone,
Grant reported favourably of Liberia: he had seen there evidence
of 'thrift, industry and enterprise', and he called upon Sierra
Leoneans to take a greater interest in and give support to the
Negro Republic.[5]

By the early 1870's Blyden's ideas and influence had already
begun to spread in English-speaking West Africa. The *Reporter*
helped further to disseminate his ideas and news of his activities.
Some of his writings on the influence of Christianity and Islam on
the Negro, which had appeared in *Fraser's Magazine* in the
1870's, were serialized in the *Reporter* and stimulated discussions
among the educated West African elite. His appointment in 1877
as the first Liberian Minister to the Court of St. James the
Reporter described as 'one of the most important occurrences in
the political history of Liberia'. It generously expressed the sentiment that 'The much abused phrase "the right man in the right
place" was at last appropriate,' and advised the Liberian Government to make permanent the legation which Blyden had
opened.[6] The respect and admiration accorded him by the highest
British circles, was duly reported by the *Reporter*, and must have
created pride among his West African compatriots.

Blyden returned from his diplomatic duties in London to Sierra
Leone in late January 1879. His activities here again show him
as thinking in terms of a West African community. After a short
visit to Liberia he took back with him to Sierra Leone Allen B.
Cooper, 'a black man of intelligence', a former member of the
Liberian House of Representatives, and the most successful coffee
cultivator in Liberia and encouraged him to start a coffee planta-

---

[4] *West African Reporter*, IV, 24 Jan. 1877
[5] *Ibid.*   [6] *Ibid.*, IV, 7 Nov. 1877.

tion there.[7] Together they made a tour of the Windward coast
visiting the island of Matacong by way of the Melakori River and
then on to the Rio Pongo. Although Blyden was an unexpected
visitor, the young men there, at short notice, delivered an address
of welcome to him praising him as a 'champion of the Negro
race' and congratulating him on being the first Liberian ambassador abroad. Blyden was gratified to see young Africans taking
such an 'interest in events affecting the welfare of their race'.
He predicted that Africans would yet play an active part in
shaping the events of the world. He stirred their racial patriotism
when he said, 'I would rather, in view of the possibilities and
probabilities, be a member of this than of any other race.' Blyden
also visited the Rio Pongo where West Indian missionaries had
been at work since 1855. Everywhere he visited on this trip he
found 'native young men educated at Sierra Leone, engaged as
clerks, book-keepers, factory keepers and independent traders',
many of them 'thoughtful and cultivated'; and he sought to
persuade them to devote their energies to Liberia.[8]

Blyden's appointment as President of Liberia College and his
attempt to have it firmly established as a West African institution
was, of course fully supported by the *Reporter*. So pro-Blyden was
the *Reporter* that it came out openly in support for the leading
blacks in their conflict with mulattoes. The issue of 22 April 1882,
charged that 'the Republican Party, now in the opposition, num-
bering among its members the few rich men—mostly men of
color' unjustly decried the Whig Government and sought to
delude the masses. The following issue again declared for Negroes
against mulattoes: 'As Negroes we feel some touch of resentment
against the class in Monrovia which is doing its best to convince
the world that a Negro Government conducted according to the
usage of civilized peoples is a farce, and that Liberia is entirely
under a mobocracy.' This dislike and distrust of Liberian
mulattoes on the part of the successful liberated African element
in Sierra Leone, in part explains the lack of co-operation between
the élite in the two territories.

But if the *Reporter* took sides in the internal politics of Liberia,
it continued to campaign for closer relationship between the

---

[7] Blyden to Coppinger, 23 April 1879. *A.C.S. Papers*, Vol. 19. Hooper never did
start his coffee plantation in Sierra Leone: he died shortly after his return to
Liberia.   [8] *West African Reporter*, V, 14 May 1879.

Negro Republic and the British colony. Thus, in 1882 it was critical of the fact that Sir Arthur Havelock, Governor of Sierra Leone, was given the added appointment of British Consul to Liberia. While the *Reporter* approved of the re-establishment of a British Consulate which had been abolished more than two decades before, it felt that there was need for a full-time resident Consul. Such a person could help to prevent misunderstandings between the two territories and facilitate solution of any problems, and thus aid in creating 'a more perfect accord between Sierra Leone and Liberia'.[9] In an editorial of 13 October 1883, at a time when the boundary dispute between the two territories was a contentious issue, the newspaper reiterated its view that 'the true interest of Liberia and Sierra Leone cannot be divergent'. Throughout, it remained loyal to Blyden, in one of its last issues describing him as 'one of the most thoughtful Negroes alive'.[10]

The newspaper itself survived Grant, its proprietor and guiding spirit, by two years. Grant had died in London on 28 January 1882 while on a business trip. He had been a splendid example of an able, hard-working and race conscious African—of whom, in Blyden's view, there were too few in West Africa. To his authorship was attributed the 'Negro creed'.

I believe in the Negro pure and simple, the ebony image of God; within 'the bounds of his habitation' equal to any, superior to many. I believe in his black skin, his crisp hair, and in all his physical, mental and moral characteristics, when normally developed . . . I believe in his restoration from barbarism and superstition to civilization and Christianity.[11]

The sudden death of 'the African patriot' at the relatively young age of fifty-one Blyden regarded not only as 'a great personal loss' but also as 'irreparable loss to the Negro Race'.[12] Shortly afterwards Blyden lost two other influential supporters: James Quaker, former Principal of the C.M.S. Grammar School at Freetown, whom in 1872 he had helped to found the *Ethiopian*, a monthly journal devoted to educational matters, and Dr. James Africanus Horton, with Blyden one of the earliest articulate champions of the interest of West Africans. Both Quaker and

[9] *West African Reporter*, VIII, 18 March 1882.   [10] *Ibid.*, X, 31 Jan. 1884.
[11] *Ibid.*, VIII, 25 Feb. 1882.   [12] *Christianity, Islam and the Negro Race*, 236.

Horton, too, died suddenly at comparatively young ages, Quaker at fifty-three, and Horton at forty-eight.

With the death of Grant, Blyden quickly found another news-paper-owner as ally. Shortly after the *Reporter* ceased publica-tion, Blyden helped the Rev. Joseph Claudius May, Principal of the Wesleyan Boys' High School to found the *Sierra Leone Weekly News*, which was edited by May's brother, Cornelius, a trained printer and journalist. Like the *Negro* and the *West Afri-can Reporter* the aim of the *Sierra Leone Weekly News* was 'to serve the interest . . . of West Africa and the race generally'.[13] The *News* became one of the most important and successful news-papers of its time in West Africa. Blyden wrote periodically for it, as well as the *Methodist Herald* (1882–8) also owned by J. C. May.

During his stay in Sierra Leone in 1884 he sought to impress upon Africans and government officials that the colony's future lay within a larger West African state. In an important lecture entitled 'Sierra Leone and Liberia,' chaired by the Hon. Samuel Lewis, and attended by leading Africans and government officials, Blyden asseverated that 'the two peoples are one in origin and one in destiny and, in spite of themselves, in spite of local preju-dices, they must co-operate'. He was of the opinion that 'Sierra Leone was really a Negro nationality under a British protectorate' and that 'sooner or later the two countries would have to unite'. Blyden urged that steps be taken to prepare for this eventuality and suggested that one of the prerequisites was a greater degree of political independence for Africans in Sierra Leone. He wanted to see established in the colony 'city corporations . . . composed chiefly of natives'. He warned Sierra Leoneans that if they continued 'in a position of social or political disadvantage, it is because they themselves wanted to acquiesce in it, and to foster those conventional opinions which suspect every attempt to push them forward in self-government, and to place upon them the responsibilities which that government involves'. He expressed the view that Africans in Sierra Leone were mature and experi-enced enough 'to move for themselves as a working social organi-zation', and that 'their political future was greatly in their own hands'. But Blyden's progressive ideas fell on 'nervous conserva-tives'.[14] It is interesting to note that this was the only recorded

[13] *Sierra Leone Weekly News*, VII, 6 Sept. 1890.
[14] *Christianity, Islam and the Negro Race*, 231–48.

occasion on which Blyden explicitly advocated political action on the part of Africans in a British colony. Perhaps, he reasoned that, after the partition of Africa, such advocacy would have been futile and dangerous.

But he continued to use every opportunity to foster raçial pride, initiative and unity among West Africans. During his stay in Sierra Leone in the late 1880's and in the 1890's, he was unencumbered by an official position, or a permanent job: his material needs were met partly from the generosity of a few wealthy African friends, partly from small stipends derived from his writings, lectures and private tutoring. In Freetown, even more so than in Monrovia, he was the social and intellectual focus. He remained close to the Muslim community, attended their festivals, overcame their objection to having their children study 'English and western subjects', and himself privately taught them these subjects. Among the educated English-speaking Africans, Blyden was forever discussing plans for enhancing the prestige of his race, the most popular of which was that of establishing African-controlled institutions of learning. He was always available to preside and speak at school functions, and for a time taught Arabic at the Wesleyan Boys' High School. A strong opponent of denominationalism, he preached from almost every pulpit in Freetown, and was, of course, a popular community lecturer. In such lectures as 'Elements of Manhood', 'Unity and Self-Respect', and 'Race and Study' he conveyed the message: 'You were not intended to ape the European; cultivate a distinct "African Personality".' Thus, in his lecture on 'Unity and Self-Respect' delivered before the Freetown Unity Club on 16 June 1891, he advised his young audience thus:

Your first duty is to be *yourselves*. . . You need to be told constantly that you are Africans, not Europeans—black men not white men— that you were created with the physical qualities which distinguish you for the glory of the Creator, and for the happiness and perfection of humanity; and that in your endeavours to make yourselves something else, you are not only spoiling your nature and turning aside from your destiny, but you are robbing humanity of the part you ought to contribute to its complete development and welfare, and you become as salt which has lost its savour—good for nothing —but to be cast out and trodden down by others.[15]

[15] *Sierra Leone Weekly News*, VII, 20 June 1891.

In one of his most famous lectures, 'Race and Study', delivered on 19 May 1893 at his residence on Free Street to members of the Young Men's Literary Association of Sierra Leone, Blyden expounded the theme of the existence of an 'African Personality' —his first recorded use of the phrase—which needed to be cultivated and developed.[16] Blyden's lecture was, in part, a rebuttal of the 'unworthy' advocacy by Renner Maxwell, a Sierra Leone-born lawyer, of miscegenation so as 'to combine the beauty of the Caucasian with the fine physique and physical strength of the Negro'.[17] For Blyden, Maxwell's opinion was tantamount to saying: 'Let us do away with the sentiment of Race. Let us do away with our *African personality* and be lost, if possible, in another Race . . .'[18] Blyden's was a humanitarian racialism: demanding to know how the Negro race could possibly make its special and distinctive contribution to humanity if it lost its identity through miscegenation.

Blyden had believed that the 'African Personality' was partly expressed through African institutions, and this led him to assume the controversial role of defender of polygamy. Of course, European missionaries had always held, at least tacitly, that polygamous practice was unchristian, but it is characteristic of the increased European arrogance which accompanied the rise of imperialism that European churchmen, as in the case of the Conference of Anglican Bishops held at Lambeth, England in 1888, could uncompromisingly pronounce against polygamy. Blyden was determined to resist what he regarded as European ignorance and effrontery. If he had ever thought of polygamy as immoral, it is likely, judging from his long sympathy with Islam, that he had discarded such a notion by the early 1860's. Moreover, since 1876, Blyden had been defying conventional Christian morality by the open liaison he had formed with a young woman, Anna Erskine, without being divorced or altogether separated from his legal wife, and this must have been partly responsible for his resignation from the Presbyterian Church in 1886. Miss Erskine, a schoolteacher from Louisiana, U.S.A., was, according to Blyden's testimony in 1877, 'a girl of first rate intellect and of

[16] *Sierra Leone Times*, 27 May 1893, for a discussion of Blyden's ideas about the African Personality', see chap. 4, 58–62.

[17] Joseph Renner Maxwell, *The Negro Question or Hints for the Physical Improvement of the Negro Race*, London 1892, preface.

[18] *Sierra Leone Times*, 27 May 1893.

remarkable energy and industry . . . but black'.[19] And although as late as 1892 he was associated with his legal wife in public, it was Anna Erskine who really played the role of wife, catering to his emotional needs, seeing to his material comfort, and bearing him altogether five children. Blyden's connubial relationship is important because, although his advocacy of polygamy was consistent with his defence of African culture, there were those Christian Africans who thought that such advocacy was merely a rationalization of his personal conduct,[20] with the probable result that his opinion did not bear the weight it might otherwise have had. Among educated articulate Africans there were probably three main views on polygamy of which Blyden's was in the minority: there were those, mainly the clergymen, who tended to support the view of their European teachers that polygamy was immoral; a second group of Christians, represented mainly by the majority of laymen, while believing monogamy to be the ideal, held that the practise of polygamy should not debar Africans from being admitted into the Christian faith; while the Blyden view was that polygamy was ideal and should be compulsory for Africans. For Blyden the arrogant and uncompromising attitude of European missionaries to polygamy was yet another example of their divisive and disruptive influence on Africans for polygamy fulfilled very important social and economic functions, especially in preventing the destitution of widows and orphans.

At any rate, he omitted no opportunity to encourage Africans to promote the welfare of their race. Thus he saw the planned celebration of the centenary of Sierra Leone in August 1887, as a fitting occasion to dramatize the need for concerted actions by West Africans to advance their race. If he could, he would have had representatives from all West Africa participate in the celebrations. He was a member of a committee comprised mainly of leading Africans which drew up an ambitious programme aimed at stimulating Negro pride and in promoting Negro initiative. It included a plan to hold an exhibition of African arts, and of the colony's industry and natural products; to erect busts of two great

[19] Blyden to Rev. J. C. Lowrie, 6 Jan. 1877, *P.B.F.M. Papers*, Vol. II; Mrs. Blyden settled in New York in 1893 and from this time there seemed to have been no contact or communication between herself and Blyden. He had three children by his wife.

[20] Some educated Africans contemptuously referred to it as 'Blyden's polygamy hobby', see *Sierra Leone Weekly News*, XIX, 2 May 1903.

Negroes and of three outstanding local Africans in the Wilber-
force Memorial Hall; and to encourage the commencement of a
model farm and industrial school. But the committee had difficulty in raising adequate funds and the celebration fell far short
of what Blyden had hoped: no public memorial was raised, no
busts of famous Africans erected.[21] However a historical play by
Blyden written especially for the occasion was successfully performed. Its obvious theme was that the various elements in West
Africa should all co-operate in building a united community.[22]
Blyden had also taken the opportunity 'of bringing Liberia and
Sierra Leone together': through his encouragement several
Liberians from Monrovia and the St. Paul's River attended the
celebrations, a few of them taking part in the play.[23]

Partly to commemorate the Sierra Leone Centennial, partly to
stimulate further interest in West Africa which its exhibits at the
Colonial and Indian Exhibition of 1886 in London had aroused,
Blyden agreed to the suggestion that Ernst Vohsen, the German
Consul and Agent for a French Company in Sierra Leone, should
pay the cost of publishing a selection of his articles in book form.
The tremendous impact which *Christianity, Islam and the Negro
Race* made both in the English-speaking and Muslim literary
world served to confirm Blyden as the intellectual focus of West
Africa. Sir Samuel Lewis, who wrote the introduction to it,
claimed that Blyden's book gave 'eloquent expression and emphasis to the sentiments and aspirations of every enlightened
member of the race'.

Blyden's ethnocentric teachings which he had used the occasion
of the Centennial Celebrations to emphasize, plus the interest
which his book had generated do seem to have succeeded in
stimulating pride in things African in Sierra Leone. This bore
immediate fruit in the form of a few individuals discarding their
European names for African ones, or adding hyphenated names
to their existing European surnames, and also in the formation of
the Dress Reform Society whose task was to recommend the
design for an appropriate 'National' dress. One of the first to

[21] *Sierra Leone Weekly News*, III, 4 Sept. 1886.
[22] *Memorial of the Celebration of the Jubilee of Her Majesty's Reign and of the Centenary of Sierra Leone*, London 1887. Appendix, 93–108. Blyden's play was called
'The Historical Representation of Sierra Leone'; he also wrote a 'Centenary Ode'
which was sung during the celebrations.
[23] Blyden to Coppinger, 14 May 1887, *A.C.S. Papers*, Vol. 24.

change his name was W. J. Davies, the first African from Sierra Leone to obtain the London University B.A. degree, and Senior Master of Wesleyan High School. From August 1887, he assumed the name of Orishatukeh Faduma. This excited considerable comment because the names Orisha-tukeh were connected with two heathen Yoruba gods; and most Creoles regarded this as a calculated affront to them as Christians.[24] But the idea of name changing soon degenerated into a farce: many replaced their European names by ones which were not necessarily African.

The first move in the attempt to replace European dress by a 'national' African dress was made on 23 May, when twelve scions of the leading families of Freetown met at the home of J. H. Spaine, Colonial Post-Master, and there formed the Dress Reform Society 'to determine and adopt a form of dress that would be more suitable to the requirement of the climate; a form that would at the same time be airy, convenient, and economical, and that would tend to the better preservation of the health of all classes'. Blyden had given his blessings to the new venture. On 13 December 1887, members of the foundation group with a few new adherents met. Among those present were Blyden himself, James Johnson, who was in Sierra Leone on his way back to Lagos from England, and Rev. J. R. Frederick, an outstanding Afro-West Indian preacher. The secretary reported that it was the 'gigantic' aim of the society 'to devise a national dress for Africa'. It was decided that a waist-coat, collar and necktie were superfluous and inconvenient articles of clothing for the tropics. These were to be replaced by a garment resembling the tunic and used together with a 'very free and airy pair of breeches'.[25] But the verbal encouragement of men like Blyden, Johnson and Frederick was not translated into example, and this attempt at originality was widely ridiculed and brought the efforts of the Dress Reform Society to nought.

The kind of cultural nationalism which Blyden was attempting to foster in Freetown was having a much healthier manifestation in Lagos. Indeed, although the youngest of the British West African colonies, Lagos had become by the 1880's the most progressive of them and Blyden began to look upon it as a possible new centre for West African nationalism. By 1890 the town itself

[24] *Sierra Leone Weekly News*, IV, 24 Sept. 1887.
[25] *Methodist Herald*, VI, 21 Dec. 1887.

was thriving and cosmopolitan, with a population of nearly 33,000. As the major seaport commanding trade routes into the Yoruba interior, Lagos had attracted liberated Africans from Sierra Leone (Saros) as well as Negro emigrants from Brazil and Cuba (Amaros).[26] British interference in Lagos affairs after 1851 culminated in its annexation as a Crown Colony in 1861, with the result that its inhabitants became British subjects. Almost a quarter of the population were by origin liberated Africans or returned exiles from Cuba and Brazil. These were usually literate and skilled, and as traders, artisans, government officials, teachers and missionaries, they formed the most enlightened and progressive elements of the Lagos community. Not surprisingly they sought political power commensurate with their commercial and social success. This resulted in the appointment to the Legislative Council in 1872 of J. P. L. Davies and George Hutchinson, two successful Saro traders; but in 1874 the Lagos Legislative Council was abolished owing to a policy of retrenchment, and the colony was administered as part of the Gold Coast. The Saros and Amaros were dissatisfied with the new political arrangement and campaigned for the separation of Lagos from the Gold Coast and the re-establishment of its Legislative Council with an increased African representation. They also demanded an increase in the number of qualified Africans in the government service. To voice their nationalist aspirations a few members of the African élite began publishing newspapers in the early eighteen eighties.[27] It was at Lagos, too, that a start was made to put Blyden's idea of an independent African Church into practice. In 1888 the Native Baptist Church established its independence from the American Baptist Union.[28]

In 1886 Lagos again became a separate colony, and was fortunate in having as its new governor Alfred Moloney, who had

[26] 'Saro' and 'Amaro' were local Yoruba corruptions used to designate the Sierra Leone and the Cuban and Brazilian African respectively.

[27] Lagos's first newspaper, *The Anglo-African*, 1862–65, was published by Jamaican-born Robert Campbell. Fifteen years elapsed before another newspaper was founded: in July 1880 the *Lagos Times and Gold Coast Colony Advertiser*, 1880–84, was started by R. B. Blaize, a prominent Saro trader; in February 1882 another Saro, J. B. Benjamin, started the *Lagos Observer*, 1882–88, and in March 1882, the *Eagle and Lagos Critic*, 1883–88, was founded by Owen Macaulay, the grandson of Bishop Crowther. See also Fred I. A. Omu, *The Nigerian Press*, 1859–1937, University of Ibadan, Ph.D., 1965, *passim*.

[28] James B. Webster, *African Churches among the Yorubas, 1888–1922*, London 1964, 55–6.

already had thirteen years of colonial service on the West Coast of Africa and was known to be enlightened and progressive. He accommodated articulate African opinion when he appointed two of them to the reconstructed Legislative Council—the Rev. James Johnson, Blyden's friend of long standing, and C. J. George, a successful Saro trader. Blyden, who had won the friendship of Moloney, encouraged him in his progressive views. Indeed, while on his way to Lagos from the Gambia in December 1885, Moloney called upon Blyden in Freetown to discuss with him ideas for the economic development of that colony, among them, encouraging Brazilian Negroes to emigrate to Lagos, and promoting 'industrial training' for Africans by starting model farms and workshops.[29]

Blyden made his first visit to Lagos in December 1890 under very special circumstances: a committee of fourteen prominent Africans[30] had invited him to give moral support in a bitter dispute between Africans and Europeans about the Niger Mission. In 1890, a party of C.M.S. missionaries led by J. A. Robinson and Graham Wilmot Brooke, two zealous but misguided young men, joined the Niger mission and with fanatical ruthlessness, condemned the work which Bishop Crowther and his African staff had been doing for almost three decades and without proper authority summarily dismissed or suspended the majority of African ministers and agents on grounds which were openly racialist.[31] This dispute was, of course reminiscent of that in Sierra Leone in 1871-3, but was much more serious: for West Africans were defending an established all-African institution against white reaction, and on this occasion they were united in protesting the high-handed actions of the Europeans as 'a direct insult and affront to Bishop Crowther, the whole African Church and the

[29] Blyden to Coppinger, 18 Dec. 1885, *A.C.S. Papers*, Vol. 22. For a discussion of Moloney's Policy of Economic Development, see A. A. B. Aderibigbe, *Expansion of the Lagos Protectorate, 1863-1900*, unpublished Ph.D. thesis, London University 1959, chap. 2.

[30] The committee was comprised of the following: James Johnson, Pastor of St. Paul's Church and member of the Legislative Council; C. J. George, J.P., and member of the Legislative Council; J. A. Otunba Payne, Chief Registrar of Lagos; John Randle, a medical doctor; N. H. Williams, Barrister-at-Law; T. A. King, druggist; and the following merchants: R. B. Blaize, J. S. Leigh, J. A. Savage, J. O. George, J. B. Williams, H. W. George, Z. A. Williams and J. W. Cole.

[31] Webster, *op. cit.*, 17-18; J. F. A. Ajayi, *Christian Missions in Nigeria, 1841-1891*, London 1965, 253.

Negro Race'.[32] Ironically, this tactless and heavy-handed attempt to 'reform missionary operation' seems in part inspired by Blyden's trenchant criticism of missionary activities in Africa in his book, *Christianity, Islam and the Negro Race*.[33]

Blyden's reputation had, of course, long preceded him to Lagos. The educated elite read his published works, followed his career as reported in the Sierra Leone newspapers, and from 1883 the Lagos papers themselves kept their readers informed about the activities of the outstanding African. An indication of the stimulus which Blyden's writings provided for the educated at Lagos is given by a report in the *Lagos Observer* of 21 June 1883 that Blyden's article, 'Mohammedanism and the Negro Race' had for the past three weeks been engendering lengthy discussions among members of 'The Lagos Mutual Improvement Society.' His proposed visit to Lagos was first publicly announced in the *Lagos Weekly Times* of 19 July 1890, and that newspaper was sure that 'the learned and patriotic gentleman' would 'receive a hearty welcome from his numerous friends and admirers'. From that issue, Blyden's name and views were kept constantly before the Lagos public. The *Lagos Weekly Times* of 4 October carried a letter by Blyden endorsing the views of Majola Agbebi, expressed in a pamphlet, *The Gospel and Africa*, comprised of sermons and speeches, in which the latter was critical of foreign missionary operations in Africa, and advocated the establishment of an independent non-denominational African Church. Agbebi had been one of the main architects of the Independent Baptist Native Church. He had also won the support of leading Africans in establishing a non-denominational institution—Hope School— which catered primarily for the children of the poor and of which he was the Headmaster. The School opened on 3 April 1888 and in July 1890 when it had an enrolment of 100, received Government assistance.[34] The *Lagos Weekly Times* of 22 November 1890, reported that the students of Hope School were planning a 'gigantic evening of amusement' in honour of 'the distinguished African Scholar'. The following issue carried a eulogistic bio-

---

[32] C.M.S. G3/A3/04, J. S. L. Davies, chairman of a Lagos Public Meeting, to Secretaries of the C.M.S., 24 Oct. 1890.

[33] Blyden himself claimed that one of the results of the discussion which his book generated was to 'rouse the C.M.S. to renewed activity' in West Africa: Blyden to Coppinger, 23 Jan. 1888, *A.C.S. Papers*, Vol. 25.

[34] *Lagos Weekly Times*, I, 31 Dec. 1890; *Lagos Times*, IV, 3 Jan. 1891.

graphical sketch of him which read in part: 'He is an oracle on both sides of the Atlantic, and . . is recognized as the highest intellectual representative and the greatest defender and uplifter of the African race . . . He breathes patriotism at every pore . . . He is . . . a man of colossal intellectual abilities and of unimpeachable moral worth.' Lagos was agog at the advent of its great African compatriot.

Blyden arrived at the Lagos pier aboard the *Matadi* on the afternoon of 20 December and was officially greeted by the Committee of Fourteen, while a throng of curious bystanders looked on. He was a guest at Orange House, the home of Otunba Payne the wealthy, generous, and public-spirited Chief Registrar of Lagos, and here received a steady stream of delegations among them 'native Ministers of Religion, the Lemomu, and several Mohammedan priests of Lagos, Brazilian and Spanish repatriates and Prince Oyekan'.[35]

Elaborate preparations had been made for Blyden's entertainment and welcome at Hope School on the evening of Tuesday, 23 December. The School was decorated to produce a festive effect. Among the decorations was 'a lantern of exquisite workmanship, the production of a (Brazilian) repatriate mechanic', mounted at the entrance of the School and displaying 'in luminous letters' the following lines:

> Africa's destiny lay hid in night,
> God said 'let Blyden be', and all was light.[36]

Inside the crowded schoolroom, James Johnson was chairman. Otunba Payne, as chairman of the Board of Hope School, read an address of welcome to Blyden, who in a brief reply praised the idea of setting up Hope School as a non-denominational institution; it was a first step in the breaking down of denominationalism and the establishment of independent African institutions.[37] Following his brief remarks, Blyden and his company were entertained by the pupils of the school in a well-rehearsed programme of songs, recitations and plays.

On the following day the Committee of Fourteen gave Blyden a formal welcome. James Johnson read the address. They had

[35] *Lagos Times*, IV, 10 Jan. 1891.
[36] *Ibid.*, IV, 27 Dec. 1890.
[37] *Lagos Weekly Times*, I, 31 Dec. 1890.

read 'with real interest, and pleasure and thankfulness his zealous
and devoted labour on behalf of the race'; it was a sign of his
love for his race that he had responded to their call. Blyden
replied that in inviting him they had shown 'evidence of self-
reliance, independence, and practical interest in the work of the
race'. They had disproved the assertion that 'the African had no
pride of race and no interest in his own people'. He briefly alluded
to the dispute on the Niger Mission: he thought the events taking
place there were 'providential'. 'The call of God had now become
clear for an African Church,' and he believed that Lagos was
fitted to take the lead, or at least play a prominent part in establishing it.[38]

But his first major pronouncement on the Niger dispute was
made on 2 January 1891 at a crowded meeting in the C.M.S.
Breadfruit School House, presided over by Governor Moloney.[39]
'The learned Doctor appeared before the reading desk with head
bowed down with submission, and in an unassuming attitude, and
voice loud enough to be heard by all in the room, commenced his
philosophical and didactic lecture.'[40] He unequivocally urged the
setting up of an independent African Church with Bishop
Crowther at its head. Blyden, like other West African Christians,
held the Bishop in the highest regard. 'Bishop Crowther', he told
his audience, 'must always stand first in the history of any
Native Church, whatever form it may take. The name must ever
be honourably identified with the history of West African Christianity.' Blyden advised that 'this present (ecclesiastical) arrangement with its foreign props and support, its foreign stimulus and
restraints' must be replaced by an arrangement where Africans
were completely in control. European missionaries, even when
they were well-meaning, contrived to do more harm than good
because of their intolerance and arrogance in dealing with Africans. Countering the European charge that Africans did not
scrupulously conform to the Christian practices they taught,
Blyden pointed out that Constantine, the first Christian emperor,
was 'half-pagan to the end', and that the success of the early

---

[38] *Ibid.*, also Edward W. Blyden, *The Return of the Exiles and the West African Church*, London, 1891, Appendix, 33.

[39] The lecture was reported in the local press, see *Lagos Times*, IV, 10 Jan. 1891, by the title 'The Questions of the Day as they Affect the Negro Race', but was subsequently published as *The Return of the Exiles and the West African Church*.

[40] *Lagos Times*, IV, 10 Jan. 1891.

Church was due to its genius for assimilation and accommodation in doctrines and rituals. With a sense of history, he urged:

We must seek to bring into the Native Church the Chiefs and other men of influence. Do not expect of them the perfection which a narrow philanthropy exacts... Had the hard conditions now imposed upon African Chiefs been required of European sovereigns and chiefs, Christianity might never have been permanently established west of the Bosphorus.

Blyden warned his audience that there would be both native and foreign opposition to the establishment of an independent African Church, and that such an institution was bound to face tremendous initial difficulties, but he felt sure that Bishop Crowther and his co-workers had provided enough 'lights and land-marks' to guide it to safety.[41]

The unanimity of the protest of West African Christians had forced the parent committee of the C.M.S. to reinstate most of the Africans dismissed or suspended; but neither that committee nor the offending missionaries offered any apologies to Bishop Crowther and his wronged associates, and so the Africans remained unappeased. And although they proved reluctant to implement Blyden's recommendation of using the opportunity to break away completely from foreign missions and set up an independent African Church, the Christians of Sierra Leone and Lagos agreed the Delta Mission should become independent, and pledged financial support for it, a decision which Bishop Crowther, although unhappy about the rift, felt compelled to endorse. As part of the Niger Mission, the Delta Mission had also been 'purged' and among the victims here was Archdeacon D. C. Crowther, son of Bishop Crowther. But Africans were especially proud of the Delta Mission and regarded it as an outstanding example of the effectiveness of Bishop Crowther's method and of the splendid work done by Africans unaided by Europeans. The first of January 1891 was the date fixed for the declaration of independence of the Delta Pastorate. Ironically, the venerable Bishop Crowther, his end undoubtedly hastened by the bitter feud, died on 31 December and was buried on the very day he had intended to declare the Delta an independent mission. This declaration of independence came on 29 April

41 Blyden, *The Return of the Exiles and the West African Church*, 25–32.

1891. However, in a final, anti-climatic end to the Niger dispute the Delta Mission resumed its connection with the C.M.S. in 1895.

Africans had failed to make the most of the Niger dispute. They had been united in their opposition to the effrontery of European missionaries, and out of this could well have come a non-denominational West African Church, but the clerical leaders, still too much swayed by European ties and opinions, hesitated to take the appropriate actions. However, Blyden's advice did not go completely unheeded. Chagrined at irresolute clerical leadership, the laymen founded the United Native African Church in August 1891, with Rev. C. W. Cole, formerly of the Methodist Episcopal Church of Liberia as President and W. E. Cole, a merchant, as Secretary.[42]

For this failure to institute an independent non-denominational African Church James Johnson was largely responsible. Next to Bishop Crowther he was the most prominent clergyman in West Africa and the one best placed to do so. Johnson had been the chairman of a series of interdenominational meetings, called as a result of Blyden's lecture, at which the decision was taken to form an independent African Church. The next step was to be a signal from Johnson on which ministers of Lagos were to switch pulpits and declare the inauguration of the African Church.[43] But he failed to take what would have been a momentous decision. It is perhaps not difficult to understand why. He had been driven by Blyden to lead in the discussion of the idea of a non-denominational African Church but as a clergyman, in Blyden's words, 'known everywhere as a rigid adherent and uncompromising supporter of his own Church', he could not have done so with alacrity: the terms of the 'Basis of Union' of the proposed African Church is not known, but in order to satisfy the divergent views of interested Africans they must have been vague or non-committal on fundamental questions, including that of polygamy, and so ultimately repugnant to Johnson's doctrinal sensibilities. Indeed, as an inflexible advocate of the view that polygamous practice was incompatible with being a Christian,[44] Johnson

[42] *Lagos Times*, IV, 8 Sept. 1891.   [43] Webster, *op. cit.*, 66.

[44] *Lagos Weekly Record*, IV, 3 March 1894. Later Johnson came to support the polygamist viewpoint. See his 'The Relations of Mission Work to Native Customs', 1908, cited in E. A. Ayandele, 'An Assessment of James Johnson and his place in Nigerian History', *Journal of the Historical Society of Nigeria*, III, Dec. 1964, 99.

could hardly have declared for an independent African Church which, if it were to succeed, would have had to accommodate the opposite view that polygamy was a time-proven social institution of Africa, and that its condemnation by European adherents of Christianity did not in fact make it unchristian. With two of the leading West African figures holding irreconcilable views on such a central issue, it was unlikely that an African Church could then have been successfully launched. When in 1871-3 in Sierra Leone, Johnson had supported Blyden's agitation for an independent African Church, the issue as to whether such a Church would admit polygamous Africans had not been openly debated, but when in the 1880's it came to the forefront the erstwhile collaborators took divergent views.

Blyden had also precipitated a rift among Christians as to the attitude to be adopted to Muslims. Johnson and the majority of West African Christians did not share Blyden's predilection for Islam nor emulate his example of easy and frequent social intercourse with the adherents of that religion. During his two months' stay in Lagos Blyden had received a constant stream of Muslim visitors to the disapproval of many Lagos Christians. It is significant that the only occasion during this visit when Blyden was 'indisposed' was on the evening he was scheduled to deliver a lecture on 'Islam and its Work in Africa'.[45] It is equally significant that Blyden waited until 13 February, the day before his departure, to respond to the repeated entreaties of Muslims to visit their principal mosque. Here Blyden, with Payne, his host, interpreting into Yoruba, addressed the Muslims in English for an hour on 'the teachings and practices of their religion which had proved useful to Africa'. The huge crowd which had come to hear Blyden had spilled over into the street, and a 'stentorian crier' had to pass 'the word from the lips of the interpreter to the surging multitude'.[46] It was the first time such an event had occurred in Lagos and Christians there were outraged the more so as Blyden had extolled Islam 'when there was only one perfect religion'— Christianity.[47] On the evening of the day of his sermon to the Muslims, Blyden was given an elaborate farewell banquet by the Committee of Fourteen and took the opportunity to answer his critics by appealing to their good sense and the interest of their

[45] *Lagos Times*, IV, 7 Feb. 1891.   [46] *Ibid.*, IV, 14 Feb. 1891.
[47] See Letter from 'Hope' in *Lagos Times*, IV, 21 March 1891.

race. He said in part: 'The Christian Negro . . . cannot afford to look upon the Mohammedans with indifference or hostility . . . It would be wisdom and good policy in Christians not to reproach them but to find out ways and means of working with them to mutual advantage.'[48]

Blyden's short stay in Lagos had been a disillusioning one. His first impression had been favourable and he had hoped that Lagos would be the dynamic centre from which to promote 'the interest of the race'. This hopefulness had been reflected in his first major address.'[49] He had been under the impression then that 'aborigines, pagans, Mohammedans and Christians live in close proximity and intimacy'. The people of Lagos, he had averred, 'had not lived . . . as islanders, but as part of a great continent, surrounded by their own people and connected with the more distant interior tribes, with whom they were in constant and unbroken intercourse'. He had spoken of Lagos as 'one of the most hopeful spots in West Africa'; he had been 'taken by exhilarating surprise' when he entered the lagoon 'and witnessed evidence of material growth. . .' Blyden, who had not long returned from America, could not help making comparisons between Lagos and the cities of the Southern United States. There was a resemblance in physical appearance: because of its black inhabitants, 'its business-like appearance, as well as the novelty of everything—the newness of its improvements—Lagos might be called an American city in Africa'. But for Blyden the comparison could not go much further; there was an important difference in the spirit and outlook of the two: there was about the latter 'an air of depression and unrest . . . a sullen acquiescence in their surroundings', while 'the visitor sees in the people of Lagos—in the openness of their countenance, the brightness of their eyes, the freedom of their movement—fullness of life'. He had been impressed, too, by the fact that the people of Lagos had not only 'retained their language but were sedulously cultivating it'. Blyden had seen the return of Brazilian Negroes as a happy augury for West Africa and praised Governor Moloney for his efforts at promoting an even greater number of Brazilian Negro emigrants, and had felt that Lagos had the qualities to excite the patriotism of Negro emigrants who returned there:

[48] *Ibid.*, IV, 21 Feb. 1891.
[49] Blyden, *The Return of the Exiles and the West African Church*, 3–5.

The natural beauty and fertility of the country, the increased development of its material resources—the noble names among their ancestors—the lives of kings and warriors of their own blood, of whom they have heard—the great deeds these heroes have performed—the legendary and historical songs and ancient dances of the tribes—all become inspirations. No suspicion haunts them that the country will ever be taken from them. They rest, not only in the conviction, but in the consciousness that it is theirs by divine right, preserved for them.

It was true that in many ways, Lagos by the early nineties was the most advanced of the British West African territories, but by the end of his first stay, Blyden had found to his disappointment that here as at Sierra Leone and Liberia were divisions and local loyalties among Africans which made co-operative effort difficult.

However, he continued to aim at promoting unity in West Africa, and he was determined to shock Christians out of their complacency and to promote social intercourse between them and the Muslims. It is noteworthy, therefore, that his second visit to Lagos, which took place between 17 April and 15 July 1894, was primarily for the purpose of the opening of a new Muslim mosque, and that during this time, notwithstanding the displeasure of Lagos Christians, he was the guest of Mohammed Shitta Bey, a wealthy Sierra Leonean-born merchant, who had contributed the entire cost of £3,000 for the construction of the new mosque.[50] For Blyden the mosque was evidence of Muslim munificence and independence of spirit. The mosque was officially opened by William H. Abdullah Quilliam, President of the Liverpool Muslim Association, on 5 July during the celebration of the great feast of Muharram. It was an impressive ceremony attended by 'sheikhs, kings, and chiefs, the Imams and chief Ulemas from all the Muslim communities on the West Coast of Africa and from many parts of the interior'.[51]

For Blyden and the Muslims one of the triumphs of the occasion was the official presence of Governor Carter and his public encouragement of Muslims. Indeed, Blyden's ideas were clearly discernible in the Governor's speech. Carter, like his predecessor, Moloney, had served on the West Coast for many years before being appointed Governor of Lagos. During these years he had

[50] See J. B. Losi, *A History of Lagos*, Lagos 1914, 110–12.
[51] *Lagos Weekly Record*, IV, 19 May 1894.

made the acquaintance of Blyden, and like Pope-Hennessy, had enthusiastically adopted the ideas of the Negro scholar. Some people might wonder, declared the Governor at the opening of the mosque, why he, a Christian, tolerated Islam: the answer was that religious dogmatism was unchristian and was, at any rate, 'fatal to the religious progress of the African'. The Governor further committed himself on what was a controversial subject: he maintained that the practice of polygamy had 'existed in Africa from time immemorial and seemed well-adapted to the needs of the people'. Christianity, he warned, had no chance of becoming an effective force in Africa so long as missionaries refused to recognize polygamy as a wholesome social institution. European missionaries, if they would be successful would do well to study carefully customs and institutions. The Governor had advice, too, for the Muslims: 'by all means continue to teach Arabic and the Koran, but do not blind yourself to the advantages of an English education'.[52] Governor Carter could not have reflected Blyden's ideas more faithfully or enthusiastically.

The mosque itself had been built by two Brazilian Negro emigrants—Senhores Martin and Porphyrio—and was 'the finest specimen of ecclesiastical architecture in West Africa'. To the *Lagos Weekly Record* the whole event was cause for immense pride:

No foreign hands reared those beautiful walls, that splendid dome, those graceful turrets. All is the work of the African. Where now is the taunt that the Negro can do nothing—that he will do nothing— that he cannot help himself? This is the noblest achievement with which the Negro of West Africa will mark the closing decade of the nineteenth century.[53]

During this stay Blyden also sought to promote the idea of the establishment of an institution of higher learning. At Lagos, as elsewhere, he had propagandized that more and 'correct' education was essential for the progress of the race. During his visit in 1891 he had discussed this question with leading Africans in several meetings held at Orange House and it was then decided that an initial sum of £2,000 should be raised to start a school which would train students 'along African lines'.[54] But no action

---

[52] *Lagos Weekly Record*, IV, 7 July 1894.
[53] *Ibid.*   [54] *Lagos Times*, IV, 31 Jan. 1891.

had been taken, and on his second visit Blyden resumed discussion of the idea with Africans and the Governor, Sir Gilbert Carter.

Blyden's educational scheme was given full publicity and support by his close associate, John Payne Jackson, editor of the *Lagos Weekly Record*; indeed, there is internal evidence that several of the editorials on this subject which appeared in the *Record* were written by Blyden himself. Jackson was born in Liberia in 1847 and received education up to the High School level at Mt. Vaughan, Cape Palmas. He emigrated to Lagos in the late 1860's, having spent some time in Accra as a trader. After an eventful career as clerk, book-keeper, trader and journalist, Payne in 1891, already with the reputation of a competent and enterprising journalist, became editor and part-owner of the *Lagos Weekly Record*, which became the most important propagator of early Nigerian nationalism.[55] Blyden was much impressed by Jackson, whom he described as 'an able man' with 'very strong race feelings'.[56]

The *Lagos Weekly Record* of 5 May, 1894, noted the need for a West African University, and recommended 'the federation of the colonies for the establishment and development of the system of education now had in view by leading natives'. But although Lagos was commercially prosperous, Blyden's scheme did not meet with the response he desired. His disappointment was reflected in an editorial in the *Record* of 30 June:

We in Lagos ... live in constant pressure of tribal affinities. We know the difficulties and stumbling blocks, the petty strifes and narrowness, engendered by what is sometimes dignified by the designation of 'local politics', which is nothing more or less than the dark, contracted and undisciplined devotion to tribal ideas. ... It is this besetting and obtrusive infirmity, which accounts, in no little degree, for the inability among us to engage in any enterprise which requires organized effort.

An editorial in the issue of 21 July deprecated 'the superficial show and glitter in the British West African Colonies', and the inability or refusal of wealthy citizens to use their money for 'constructive purposes'.

[55] Lloyd Gwam, 'John Payne Jackson: Journalist', *Nigeria Sunday Times*, 17 Jan. 1965; James S. Coleman, *Nigeria: Background to Nationalism*, Berkeley 1963, 184; Omu, *Nigerian Press*, 70. Jackson's parents were Afro-American.
[56] Blyden to Wilson, 25 Aug. 1897, *A.C.S. Papers*, Vol. 27.

At the request of Governor Carter, and after an interview with Joseph Chamberlain at the Colonial Office, Blyden returned to Lagos on 9 March 1896, to assume the position of Agent for Native Affairs.[57] Blyden's duties were not specific: his appointment was a special one and could only have been filled by someone of his prestige and influence. In his new capacity, Blyden, undaunted by its initial cool reception, again sought to promote the idea of an institution of higher learning in Lagos for West Africans. The 'educational drama' enacted in Lagos in 1896 was almost identical with that played in Sierra Leone in 1872–3.[58] After preliminary discussions with leading Africans and the Governor, Blyden wrote his first formal letter to Carter on 14 May, pointing out the disadvantages for Africans of a purely missionary education, or of education in Europe, and stressed the need for an institution of higher learning in West Africa, Carter replied that he was very sympathetic to the idea, but warned that unless Africans took the initiative in founding such an institution no aid could be expected from the Government. In late May Blyden convened a meeting of leading Africans at his residence; here a prospectus for the College was drawn up and the decision taken to launch a campaign for funds.

This new educational project received publicity from all the West African newspapers. *The Sierra Leone Weekly News* recalled the attempt in 1872–3 to found a Negro University and hoped that the new effort would be more successful. The *Lagos Weekly Record* of 2 May, attempted to stir public interest by using the now familiar arguments against European missionary education in persuasive and patriotic language:

It has produced upon us this unhappy result, that we are ashamed of the rock whence we were hewn, and the whole of the pit whence we were digged—ashamed of the root whence we get whatever of our vital strength we have—ashamed to recollect that our fathers and mothers or grandfathers and grandmothers were Egbas, Jebus or Ijeshas—ashamed again of our forty or fifty cousins at Abeokuta,

[57] C.O. 147/104, Carter to Chamberlain, 16 March 1896; *Liberia Bulletin*, No. 8, Feb. 1896, 13.

[58] C.O. 147/110, Carter to Chamberlain, 3 Aug. 1896, enclosures: Blyden to Carter, 14 May and 3 June 1896, also Colonial Office Minutes; *Liberia Bulletin*, No. 9, Nov. 1896, 81; *Lagos Weekly News*, XII, 2 May 1896 and 30 May 1896; *Sierra Leone Weekly News*, XII, 2 May 1896.

Jebu and Ilesha, who are remarkable for nothing but their half-naked, robust bodies in spite of our excellent European equipment... Through this contempt and neglect of our antecedents we display a certain affectation, despicable alike to European and thinking natives. We do not for one moment condemn the energy and desire for improvement which makes us strive to emulate the enterprise, activity and thrift of the European; for such desire and emulation are not without their uses to us; they give us a stimulus which we need and drive us on the road to advancement. But what we object to is making the attainment of European things the end of our efforts, and resting on them as making us superior to our interior brethren. The culture or the wealth or the success of any kind which hinders a man from honouring his father and his mother and places him out of sympathy with his people is a curse to him and them; and we go further and say that the religion which separates a man from his people and makes him stand off from them in contemptuous scorn, is a religion not from God but from the devil.

An editorial of 4 July stated the purpose of the projected institution in language that would have been familiar to anyone acquainted with Blyden's previous efforts at promoting higher education in West Africa: it was intended to produce Africans who would be qualified to interpret Africa to the rest of the world. A preliminary prospectus of an institution to be called 'The Lagos Training College and Industrial Institute' was issued in mid-July 'with a view of calling the attention of the Lagos and other portions of the West African public to the important effort now being made on behalf of Africa and the Negro race and to solicit their interest and co-operation towards the initiation of the scheme'.

The institution itself was to comprise of a 'literary' and an industrial department; in the former would be taught 'ancient and modern languages, mathematics, history, mental and moral philosophy and natural science'; in the latter, 'various handicrafts and scientific and practical agriculture. To facilitate the practice of agriculture, Blyden recommended that the institute be built in the mainland in the vicinity of the Government Botanic Garden at Ebute Metta.

Governor Carter had duly transmitted his correspondence with Blyden to the Colonial Office. Officials there agreed with Carter that the 'Lagos Government should support the scheme as far as possible and give financial assistance when it is certain that the natives are in earnest'. But they were confident that such a scheme would not succeed if left to African initiative. H. J. Read, Principal Clerk minuted: 'There is not much public spirit in the West African and Mr. Blyden will be a very clever man if he can extract much in the way of subscriptions from his fellow countrymen, who, moreover, dislike anything in the shape of direct contribution.' Sir John Bramston, the Assistant Under-Secretary, supported this point of view: 'Dr. Blyden is doubtless quite right as to the futility of sending home a few youths to get a smattering of education and European habits ... we may wish him every success but I fear it will be uphill work.' The Colonial Office was correct. In a letter of 10 November a bitterly disappointed Blyden admitted to Governor Carter that he had failed to win adequate African support for his scheme, and expressed his 'disgust at the lamentable incapacity of the people and their invincible apathy to anything but the accumulation ... of money which they know not how to use.'[59]

Blyden was further discouraged by the fact that his sympathetic associate, Governor Carter, was forced to retire prematurely in October 1896 because of ill-health. He confided to Carter that he did not feel he could work 'under another Governor less acquainted with African matters and less alive, through ignorance of the country and people, to the methods best adapted to their welfare'. But so well was Blyden thought of at the Colonial Office that Sir John Bramston instructed the newly appointed Governor, Henry E. McCallum to write allaying his fears. In a 'gushing' letter, McCallum assured Blyden he would depend for his 'light and leading upon advisers such as yourself who have taken up the question of the improvement of the African with enthusiasm'.[60] Blyden accepted this assurance and decided to keep his position.

But McCallum, a newcomer to West Africa, proved to be unreceptive to African advice. The *Record* soon discovered that he was a man 'with palpable lack of tact and ordinary prudence'. It criticized him for introducing a house tax without first making an attempt to explain it to Africans, and for his wholesale condemnation of African officials as corrupt. Africans protested at public meetings and to the Colonial Office that McCallum's actions were 'prejudicial in their effects upon the character and

---

[59] C.O. 147/107, Blyden to Carter, 10 Nov. 1896.
[60] *Ibid.*, McCallum to Blyden, 26 Jan. 1897.

reputation of the native community'.[61] Blyden himself disapproved of the 'inflammatory' notes McCallum wished him to send to the Muslim chiefs of the interior and refused to translate them.[62] Perhaps mainly because he found it difficult to co-operate with McCallum, but ostensibly on the ground of ill-health, Blyden resigned from his position as Agent for Native Affairs at the end of 1897.

As Agent for Native Affairs, Blyden did achieve a major success in breaking down the traditional Muslim distrust of 'western education' and in establishing the first school in West Africa for the training of Muslim children in secular English education. Blyden met the leaders of the Muslim community on 13 April 1896, and outlined his plan of education for their children, taking pains to emphasize that all their teachers would be Muslims who were English-speaking, and that no attempt would be made to interfere with the children's religion, customs or dress.[63] But despite these disarming concessions, the older and more conservative men at first opposed Blyden's plans and only reluctantly gave way to the views of the younger and more progressive leaders. A week after Blyden's proposals, a delegation of Muslim leaders headed by Yusufu Shitta Bey, agreed to plans for an 'English' school for their children on conditions which would permit them to abandon the experiment if they thought that it operated against the interest of their community: they refused to construct a school building, or have the Government do so, but instead they rented premises on Bankole Street for a year and insisted on paying the rent themselves; their choice of headmaster, Idrisu Animasaun, a progressive young Muslim, refused to accept a salary from the Government. It was clear that the Muslim community entered the scheme with scepticism, and had taken adequate precautions to make disentanglement easy if it was necessary. The school opened on 15 June, with an enrolment of forty boys and forty-six young men, which soon increased to 115, but attendance especially among the young men, many of whom were part-time employees, was irregular. To assist Animasaun,

[61] *Lagos Weekly Record*, VIII, 14 and 28 Aug. 1897.

[62] C.O. 267/491, Blyden to Antrobus, 19 Feb. 1906.

[63] The Macaulay Papers, Vol. II, at the University of Ibadan, Nigeria, contain copies of the official letters and documents which pertain to Blyden's opening of the first 'English' School for Muslims. Unless otherwise stated, the information on this school is taken from this source.

Blyden secured two young Muslims from Sierra Leone. A year later, Blyden reported to Governor McCallum that the scheme was a success. He wrote: 'The enterprise may now be considered established in the minds of the Mohammedans. Instruction in English is given daily to about eight boys in Yoruba. They are taught Reading, Writing, Arithmetic and Grammar, they also study Arabic and Yoruba Books. Parents are ... very much pleased with what is to them the astonishing progress made by their children in the English language.' At the end of the experimental year, the Muslims gave consent to the Government to erect a building for the school, and Animasaun remained as a Government-paid headmaster. When Blyden left Lagos at the end of 1897, 'English education' for Muslim children was no longer a novelty: the success of the Lagos school had led to requests for the establishment of similar schools at Epe, Ibadan and Badagry.[64]

As Director of Mohammedan Education in Sierra Leone from 1901–6, Blyden had continued his attempt to build a bridge of communication between Muslims and English-speaking Africans for him an indispensable prerequisite for any attempt to create a West African community and nation.

In February 1906 another educational idea which Blyden had advocated since the 1870's was implemented when the Sierra Leone Government started a school at Bo—a town in Temne country 136 miles from Freetown—for the sons and nominees of African chiefs.[65] It started as a primary school and met most of Blyden's requirements. Although 'sound ethical training' was to be 'inculcated' into the students, the school was to be secular. Pupils were to be trained in technical as well as academic subjects. They were to be encouraged to retain their own dress, customs and games, and cultivate the use of their African instruments of music. It was stipulated that on completion of their training, pupils were not to be employed in the service of the Government but were to return as leaders to their own communities. In all these respects, the scheme implemented Blyden's ideas. But he was greatly disappointed that a C.M.S. missionary, the Rev. Mr. Proudfoot, was appointed as the first Principal of the School. He wrote to the Colonial Office strongly opposing Proudfoot's appointment arguing that experience in West Africa had shown that missionaries had failed as teachers because they had been con-

[64] *Lagos Weekly Record*, IX, 14 May 1898.   [65] Hilliard, *op. cit.*, 25.

temptuous of African customs and institutions,[66] but his plea was in vain.

That Bo School was associated in the minds of the people of Bo—the largest town in the Sierra Leone Protectorate—with Blyden can be seen from the fact that on 26 December 1907, the young men of the town formed the Blyden Club, the aim of which was to cultivate and project 'the African Personality'.[67] Prince Momolu Massaquoi, a distinguished Vai Chief educated in the United States, was chairman at the inauguration of the Club and warned its members in the spirit of their great patron: 'We want no veneering. We want men who are themselves in their own thought.'[68] The Club thrived, and on its first anniversary, the Rev. D. A. Davies, an African University graduate, exhorted its members to 'strive always to be Blydenic'. He wished members 'to conduct themselves Blydenically' so that they might be an example 'not only to the young men of Sierra Leone and Africa, but throughout the world'.[69]

The Blyden Club was symbolic of his continued propagation of cultural nationalism. If after leaving Liberia College in June 1901, he regretted that there was no West African institution from which he could direct the study of African social life, he omitted no opportunity to urge this upon educated West Africans. By 1900 there were only two works by West Africans which could be said to be of a sociological nature: J. Augustus Cole's, *A Revelation of the Secret Orders of West Africa* (1886), and John Mensah Sarbah's *Fanti Customary Law* (1897). But to Blyden's chagrin, Cole's work, although it provided useful sociological data, was mainly concerned to have secret societies abolished because they were 'in direct opposition to Christianity and contrary to the principles of morality and truth'.[70] To Blyden, Cole's book was further proof of Christianity destroying pride of race among Africans. On the other hand, Sarbah's book, in Blyden's view, set an example for other educated West Africans. Sarbah and his associates in the Gold Coast had been 'dissatisfied with

---

[66] C.O. 267/491, Blyden to Antrobus, 2 Feb., 19 Feb., 3 March and 10 March 1906.
[67] *Sierra Leone Weekly News*, XXIV, 11 Jan. 1908.
[68] *African Mail*, 1, 7 Feb. 1908.
[69] *Sierra Leone Weekly News*, XXV, 14 Nov. 1908.
[70] J. Augustus Cole, *A Revelation of the Secret Orders of Western Africa*, Dayton, Ohio 1886, 9.

the demoralising effects of certain European influences, [and were] determined to stop further encroachment into their nationality'. The purpose of his book was both to stimulate pride among Africans in their social institutions as well as provide European officials with 'a correct picture' of Fanti laws and customs.[71]

Blyden was also heartened that in Majola Agbebi and J. E. Casely Hayford, his two staunchest disciples, were exemplified the spirit of keen race pride and African assertion. During Blyden's stay in Lagos in the 1890's his friendship with Agbebi had grown; in addition, they visited Liberia together for a few weeks in 1894 and London, England, in April 1895 where Blyden proudly introduced him to his influential friends. Agbebi had continued to strive for an African Church free of 'foreign trappings'; thus in 1898 he excluded the use of wine as a sacrament in the services of the Native Baptist Church, partly as a protest against the trade in liquor in West Africa.[72]

Agbebi rightly saw that if there was to be a truly African Church, it had to be self-supporting and an aggressive missionary agency. Not surprisingly, he preached 'the gospel of coffee, cocoa and cotton'. In 1895 he persuaded a West Indian couple, the Rev. J. E. Ricketts and his wife, to join his Church as 'Industrial Missionaries', and they worked first in Lagos and later in Ijebu territory.[73] In 1898 the Native Baptist Church became a missionary agency when Agbebi started a branch in New Calabar. From January to April 1902 he visited forty-five towns and villages in Southern Nigeria—Yorubaland, Benin and Ijaw country—organizing small congregations and opening schools.[74] In his missionary and educational work Agbebi refused to recognize the territorial boundaries drawn by the European imperialist powers: in August 1902 his work was extended into the Western Cameroons. Agbebi's method of operation is instructive. On a visit to new territory he first sought to win the confidence of the ruling element and convert them. He pointed out to prospective converts that conversion to Christianity would not entail the disruption of the social fabric by the giving up of such wholesome customs as polygamy. Agbebi wanted Christianity to serve and elevate his

[71] John Mensah Sarbah, *Fanti Customary Laws*, London 1897, preface.
[72] *Anti-Slavery Reporter*, Series IV, Vol. XVIII, Sept.–Dec. 1898.
[73] *Sierra Leone Weekly News*, XX, 2 Nov. 1895.
[74] See Mojola Agbebi, *An Account of Mojola Agbebi's Work in West Africa*, New Calabar, 1904.

African communities rather than inflict hardship upon them, as he believed the dogmatic form of European Christianity did. Agbebi's methods brought efficacious results: several chiefs became Christian converts and placed their sons and nominees under his instruction. Agbebi's drive and organizing ability can be estimated by the fact that by 1903 he had organized and become President of the Native Baptist Union of West Africa which included churches in Sierra Leone, Ghana (Gold Coast), Nigeria, and the Cameroons.

Earlier, in 1901, Agbebi had been instrumental in bringing about a merger between the Native Baptist Church and the United Native African Church to form the African Church of Lagos. On the occasion of its first anniversary, Agbebi again stressed the need for a united West African Church 'untrammelled by the trappings of European sectarianism'.[75] A 'delighted' Blyden wrote to Agbebi expressing his whole-hearted approval that he had 'uttered views so radically different from the course of his training, but intrinsically African and so valuable for the guidance of his people'. Blyden's letter continued: 'No one can write on the religion of the African as an African can ... and you have written thoughtfully and with dignity and impressiveness ... "Africa is struggling for a separate personality" and your discourse is one of the most striking evidences of this. The African has something—a great deal to say to the world— ... which it ought to hear.'[76]

Nothing better illustrates the coincidence of views between Blyden and Agbebi than the paper the latter gave at the First Universal Race Congress held at the University of London between 26 and 29 July 1911.[77] Blyden, who was very ill and near the end of his life, could not attend, but in Pastor Agbebi he could not have had a more faithful representative of his viewpoint. While most members of the Conference reflected the generally accepted current view that culture was a learned process, and that there was no essentially innate qualitative differences in the ability of races, Agbebi put forward the view held by Blyden that each race had inherent and distinct attributes. From this he went

[75] See Mojola Agbebi, *Inaugural Sermon*, New York 1903.

[76] *Ibid.*, 17.

[77] See Mojola Agbebi, 'The West African Problem', *Papers on Inter-Racial Problems Communicated to the First Universal Congress. . . . Edited by G. Spiller*, London 1911, 341-7.

on to argue that social organizations were, in large part, manifestations of unique racial characteristics and hence should not be unduly tampered with; he deprecated the 'disordering and dislocation of the African social system' caused by the impact of European culture, pleaded with European imperialists to 'exercise sympathy and patience and to study and understand' African social institutions if they were to rule well; he regretted the 'fatal mistake on the part of Europeanized Africans of abnegating African social laws'. Blyden-like, Agbebi opposed miscegenation, defended secret societies of Africa as more useful than those of Europe, spoke up for polygamy as 'the basis of political economy and human happiness', extolled Islam as 'a demonstrative and attractive faith' which had adapted itself 'to the social laws, domestic arrangements, religious aspiration, political ambition, intellectual aptitude, mental energy, and racial instincts' of Africans; and patiently explained, without condoning, that human sacrifice, ancestral worship, and witchcraft served useful functional purposes in Africa.

To Blyden, J. E. Casely Hayford, like Agbebi, was an outstanding 'African Personality'. They had first made each other's acquaintance in Sierra Leone in the early 1870's when Hayford was a student at the Wesleyan Boys' High School, and Blyden was vigorously advocating cultural ethnocentrism. Blyden made a profound impression on Hayford who became his life-long follower and probably his most devoted disciple. Hayford, like Sarbah, was a trained lawyer, and became active in the then Gold Coast defending the interests of Africans. In 1897, at the request of the Gold Coast Aborigines Rights Protection Society, Casely Hayford undertook a study of the western peoples of the Gold Coast for the practical purpose of opposing the Lands Bill of 1897 which invested in the Crown the right to administer public lands; through the efforts of Hayford and the A.R.P.S., the bill was repealed.[78] In 1903, Hayford's researches were published in a book entitled *Gold Coast Institutions*, and in it he made a plea for the retention of wholesome African customs and institutions. Like Blyden, Hayford was especially critical of the 'de-Africanizing influence' of European missionaries.[79]

[78] David Kimble, *A Political History of Ghana, 1850–1928*, London 1963, 158–60.
[79] J. E. Casely Hayford, *Gold Coast Native Institutions*, London 1903, 105.

If Hayford derived his inspiration from Blyden, he, in turn, encouraged his penurious mentor, and helped to ensure that his writings appeared in print: in 1905 Hayford made a substantial financial contribution towards the publication of lectures which Blyden had delivered in England in 1901 and 1903. In an introduction to the work, Hayford gave the most enthusiastic endorsement of Blyden's work and ideas that he ever received in his lifetime:

The claims of Edward Wilmot Blyden to the esteem and regard of all thinking Africans rests not so much upon the special work he has done for any particular people of the African race, as upon the general work he has done for the race as a whole.

The work of men like Booker T. Washington and W. E. Burghardt Du Bois is exclusive and provincial in a sense. The work of Edward W. Blyden is universal, covering the entire race and the entire race problem.

What do I mean? I mean this, that while Booker T. Washington seeks to promote the material advancement of the black man in the United States, and W. E. Burghardt Du Bois his social enfranchisement amid surroundings and in an atmosphere uncongenial to race development, Edward W. Blyden has sought ... to reveal everywhere the African unto himself; to fix his attention upon original ideas and conceptions as to his place in the economy of the world; to point out to him his work as a race among the races of men; lastly, and most important of all, to lead him back to self-respect. He has been the voice of one crying in the wilderness of all these years, calling upon all thinking Africans to go back to the roots whence they were hewn by the common Father of the nations—to drop metaphor, to unlearn all that foreign sophistry has encrusted upon the intelligence of the African.[80]

Blyden's own greatest single effort at 'unfolding the African ... through a study of the customs of his fathers', and also of assisting the European political overlord ruling in Africa, to arrive at 'a proper appreciation of conditions' was made in 1908 with the publication of his work, *African Life and Customs*, which had first appeared as a series of articles in *Sierra Leone Weekly News*. And to this Hayford had given enthusiastic public approval, claiming that 'it was the learned Doctor who first pointed out that Africa needs no spiritual interference from without; but that

[80] Blyden, *West Africa before Europe*, Introduction, I–IV.

she requires emancipation from the thraldom of foreign ideas inimical to racial development'.[81]

In 1911, Casely Hayford published his second book, *Ethiopia Unbound*, a rambling semi-autobiographical work which, however, contained another sterling defence of African culture. In it Hayford, once again, paid admiring tribute to Blyden and his work. He wrote: 'He was . . . a god descended upon earth to teach the Ethiopians anew the way of life. He came not in thunder, or with sound, but in the garb of a humble teacher, a John the Baptist among his brethren, preaching rational and national Salvation. From land to land and shore to shore his message was the self-same one, which, interpreted in the language of Christ was: "What shall it profit a race if it shall gain the whole world and lose its soul?"'[82] After reading this work, the old race patriot felt certain that his mantle had fallen on Casely Hayford. On 22 October 1911, Blyden wrote to Hayford: 'The more I read *Ethiopia Unbound*, the more I see it is not your book, but an inspiration. It has given me more joy and encouragement than anything I have seen for many years.'[83]

But it is true that although Agbebi and Casely Hayford were staunch disciples of his, Blyden had become increasingly estranged from the younger generation of educated West Africans. This was because of his conservative cultural nationalism coupled with his opposition to what he considered a premature challenge to European political overlordship. While educated Africans had no wish to lose altogether their African heritage they found it difficult to support Blyden in his strong emphasis on the need to retain traditional culture; they saw much in western culture which appealed to them, as exemplified, paradoxically, in the life of Blyden himself, the most westernized of West Africans. Blyden was content, too, that Africans should submit uncomplainingly to European political rule and actually dubbed as ingratitude African agitation for greater political representation, and their protests against growing discrimination in the administration of the colonies. This estrangement in the views of Blyden and the young, politically conscious West Africans can be illustrated in

[81] Blyden, *African Life and Customs*, Appendix A, 77.
[82] Casely Hayford, *Ethiopia Unbound: Studies in Race Emancipation*, London 1963, 163.
[83] Quoted in Hayford, *The Truth about the West Africa Land Question*, London. 1913, 113.

their attitude to the exclusion of African doctors from the West
African Medical Service after 1902 and to the South African Act
of Union (1910). African doctors were excluded from entering
the West African Medical Service on the grounds that British
officers and their families would have no confidence in them.[84]
Moreover, in the colonies proper, the Colonial Office had, by the
late 1890's, decided against appointing Africans to the highest
medical positions; further, they were paid at a lower rate than
Europeans, the most junior of whom was regarded as their
senior.[85] Africans had naturally protested against this and other
blatant discriminations in the Colonial Service, but Blyden felt
that there was no justification for their protests.

The South African Act of Union had given independence to
South Africa under white minority rule but had failed on many
important issues to protect the interests of Africans. At this, too,
West Africans voiced their protests. Their sentiments were expressed by the *Sierra Leone Weekly News* thus: 'The South
African Union Act has sent a shock throughout the whole British
Empire. It has raised a solid doubt in the minds of the 360 millions of British subjects who are not of European descent, concerning the ultimate intentions of 60 millions of British subjects,
who are of European descent.'[86] This discrimination against
Africans everywhere on their continent prompted the *News* to
call for the formation of a British West African Civil Rights Defence Association for the purpose of seeing that Africans secure
'fair play'; and for the conversion of Fourah Bay College into a
West African University which would 'train up sons of Africa . . .
to become the rulers and governors of the West African Nations
and of the Commonwealth of West Africa . . . embracing all
British West African territories'.[87] A 'Marxist' correspondent of
the newspaper called on the British West African Colonies to
adopt his programme for obtaining 'freedom' in three stages.[88]
The first was to be one of 'Moral, intellectual and Industrial
Preparation'. The second would see 'a rigorous boycott of foreign
goods and a bloody war'. What was needed, he urged, was
'Propaganda and suffering at the beginning, heroism and valour
in the middle, wisdom and constructive genius at the end.' He

[84] Kimble, *A Political History of Ghana*, 98.
[85] Fyfe, *op. cit.*, 614.   [86] *Sierra Leone Weekly News*, XXVI, 15 Jan. 1910.
[87] *Ibid.*   [88] *Sierra Leone Weekly News*, XXVI, 22 Jan. 1910.

exhorted: 'Awake Sierra Leone and West Africa! Awake and take your place among the nations of the world!'

But to Blyden in his old age the expression of the above nationalist sentiments merely showed the 'short-sightedness and ingratitude' of the Africans of Sierra Leone.[89] It was not that Blyden had eschewed political independence for Africans, but rather that his experience of a life-time of agitation for African assertion in cultural and educational matters without any enthusiastic response had convinced him that as yet African assertion in the political sphere was premature. To him, it mattered not that Africans were discriminated against on their own continent: he believed that European political overlordship was temporary, and that discrimination was merely part of the price Africans had to pay to have their continent brought unto the world stage. However, Blyden's philosophic optimism appears naïve even with regard to developments then taking place in South Africa.

His political alienation from the majority of educated West Africans resulted in comparative physical seclusion during the last five years of his life. During these years he was needy and in poor health, yet he would not tolerate having his views challenged by the 'hot-headed' young Africans of Sierra Leone, who were thus forced to shun him. And he had outlived his former close associates in Sierra Leone. The death of Grant and Quaker in the 1880's was followed by that of T. J. Sawyerr in 1894, Moses Blyle in 1896, J. C. May in 1902 and Sir Samuel Lewis in 1903. The death of the last two Blyden had felt particularly keenly as he regarded them as outstanding 'African Personalities' who had died at the height of their powers. As Principal of the Wesleyan Boys' High School from 1874, May had educated African boys from all English-speaking West Africa, and had implanted in them a love of race and respect for their own culture; and it is not surprising that among his students were the future Gold Coast and West African nationalists, J. E. Casely Hayford and T. Hutton Mills. Lewis, as has already been noted, had unequivocally associated himself with Blyden's views in his introduction to the latter's book, *Christianity, Islam and the Negro Race*; and had been the most regular chairman at Blyden's public lectures in Freetown. Indeed, one of Blyden's most famous lectures, 'Race and Study', was dedicated to Lewis. In an obituary on Lewis,

[89] C.O. 267/528, Blyden to Antrobus, 16 Jan. 1910.

Blyden stated that 'a friendship of thirty years' standing and community of views made us constant companions, and we freely associated in all social and domestic matters'.[90]

Already needy and lonely, in 1909 Blyden suffered the added misfortune of having to undergo an operation for aneurysm in the knee at the Royal Southern Hospital, Liverpool, where he was confined for fifteen weeks.[91] After the operation he found himself more penurious than ever. He wrote to his old friend, Sir Reginald Antrobus, a former Assistant Under-Secretary at the Colonial Office (1898–1909) thus: 'I am now in feeble health and living from hand to mouth. The Sierra Leoneans, among whom I have hitherto received sympathy and help, are now indifferent because I cannot encourage them in their misguided course.'[92] In a later letter he complained that 'The Natives now avoid me as the Liberians do, because I am pointing out the way of life and prosperity for them . . . My expenses of fifteen weeks in the hospital have left me in debts, and the Liberians, men whom I have taught and in other ways assisted, seem to have no idea of restoring my pension. History repeats itself; the people kill the prophets: Cicero, Desmosthenes, Socrates, must go if the unprincipled demagogues so will.'[93] Antrobus successfully interceded at the Colonial Office on Blyden's behalf: he recommended a small pension for the Negro patriot, at the same time pointing out that Blyden was not likely to live much longer. Accordingly the Colonial Secretary instructed the Governors of Sierra Leone, Lagos and the Gold Coast to secure the passage of a pension of £25 for Blyden in each of the Legislatures. This pension Blyden obtained for somewhat less than two years before his death on 7 February 1912.

His attempt to foster unity among Africans bore fruit even at his funeral service: Muslims and Christians, traditionally antagonistic, attended in large numbers. Perhaps it was the Muslims who did him greater honour: Muslim men bore his coffin from his residence at Rawdon Street, Freetown, to the graveyard at the Race Course, while in the procession school children marched from all the Muslim schools of the city.[94] The funeral service was, however, conducted according to Christian rites by the Rev. J. R.

[90] *Sierra Leone Weekly News*, XIX, 1 Aug. 1905.
[91] *Sierra Leone Weekly News*, XXV, 21 Aug 1909.
[92] C.O. 267/528, Blyden to Antrobus, 16 Jan. 1910.
[93] *Ibid.*, Blyden to Antrobus, 24 Jan. 1910.
[94] *Sierra Leone Guardian and Foreign Mails*, VII, 16 Feb. 1912.

Frederick, a devoted Afro-West Indian friend of Blyden's. Memorial services were held in his honour throughout English-speaking West Africa, and soon committees were set up to decide on a suitable memorial for him.[95]

From the 1870's Blyden had striven to create the consciousness among West Africans of belonging to one community. He had sought to do so by emphasizing the need for Africans to unite in order to improve the lot of the Negro race, by fostering cultural ethnocentrism, and by seeking to bring about communication and co-operation between Christians and Muslims. But if in the concept of a united West Africa, and if in the means of achieving it he showed creative imagination, Blyden disappointed West Africans in failing to be a practical leader. By the 1880's he had established an intellectual ascendancy in West Africa, and many West Africans were prepared to follow where he led, but they looked to him in vain for a firm and sustained lead, or for clear directives. Many of them thought his ideas sophistical or contradicted by his actions. Thus, although a staunch advocate of the retention of traditional culture, he was himself a most 'westernized' African, and never seemed even to have adopted African dress. Further, although he had been long and harshly critical of the operations of Christianity in Africa, and as he grew older seemed to show a distinct partiality for Islam, he himself never became a Muslim. What were his admirers, looking for a lead in religious matters, to do? Finally, his fatalistic acceptance of European imperialism and his denunciation of the political aspirations of the younger generation of Africans had served to discredit him as an effective West African leader. Nonetheless, by his outstanding literary and scholastic achievements, by his attempt to foster

[95] Among the suggestions for a Blyden Memorial were busts, schools and scholarships. In 1913 a huge bust of Blyden was erected on Water Street, Freetown, but this was by some of his European admirers with West African interests: Sir Owen Phillips, Sir William H. Lever, Sir Harry Johnston and Leo Weinthal. In Freetown his African friends and admirers placed a headstone, with the inscriptions in gold, over his grave. The headstone was signed by the J. J. Thomas, Archdeacon Macaulay, Rev. C. Marke, Rev. J. R. Frederick, C. May, Casely Hayford, Hadir-Ud-Deen, W. T. G. Lawson and J. S. T. Davies. In Lagos, Blyden's admirers erected stained glass windows in his honour in the Old Glover Memorial Hall, on each of which was the inscription 'This window was presented to the Glover Hall by admirers of Dr. Blyden to commemorate the eminent service he rendered to the people of British West Africa.' In the old Hall (which has been demolished), as in the present one, has hung a large photograph of Blyden with the caption: 'Greatest Defender of the Negro Race.'

African assertion and independence in cultural affairs (which he saw as the prerequisite to political independence), and by his striving after unity, he left West Africans a rich legacy and for this they have always honoured his name.

Epilogue

As the most articulate and brilliant vindicator of Negro and African interests in the nineteenth century, Blyden's ideas have contributed greatly to the historical roots of African Nationalism, Pan-African and Negritude, and have been a source of inspiration and pride to modern exponents of these ideologies, as well as to English-speaking New World Negro intellectuals in their continuous quest for dignity and equality for members of their race.[1]

In West Africa his influence among nationalists in the first three decades of the twentieth century was direct and pervasive, and was most obvious in their efforts at establishing a British West African Federation, in their search for better and increased educational facilities, and in their attempts to foster pride in African history and culture. It was J. E. Casely Hayford who most actively carried on Blyden's work. In 1913, a year after Blyden's death he wrote: 'One touch of nature has made all West Africa kin', and wished to see 'a United West Africa ... take her true part among the nations of the earth.'[2] Calling publicly in 1919 for a United West Africa, Casely Hayford admitted the inspiration he derived from Blyden. 'I have adopted the suggestion', he wrote, 'that in the promotion of race unity, it must be, as the late doctor Blyden was wont to say, line upon line, precept upon precept, here a little, and there a little'.[3] In March 1920, at the invitation of Casely Hayford, delegates from the Gambia, Sierra Leone, Nigeria and Gold Coast (Ghana) met in Accra and formally established the National Congress of British West Africa. And until his death in 1930 Casely Hayford remained the most active advocate of British West African Unity.[4]

[1] See John Henrik Clarke, ed., *Harlem*, New York 1964, article by Richard B. Moore, 'Africa Conscious Harlem', p. 78; in the New World Blyden's name has been used in the naming of Negro organizations and institutions: e.g. there is a Blyden Club of New York and an Edward Wilmot Blyden Library in Norfolk, Virginia: Holden, *Blyden of Liberia*, 900.

[2] Casely Hayford, *The Truth about the West African Land Question*, London 1913, preface.

[3] Casely Hayford, *United West Africa*, London 1919, 27.

[4] See David Kimble, *A Political History of Ghana*, London 1963, 374–403.

Hayford's mantle as a champion of West African unity fell on the Nigerian, Nnamdi Azikiwe, who in 1934 returned to West Africa as a newspaper owner and editor after ten years of higher education in the United States.[5] Azikiwe, like Kwame Nkrumah of Ghana, became fully acquainted with Blyden's writings at the Negro Universities he attended in the United States. And he, too, has admitted being influenced and inspired by Blyden whom he regards as one of the men 'who laid the foundation upon which West African history was built'.[6] Intelligent, sensitive and race-proud, Azikiwe's experience of colonialism in Africa and discrimination in America led him to subscribe to pan-Negro nationalism. Thus, there is a marked similarity between Azikiwe's views, particularly as expounded in *Renascent Africa* (1937), and those of Blyden: the denial that the Negro race was 'inferior or backward', and the affirmation that it has made a 'definite contribution to history'; the claim that the African was 'mis-educated', and the call for 'an African endowed and operated University' which would bring about African 'mental emancipation' from the enslavement of false or misleading European ideas; the contention that Islam is a more humane and practical religion than Christianity and hence more suited to the African; and the expression of the need for educated Africans to 'bridge the linguistic and cultural gaps' in order to promote greater unity in Africa.[7] Like Blyden too, Azikiwe in his early nationalist years regarded Liberia, the then lone independent Republic in Africa, as the symbol of Negro-African freedom, and wished to see it have full Negro support so that it could attain 'a more glorious destiny'.[8] It is not surprising that Azikiwe's first major scholarly work was on Liberia; in this he undertook 'an analysis of the backgrounds and the contributing factors to the contemporary problems of the Republic of Liberia'.[9]

[5] Dr. Nnamdi Azikiwe, who became Nigeria's foremost nationalist, was President of an Independent Nigeria from 1960 until January 1966. There are two useful biographies of him: Vincent C. Ikestuonye, *Zik of New Africa*, London 1961; and K. A. B. Jones Quartey, *A Life of Azikiwe*, London 1964.

[6] Nnamdi Azikiwe, *Renascent Africa*, Lagos 1937, 169. In a foreword to Holden's *Blyden of Liberia*, Dr Azikiwe wrote that 'Dr Blyden rightly has been referred to as a father of African nationalism.' Dr. Azikiwe kept on display a portrait photograph of Blyden at the Presidential statehouse in Lagos. So did ex-President Nkrumah at the Presidential Palace in Accra.

[7] *Ibid.*, passim.   [8] *Ibid.*, 173.

[9] Nnamdi Azikiwe, *Liberia in World Politics*, London 1934, preface.

If Blyden was the ideological father of the idea of West African unity, he also inspired nationalism in the individual territories. Of such post World War I nationalists as T. Hutton Mills, A. Sawyerr and Dr. V. Nanka-Bruce of Ghana; F. W. Dove, L. E. M'Carthy and Dr. H. C. Bankole-Bright of Sierra Leone; Patriach J. G. Campbell, J. Egerton Shyngle, Herbert Macaulay and Professor Eyo Ita of Nigeria;[10] and E. F. Small of the Gambia, most knew Blyden personally; all were well-acquainted with his ideas. Indeed for nationalists and educators of British West Africa the life and achievements of Blyden was a popular subject of public lecture.[11]

Blyden's pan-Negro ideology was undoubtedly the most important historical progenitor of Pan-Africanism, which term first gained currency during and after the first Pan-African Conference held in London in July 1900. [12] Yet it is interesting to note that he did not attend that conference, and perhaps deliberately boycotted it. Although there seems to be no recorded statement of his attitude to the Conference, it is reasonable to assume that he was opposed to it on the grounds that a meeting of Negroes in a 'foreign capital' could serve no useful purpose: if they really wanted to help Africa and the Negro race, they

---

[10] Professor Eyo Ita, one of the most outstanding Nigerian nationalists (see Coleman, *op. cit.*, 218–21), in a letter to the author dated 28 February 1966, stated that Blyden's writings was one of the major formative influences on him. In part he wrote: 'I came to read books by and about Edward Wilmot Blyden and Du Bois in the late twenties. In December 1920 Dr. Kwegyir Aggrey of Ghana already wakened in my heart the vision of Africa as a great homeland with a unique divine mission on earth. On such a soil the great ideas of Blyden bloomed and flourished luxuriantly.'

[11] For example, see A. Deniga, *Blyden, the African Educationalist*, Lagos 1923; Julius Ojo Cole, *Dr. Edward Wilmot Blyden, an interpretation*, Lagos 1935; Herbert Macaulay, 'The Life History of Edward Wilmot Blyden... one of the greatest African Negroes of his Age'. *West African Pilot*, 15–19, 23, 25 and 26 Nov. 1943. In 1953 Dr. K. Onwuka Diké, the distinguished historian, and the first Nigerian Vice-Chancellor of the University of Ibadan, in arguing the need for Africans, to develop confidence in themselves approvingly quoted Blyden; *West Africa*, 11 March 1953, 251. Blyden has at least two primary schools named after him—the Edward Wilmot Blyden Memorial School—established in Lagos, Nigeria, in 1938 by J. S. Albert for young under-privileged students, and the Edward Blyden School of Abeokuta, Western Nigeria.

[12] *The Times*, 24, 25 and 26 July. The Conference was organized by Henry Sylvester-Williams, a barrister-at-law from Trinidad, and was attended by some thirty delegates, mainly from the West Indies and the United States, with one delegate each from Liberia and Ethiopia.

could best do this by employing their talents in Liberia or even one of the African colonial territories. In addition, Blyden either knew or suspected that the conference would be dominated by such mulattoes as Dr. W.E.B. Du Bois and Bishop Alexander Walters, and, of course, his hatred of mulattoes had remained unabated. Thus, there were probably two important differences between Blyden's pan-Negro ideas and those of the Pan-African movement in its pre-African phase with Du Bois as its guiding spirit:[13] if they were both racially based, Blyden's was even of a more exclusive nature in that he wanted only 'pure Negroes' to participate; secondly, he never quite reconciled himself to Negroes living permanently in the New World, and insisted that any major efforts to improve the lot of the Negro race must be made on the African continent. But these differences do not nullify the obvious affinity between Blyden's pan-Negro nationalism and the ideology of Pan-Africanism; George Padmore, a West Indian from Trinidad, and the foremost theoretician of Pan-Africanism in the twentieth century, was a great admirer of Blyden.[14]
great admirer of Blyden.[14]

If Blyden's pan-Negro ideas are one of the main historical progenitors of Pan-Africanism, it was perhaps in Marcus Garvey's Back-to-Africa Movement that the greatest heritage of his ideas is to be found. When Blyden died, Garvey was a young man of twenty-five, and although so far no reference has been found to Blyden by Garvey, it is known that the latter, who was a voracious reader of works on or by Negroes, was well-acquainted with the writings and ideas of the former.[15] At any rate, there is a marked identity of views between the two West Indians: both claimed to be 'pure Negroes' and were intensely race-proud; both supported New World Negro 'repatriation'

[13] See W. E. B. Du Bois, *The World and Africa*, New York 1947, 7–12, 236–45; Colin Legum, *Pan-Africanism*, London 1962, 24–32; and American Society of African Culture, *Pan-Africanism Reconsidered*, Los Angeles 1962, 37–52.

[14] George Padmore, *Pan-Africanism or Communism?* London 1965, 54–5. Padmore regarded Blyden as 'the greatest Negro of his time' and expressed his profound admiration for him by naming his first child – a daughter – Blyden; communication of Mrs. Blyden Nurse Cowart of California to author, December 1966. Professor J. R. Hookes, recent biographer of Padmore, has in conversation confirmed that Padmore greatly admired Blyden.

[15] Richard Moore, a well-known Harlem nationalist, has told the author that Garvey bought Blyden's *Christianity, Islam and the Negro Race* from his bookstore in 1917.

to Africa and envisaged that continent as the scene of future glory for the Negro. Garvey's mass movement collapsed in the mid-1920's but nonetheless served as a powerful stimulant to African nationalism.[16]

Like that of Pan-Africanism, the modern concept of Negritude as expounded by such writers as Aimé Césaire of Martinique and President Léopold Senghor of Senegal can find respectable historical roots in the writings of Blyden. Indeed Blyden's pan-Negro ideology rested on Negritude—the affirmation that there was an innate Negro character or 'Personality'—characterized by emotion, intuitiveness and empathy with nature; and the rejection, at least partial, of European culture and values. The object of Blyden was the same as that of the more recent exponents of Negritude to create among Negroes, long demoralized in a contemptuous white-dominated world, pride, confidence and a cultural identity by assigning them a special and significant role.

[16] For example, both Nnamdi Azikiwe of Nigeria and Kwame Nkrumah of Ghana have freely admitted that Garvey's ideas greatly stimulated their budding nationalism. See Azikiwe, *Renascent Africa*, 98; Kwame Nkrumah, *Autobiography*, Edinburgh 1957, 45; also George Shepperson, 'Notes on Negro American Influences on the Emergence of African Nationalism', *Journal of African History*, 1, 2, 1960, 303.

Select Bibliography

I MANUSCRIPTS IN THE UNITED STATES

a Papers of the American Colonization Society, Library of Congress, Washington, D.C.

Apart from his own published writings, this is easily the most important source for any study of Blyden. This collection contains his regular correspondence with the Secretary of the American Colonization Society over a period of almost forty years 1864–1891. Copies of the Secretary's replies are also in this collection.

b Papers of the Presbyterian Board of Foreign Missions, 375 Riverside Drive, New York City.

This collection contains letters and memoranda written by Blyden to the Secretary of the Board between 1851 and 1882. This was not a continuous correspondence—there are some gaps of more than a year—but there are periods when it was regular. It is a useful supplement to the above.

c The Hemphill Papers, Duke University, Durham, North Carolina.

d The John E. Bruce Papers, Schomburg Collection, Harlem Branch of the New York Public Library.

Each of the two above collections has about a dozen relevant items.

e Edith Holden, *The Story of Blyden* 1940, Schomburg Collection, Harlem Branch of the New York Public Library.

The title is misleading. This is, in fact, a small unpaginated bound volume of manuscripts comprising relevant entries from the Journal of the Rev. John Knox (one of Blyden's early mentors and the grandfather of Miss Holden); letters to Knox from or about Blyden; and a few clippings from the *Presbyterian*.

f Papers of the Trustees of Donations for Education in Liberia, Massachusetts Historical Society, Boston.

Relevant for Blyden's connexion with Liberia College.

g The John Miller Papers, Princeton University.

This collection contains four letters written by Blyden to the Rev. John Miller between Nov. 1888 and April 1889.

2   MANUSCRIPTS IN ENGLAND

a Anti-Slavery Papers, Rhodes House Library, Oxford.

b Brougham Papers, University College, London.

c Gladstone Papers, British Museum Add. Mss.

d John Holt Papers, Liverpool.

e Lugard Papers, Rhodes House Library, Oxford.

f Morel Papers, London School of Economics.

The above Papers contain a limited number of Blyden's letters — ranging from one in the Lugard Papers to a dozen in the Gladstone Papers.

g Papers of the West African Mission of the Church Missionary Society, Salisbury Court, London, E.C.1.

These are indispensable for any discussion of the controversy between Africans and Europeans (in which Blyden was involved) at Sierra Leone between 1871 and 1874 and on the Niger, 1890–1892.

FROM THE PUBLIC RECORD OFFICE

a C.O. 267. Governors' despatches from Sierra Leone.

b C.O. 147. Governors' despatches from Lagos.

Blyden was employed by the British Government in Sierra Leone in 1872/3 as Agent to the Interior and in 1901–6 as Director of Muslim Education, and in Lagos in 1896–7 as Agent for Native Affairs. His reports and letters are to be found as enclosures in the despatches of Governors. These include two important reports on two major expeditions to Falaba and Timbo: C.O. 267/316, and 267/320, respectively.

c C.O. 806/46. African No. 82.

Contains letters by James Johnson and Bishop Cheetham relevant to the dispute between Africans and European missionaries in Sierra Leone in 1873–4.

d C.O. 806/195. African No. 251. Boundary Negotiations with Liberia, 1881–3.

e F.O. 403/6–7. Confidential Prints. Correspondence Respecting the Boundaries of the Republic of Liberia, 1861–71.

f   F.O. 403/9–11. Confidential Prints. Further Correspondence Respecting the Liberian Boundary, 1878–79.

g   F.O. 403/129. Confidential Prints. Memorandum Respecting the Safeguard of the Independence of Liberia.

h   F.O. 403/363. Memoranda on a Protectorate for Liberia.

3   MANUSCRIPTS IN NIGERIA

The Herbert Macaulay Papers, Vol. 11, University of Ibadan. This volume contains copies of the correspondence pertaining to Blyden's founding of the first Government School for Muslim students in Lagos.

4   NEWSPAPERS

African Times London
Frederick Douglass's Paper Rochester, New York
Freedom's Journal New York
Lagos Times
Lagos Weekly Record
Lagos Weekly Times
Liberia Herald Monrovia
Methodist Herald Freetown
Monrovia Observer Monrovia
Sierra Leone Times Freetown
Sierra Leone Weekly News Freetown
The Times London
Weekly Anglo-African New York
West African Reporter Freetown
West African Pilot Lagos

5   JOURNALS

African Repository Washington
American Colonization Society, Annual Reports Washington
Anti-Slavery Reporter London
Journal of the Maryland Colonization Society Baltimore
Journal of the New York Colonization Society New York
Journal of the African Society London
Liberia Bulletin Washington

6   THE PUBLISHED WRITING OF EDWARD WILMOT BLYDEN

a   Pamphlets and Books:

Africa and the Africans. Proceedings on the Occasion of a Banquet ... for Edward W. Blyden, LL.D. ... by West Africans in London London, 1903

African Colonization. An Address at the Annual Meeting of the Maine Colonization Society Portland, Maine, 1862

African Life and Customs London, 1908

The African Problem and Other Discourses Delivered in America in 1890 London, 1890.

The Aims and Methods of a Liberal Education for Africans Cambridge, Mass., 1882

The Arabic Bible in the Soudan: A Plea for Transliteration London, 1910

A Brief Account of the Proceedings on the Retirement of President J. J. Roberts and the Inauguration of Hon. S. A. Benson Monrovia, 1856.

The Call of Providence to the Descendants of Africa in America New York, 1862.

A Chapter in the History of Liberia Freetown, 1892

A Chapter in the History of the Slave Trade New York, 1859

Christianity, Islam and the Negro Race London, 1888

A Eulogy Pronounced on the Rev. John Day Monrovia, 1859

From West Africa to Palestine Freetown, Manchester and London, 1873

Hope for Africa, A Discourse Delivered in the Presbyterian Church, 7th Avenue, N.Y., July 21, 1861 Washington, 1861

The Jewish Question Liverpool, 1898

Liberia's Offering New York, 1862

The Origin and Purposes of African Colonization Washington, 1882

The Pastor's Work London, 1866

The Problems Before Liberia London, 1909

Proceedings at the Banquet in Honour of E. W. Blyden ... on the Occasion of his Retirement from his Official Labours in the Colony of Sierra Leone London, 1907

Proceedings at the Inauguration of Liberia College at Monrovia, January 23, 1862 Monrovia, 1862

Report of the President of Liberia College to the Board of Trustees Cambridge, Mass., 1882

The Return of the Exiles and the West African Church London, 1891

The Significance of Liberia Monrovia, 1906

The Three Needs of Liberia London, 1908

Vindication of the Negro Race Monrovia, 1857

A Voice from Bleeding Africa on behalf of her exiled children Monrovia, 1856

West Africa before Europe and Other Addresses London, 1905

West African University: Correspondence between E. W. Blyden and His Excellency, J. Pope-Hennessy ... Freetown, 1872

b *Articles*

'Address at the Opening of a New Library', *Liberia Bulletin*, No. 23 November 1903, 24–30

'Africa and the Africans', *Fraser's Magazine*, New Series, XVIII August 1878, 178–96

'The African in America', *Liberia Bulletin*, No. 16 February 1900, 91–4

'The African Problem', *North American Review*, CLXI September 1895, 327–39

'Christianity and the Negro Race', *Fraser's Magazine*, New Series, XIII May 1876, 554–68

'Christian Missions in West Africa', *Ibid.*, XIV October 1876, 504–22

'The Education of the Negro', *Liberia Bulletin*, No. 11 November 1897, 68–70

'Islam in the Western Soudan', *Journal of the African Society*, No. 5 October 1902, 11–37

'The Koran in Africa', *Ibid.*, No. XIV January 1905, 157–71

'Liberia's First Jubilee', *Liberia Bulletin*, No. 11 November 1897, 39–43

'The Liberian Scholar and the Work Before Him', *Liberia Bulletin*, No. 17 November 1900, 11–22

'Mixed Races in Liberia', *Smithsonian Institute Annual Report* Washington, 1870, 386–89

'Mohammedanism and the Negro Race', *Fraser's Magazine*, New Series, XII November 1875, 598–615

'Mohammedanism in West Africa', *Methodist Quarterly Review*, LIII January 1871, 62–78

'The Native African—His Life and Work', *Liberia Bulletin*, No. 24 February 1904, 61–72

'The Negro in Ancient History', *Methodist Quarterly Review*, LI January 1869, 71–93

'The Negro in the United States', *African Methodist Episcopal Review*, XVI 1900, 308–31.

'Race and Study', *Sierra Leone Times* May 27, 1873

7   OTHER PUBLISHED WORKS

a   Pamphlets and Books:

Agbebi, Mojola, *An Account of Mojola Agbebi's Work in West Africa* New Calabar 1904

—*Inaugural Sermon delivered at the celebrations of the first anniversary of the African Church* Lagos 1902

Ajayi, J. F. A., *Christian Missions in Nigeria: 1841–91* London, 1965

Allen, Gardner W., *The Trustees of Donations for Education in Liberia: A Story of Philanthropic Endeavour, 1850–1923* Boston, 1923

Alexander, Archibald, *A History of Colonization in the Western Coast of Africa* Philadelphia, 1846

Amery, Julian, *Life of Joseph Chamberlain* London, 1951, Vol. IV

Armistead, Wilson, *A Tribute to the Negro* Manchester and New York, 1848

An Appeal to Pharaoh, The Negro Problem and its Radical Solution New York, 1889

Ayandele, E. A., *The Missionary Impact On Modern Nigeria 1842–1914* London, 1966.

Azikiwe, Nnamdi, *Liberia in World Politics* London, 1934

— *Renascent Africa* Lagos, 1937

Bank Henries, A. Doris, *The Life of Joseph Jenkins Roberts* London, 1964

—*Presidents of the First African Republic* London, 1963

Barrow, A., *Fifty Years in Western Africa: Being a Record of the West Indian Church on the Banks of the Rio Pongo* London, 1900

Bennett, Lerone, *Before the Mayflower* Chicago, 1962

Bowen, John W. E., (ed.), *Africa and the American Negro: Addresses and Proceedings of the Congress on Africa* Atlanta, 1896

Buell, L. R., *Liberia: A Century of Survival, 1847–1947* Philadelphia, 1947

— *The Native Problem in Africa* New York, 1928, Vol. II, Section 16: 'The Liberian Republic'.

Burton, R. F., *Wanderings in West Africa* London, 1863

Campbell, Robert, *A Pilgrimage to my Motherland* New York, 1861

Clowes, W. Laird, *Black America: A Study of the ex-slave and his late master* London, 1891

Cole, Julius Ojo, *Edward Wilmot Blyden, An Interpretation* Lagos, 1935

Constitution of the African Civilization Society New Haven, 1861

Crummell, Alexander, *The Duty of a Rising Christian State to the World's Well-being and Civilization* London, 1856

—*The Relations and Duties of the Free Colored Men in America to Africa* Hartford, 1861

Delany, Martin R., *The Condition, Elevation, Emigration and Destiny of Colored People of the United States: Politically Considered* Philadelphia, 1852

—*Official Report of the Niger Valley Exploring Party* New York, 1861

— 'Political Destiny of the Coloured Race in the American Continent', Appendix No. 3, in *Report of the Select Committee on Emancipation and Colonization* Washington, 1862

Deniga, A., *Blyden, The African Educationalist* Lagos, 1923

Douglass, Frederick, *Life and Times* New York, 1962

Durham, Frederick Alexander, *The Lone Star of Liberia: Being the Outcome of Reflection on Our Own People* London, 1892

Franklin, John Hope, *From Slavery to Freedom* New York, 1956

Frazier, E. Franklin, *The Negro Church in America* New York, 1963

— *The Negro in the United States* New York, 1963

Fyfe, C. H., *A History of Sierra Leone* London, 1962

Gollock, Georgina, *Sons of Africa* London, 1928

Grogan, Lady Louise, *R. Bosworth Smith* London, 1901

Gwynn, Stephen D., *The Life of Mary Kingsley* London, 1933

Hargreaves, J. D., *Life of Sir Samuel Lewis* London, 1958

Hayford, J. E. Casely, *Ethiopia Unbound: Studies in Race Emancipation* London, 1911

— *The Truth About the West African Land Question* London, 1913

—*United West Africa* London, 1919

Hayford, Mark, *Mary Kingsley from an African Standpoint* London, 1901

— *West Africa and Christianity* London, 1900

Horton, J. A. B., *West African Countries and Peoples* London, 1868

— *Letters on the Political Condition of the Gold Coast* London, 1870

Holly, James T., *A Vindication of the Capacity of the Negro Race for Self-Government* ... New Haven, 1857

Huberich, Charles H., *The Political and Legislative History of Liberia* New York, 1947

Johnston, Harry, H., *The Story of My Life* London, 1923

— *Liberia* London, 1906, Vol. 1.

Kimble, David, *A Political History of Ghana: 1850–1928* London, 1963

Kopytoff, Jean H., *A Preface to Modern Nigeria: The 'Sierra Leoneans' in Yoruba, 1830–1890* Madison, 1965.

Logan, Rayford, *The Negro in American Life and Thought: The Nadir, 1877–1901* New York, 1954

Maxwell, Joseph Renner, *The Negro Question, or Hints for the Physical Improvement of the Negro Race* London, 1882

Memorial of the Jubilee of Her Majesty's Reign and the Centenary of Sierra Leone London, 1887

Meier, August, *Negro Thought in America, 1880–1915* London, 1964

Milne, A. H., *Alfred Lewis Jones* Liverpool, 1914

Padmore, George, *Pan-Africanism or Communism?* London, 1956

Reade, W. W., *The African Sketch-book* London, 1873

Sampson, Magnus J., *West African Leadership* Ilfracombe, N. Devon, 1951

Thomas, Isaac B., *A Life History of Herbert Macaulay* Lagos, 1946

Washington, Booker T., *Up From Slavery* New York, 1901

Woodson, Carter G., *The Mind of the Negro as Reflected in Letters Written During the Crisis, 1800–1860* Washington, 1926.

— (ed.), *The Works of Francis Grimké* Washington, 1942, Vol. IV.

b   *Articles:*

Ayandele, E. A., 'An Assessment of James Johnson and His Place in Nigeria History', Parts I and II, *Journal of the Historical*

Society of Nigeria, II December 1963, 418–516 and II December 1964, 73–102 respectively.

Gwam, L. C., 'Dr. Edward Wilmot Blyden', *Ibadan*, No. 15 March 1963, 8–10.

July, Robert, 'Nineteenth-Century Negritude: Edward W. Blyden', *Journal of African History*, V, 1 1964, 73–86

Lynch, Hollis R., 'Edward W. Blyden: Pioneer West African Nationalist', *Journal of African History*, VI, 3 1965, 373–88

— 'The Native Pastorate Controversy and Cultural Ethnocentrism in Sierra Leone, 1871–174', *Journal of African History*, V, 3 1964, 395–413

—'Pan-Negro Nationalism in the New World before 1862', *Boston University Papers on Africa*, Vol. 11 1966, 149–79

Nicol, A., 'Great Sons of Africa: Dr. Edward Blyden', *Africana, the Magazine of the West African Society*, I, April 1949, 19–20

Shepperson, George, 'Notes on Negro American Influences on the Emergence of African Nationalism', *Journal of African History*, 1, 2 1960, 299–312

8 UNPUBLISHED THESES:

Aderibigbe, A. A. B., *Expansion of the Lagos Protectorate, 1863–1900* Ph.D. London, 1959

Jones, Hannah A. B., *The Struggle for Political and Cultural Unification in Liberia, 1847–1930* Ph.D., Northwestern, 1962

Omu, Fred I. A., *The Nigerian Press, 1859–1937* Ph.D., Ibadan, 1965.

Index